AF668833

ANCIENT INDIAN TRADITION & MYTHOLOGY

TRANSLATED BY

A BOARD OF SCHOLARS

AND EDITED BY

Dr. G.P. BHATT

VOLUME 72

ANCIENT INDIAN TRADITION AND MYTHOLOGY SERIES

[PURĀṆAS IN TRANSLATION]

Volumes Released

ŚIVA 1-4
LIṄGA 5-6
BHĀGAVATA 7-11
GARUḌA 12-14
NĀRADA 15-19
KŪRMA 20-21
BRAHMĀṆḌA 22-26
AGNI 27-30
VARĀHA 31-32
BRAHMA 33-36
VĀYU 37-38
PADMA 39-48
SKANDA, PARTS I-XXII, 49-71
VĀMANA 72-73

Volumes Under Preparation

BHAVIṢYA
BRAHMAVAIVARTA
DEVĪBHĀGAVATA
GANESH
KĀLIKĀ
MĀRKAṆḌEYA
MATSYA
VIṢṆU
VIṢṆUDHARMOTTARA

THE VĀMANA-PURĀṆA

PART- I

Translated and annotated by

DR. R. S. SHIVA GANESHA MURTHY

MOTILAL BANARSIDASS PUBLISHERS
PRIVATE LIMITED • DELHI

First Edition: ***Delhi, 2013***

© MOTILAL BANARSIDASS PUBLISHERS PVT. LTD.
ALL RIGHTS RESERVED

ISBN: 978-81-208-3224-4

MOTILAL BANARSIDASS
41 U.A. Bungalow Road, Jawahar Nagar, Delhi 110 007
8 Mahalaxmi Chamber, 22 Bhulabhai Desai Road, Mumbai 400 026
120 Royapettah High Road, Mylapore, Chennai 600 004
236, 9th Main III Block, Jayanagar, Bangaluru 560 011
Sanas Plaza, 1302 Baji Rao Road, Pune 411 002
8 Camac Street, Kolkata 700 017
Ashok Rajpath, Patna 800 004
Chowk, Varanasi 221 001

UNESCO COLLECTION OF REPRESENTATIVE WORKS—*Indian Series*
This book has been accepted in the Indian Translation Series
of the UNESCO Collection of Representative Works,
jointly sponsored by the United Nations Educational,
Scientific and Cultural Organization
(UNESCO) and the Government of India

Printed in India

by RP Jain at NAB Printing Unit,
A-44, Naraina Industrial Area, Phase I, New Delhi–110028
and published by JP Jain for Motilal Banarsidass Publishers (P) Ltd,
41 U.A. Bungalow Road, Jawahar Nagar, Delhi-110007

PUBLISHER'S NOTE

The purest gems lie hidden in the bottom of the ocean or in the depth of rocks. One has to dive into the ocean or delve into the rocks to find them out. Similarly, truth lies concealed in the language which with the passage of time has become obsolete. Man has to learn that language before he discovers that truth.

But he has neither the means nor the leisure to embark on that course. We have, therefore, planned to help him acquire knowledge by an easier course. We have started the series of Ancient Indian Tradition and Mythology in English Translation. Our goal is to universalize knowledge through the most popular international medium of expression. The publication of the Purāṇas in English Translation is a step towards that goal.

Acknowledgement

It is our pleasant duty to put on record our sincere thanks to Dr. R. N. Dandekar and the UNESCO authorities for their kind encouragement and valuable help in the publication of the volumes in this series.

CONTENTS

ABBREVIATIONS

Common and self-evident abbreviations such as Ch(s)—Chapter(s), p—page, pp.—pages, v—verse, vv—verses, Ftn—Footnote, Hist. Ind. Philo.—History of Indian Philosophy are not included in this list.

ABORI	*Annals of the Bhandarkar Oriental Research Institute*, Poona
AGP	S.M. Ali's The Geography of *Purāṇas*, PPH, New Delhi, 1973
AIHT	*Ancient Indian Historical Tradition*, F.E. Pargiter, Motilal Banarsidass (MLBD), Delhi
AITM	*Ancient Indian Tradition and Mythology Series*, MLBD, Delhi
AP	*Agni Purāṇa*, Guru Mandal Edition (GM), Calcutta, 1957
Arch. S. Rep.	*Archaeological Survey Report*
AV	*Atharva Veda*, Svādhyāya Maṇḍal, Aundh
BdP	*Brahmāṇḍa Purāṇa*, MLBD, Delhi 1973
BG	*Bhagavadgītā*
BhP	*Bhāgavata Purāṇa*, Bhagavat Vidyapeeth, Ahmedabad
Br	*Brāhmaṇa* (preceded by name such as Śatapatha)
BsP	*Bhaviṣya Purāṇa*, Vishnu Shastri Bapat, Wai
BVP	*Brahma Vaivarta Purāṇa*, GM, 1955-57
CC	*Caturvarga Cintāmaṇi* by Hemādri
CVS	*Caraṇa Vyūha Sūtra* by Śaunaka, Commentary by Mahīdāsa

DB	*Devī Bhāgavata, GM,* 1960-57
De or GDAMI	*The Geographical Dictionary of Ancient and Mediaeval India,* N.L. De, Oriental Reprint, Delhi, 1971
DhS	*Dharma Sūtra* (preceded by the author's name such as Gautama)
ERE	*Encyclopaedia of Religion and Ethics* by Hastings
GP	*Garuḍa Purāṇa,* ed. R.S. Bhattacharya, Chowkhamba, Varanasi, 1964
GS	*Gṛhya Sūtra* (preceded by the name of the author such as Āpastamba)
HD	*History of Dharma Śāstra,* P.V. Kane, G.O.S.
IA	*The Indian Antiquary*
IHQ	*The Indian Historical Quarterly*
JP	*Purāṇa* (Journal of the Kashiraj Trust), Varanasi
KA	*Kauṭilya Arthaśāstra*
KP	*Kūrma Purāṇa,* Veṅkaṭeśvara Press Edn., Bombay; also Kashiraj Trust Edn., Varanasi, 1971
LP	*Liṅga Purāṇa,* GM, 1960; also MLBD, Delhi, 1981
Manu	*Manusmṛti*
Mbh	*Mahābhārata,* Gītā Press, Gorakhpur, VS 2014
MkP	*Mārkaṇḍeya Purāṇa*
MN	*Mahābhārata Nāmānukramaṇi,* Gita Press, Gorakhpur, VS 2016
MtP	*Matsya Purāṇa,* GM, 1954
MW	Monier Williams' *Sanskrit-English Dictionary,* MLBD, Delhi 1976
NP	*Nāradīya* or *Nārada Purāṇa,* Veṅkaṭeśvara Press, Bombay

PCK	*Bhāratavarṣīya Prācīna Caritrakośa*, Siddheshwar Shastri, Poona, 1968
PdP	*Padma Purāṇa*, GM, 1957-59
PE	*Purāṇic Encyclopaedia*, V. Mani, English version, MLBD, Delhi, 1975
PR or PRHRC	*Puranic Records on Hindu Rites and Customs*, R.C. Hazra, Calcutta, 1948
ṚV	*Ṛg-Veda*, Svādhyāya Maṇḍal, Aundh
Śat Br	*Śatapatha Brāhmaṇa*
SC or SMC	*Smṛti Candrikā* by Devanna Bhaṭṭa
SEP	*Studies in Epics and Purāṇas*, A.D. Psalkar, Bharatiya Vidya Bhavan (BVB), Bombay
SkP	*Skanda Purāṇa*
SP	*Śiva Purāṇa*
VāP	*Vāyu Purāṇa*
VR	*Vālmīki Rāmāyaṇa*
VdP	*Viṣṇudharmottara Purāṇa*
VmP	*Vāmana Purāṇa*
VP	*Viṣṇu Purāṇa*
VrP	*Varāha Purāṇa*

INTRODUCTION

Vāmana is assigned fourteenth position in the list of eighteen *Mahāpurāṇas* or major Purāṇic texts, preceded by *Skanda* and succeeded by *Kūrma.* It gets its name after Vāmana or the dwarf incarnation of God Viṣṇu, which is the first human incarnation preceded by the "Fish", "Tortoise", "Boar" and "Man-Lion" incarnations that can, by the way, be seen as corresponding to the earlier stages of the evolution of life on the earth, the main purpose of the *Purāṇa* being a description of the legend of the demon Bali, grandson of Prahlāda, the Viṣṇu devotee *par excellence,* suffering a great discomfiture due to a very tactful manoeuvre resorted by God Viṣṇu as the dwarf.

The extant text of *Vāmana* has 95 chapters and approximately 6,000 *ślokas,* though *Bhāgavata* and some other *Purāṇas* state that *Vāmana* had an *Uttarabhāga* also containing four *Saṁhitās* of 1000 *ślokas* each, which, however, has not been discovered so far.

Pulastya and Nārada are the interlocutors of the *Purāṇa.* In the beginning Nārada questions Pulastya about the assumption of the form of Vāmana by Viṣṇu, waging of war by Prahlāda against gods, Satī's agreement to be the wife of Śiva, Satī's self-immolation at the *yajña* of Dakṣa and her being reborn as the daughter of Himālaya with a desire of becoming the spouse of Śaṅkara, the glory of the places of pilgrimage, account of *dāna, vrata, upāsanā,* etc.

As the title indicates, this *Purāṇa* has mainly a Vaiṣṇava theme but Śaiva material also forms an integral part of it, e.g. Śiva's killing of the demon Andhaka, marriage of Śiva and Pārvatī, birth of Gaṇeśa and Kārttikeya, defeat of

Mahiṣāsura by Devī, glorification of *Śivaliṅgas* and their installation.

The legends, stories and episodes included in this *Purāṇa* are generally of the same type as found in other *Purāṇas.* Here we may call attention to some noteworthy features of the *Purāṇa.* One is that it was composed in the Kurukṣetra region of North India, to the glorification of which it gives special attention, particularly to the *tīrthas,* rivers, hills and other geographical features of the area.

Secondly, the *Purāṇa* gives equal prominence to Vaiṣṇavism and Pāśupata Śaiva-sect in its description and exhibits a spirit of tolerance and magnanimity in its treatment of both, as is evidenced in its representation of Śiva as saying, "Ẹven if you cuṭ me into twain, you will find the presence of Viṣṇu in my heart" (67.37), and of Viṣṇu as telling the *Devas,* "Śiva is present here in my heart in the form of *Liṅga* where you may worship him" (62.21-23).

Thirdly, a very much noteworthy feature of this *Purāṇa* is the preponderance of the *asura* motif. No other *Purāṇa* gives the accounts of so many *asura* heroes in so liberal and zestful manner as this *Purāṇa* does. So many *asuras* are represented in an edifying way as following the ideals of *Dharma,* righteousness, e.g. Prahlāda, a great devotee of Viṣṇu and his grandson Bali who, despite the warning given by the preceptor Śukrācārya, prominently exhibits the spirit of a liberal donor and quite unmindful of his personal interest ungrudgingly accepts underworld status to which he is reduced by God Viṣṇu. Perhaps one of the reasons is that the narrator of the *Purāṇa* is Pulastya, the grandfather of demon Rāvaṇa.

As to the date of the *Purāṇa,* it was some time between 5th and 10th centuries CE, probably the first half of the seventh century CE when Harṣavardhana was the king in North and Mahendravarman Pallava in the South, when the assimilative spirit, religious tolerance and the intellectual fertility characterising the Gupta Age permeated the society.

As to the contents of the *Purāṇa,* it is found that in addition to the legends, myths, stories, etc. of the gods, *asuras, ṛṣis,* etc. which belong to the *Purāṇas* generally *Vāmana* is rich in the description of pilgrimage centres, i.e. *tīrthas,* in the stotras or eulogies to the gods, geographical materials, description of the mountains, rivers, Janapadas, etc. Here we make a brief survey of more interesting items of the contents—

Chapter 6 mentions four schools of Śaivism, viz. *Śaiva, Pāśupata, Kāladamana* and *Kāpālika.* The *Kāladamana* sect is better known by the name *Kālāmukha.*

Chapter 7 has a short inset showing the birth of the nymph Urvaśī from the thigh of Nārāyaṇa, the *ṛṣis* who together with another one, Nara, was performing penance in Himālayas.

Chapter 9 describes the vehicles of the different gods as follows:

Indra	- White elephant
Yama	- Bufallo named Pauṇḍraka
Varuṇa	- Śiśumāra
Kubera	- Nara
Eleven Rudras	- White bulls
Candramā	- Haṁsa
Twelve Ādityas	- Chariots yoked with horses and camels
Eight Vasus	- Elephant
Yakṣa	- Nara
Kinnara	- Serpent
Twin Aśvins	- Horse
Maruts	- Antelope
Bhṛgus	- Parrot
Gandharvas	- Walking on foot

Twelve kinds of *dharmas* are described in chapter 11 including that of humans in whose case it is self-study of *Vedas, Brahmacarya, Dāna, Yajña, Compassion,* etc. and devotion to Viṣṇu, Śiva, Sūrya and Devī. The seven continents (*Dvīpas*) of the Earth are also described, the seventh, Puṣkara Dvīpa, contains 21 hells (*narakas*).

Chapter 12 gives a list of bests (*Pravara-sūcī*) in the case of 56 classes of deities, mountains, etc. naming, e.g. *Matsya Purāṇa* as the best among *Purāṇas, Kuru-Jāṅgala* as the best of *kṣetras,* Pṛthūdaka as the best of tīrthas, etc.

Chapter 13 gives nine geographical divisions of Bhāratavarṣa, which is the name of what we now call greater India. Eight islands, several *Kula-parvatas, Varṣa-parvatas* and *Viṣkambha-parvatas* and 21 hills are also described. Rivers are classified according to their sources. *Janapadas* (political units) of the seven divisions of the country constitute a long list.

Various *Dharmas* including *Sāmānya* and *Āśrama Dharmas* are discussed in chapter 14. They include rules of health and hygiene, purification, food, clothing, ethical and social conduct, *Śrāddha,* worship of gods, performance of Sandhyā, etc. in daily routine.

In chapter 17 the birth of Mahiṣāsura, that of Raktabīja and of Kātyāyanī Durgā are described. The episode of the Vindhya Mountain, bowing to Ṛṣi Agastya, is also related. The death of Mahiṣāsura is described in chapter 20.

Chapter 21 describes the story of Saṁvaraṇa, son of *Ṛkṣa* who lived in *Kṛtayuga,* and of his marriage with Tapatī, daughter of Sūrya, and of the birth, from their wedlock, of Kuru, the king after whom the place is named as Kurukṣetra. It is also explained why it is called Dharmakṣetra.

Chapter 32 has a description of the Vedic river *Sarasvatī* in Kurukṣetra, its source and *Māhātmya.* Its source is given as *Plakṣa* or *Plakṣa-Prasravaṇa,* i.e., the glacial water-flow of *Plakṣa.*

Chapter 33 describes the source of Sarasvatī in Kurukṣetra. She came to Avantika which was in Pṛthūdaka. After sanctifying Kurukṣetra by her waters she took a westerly course to meet the western sea.

The region between *Sarasvatī* and *Dṛśadvatī,* another great river which forms the southern boundary of Kurukṣetra, was known as *Brahmāvarta.*

Chapter 34 gives the names of seven forests and seven rivers of Kurukṣetra. The forests are: *Kāmyaka Vana, Aditi Vana, Vyāsa Vana, Phalakī Vana, Sūrya Vana, Madhu Vana and Puṇyaśīta Vana.* The rivers are: *Sarasvatī, Vaitaraṇī, Āpagā, Amlu Nadī, Kauśikī, Dṛśadvatī* and *Hiraṇvatī.*

Chapters 35-37 give accounts of various *tīrthas* of Kurukṣetra, their glory and their efficacy. The *tīrtha* named Brahmodumbara is associated with the penances of Brahmā and the seven *ṛṣis.*

Chapter 38 contains the episode of sage Maṅkaṇa, his ecstatic dance on seeing the sap of plants issuing forth from his injured hand, his being humbled by Śiva, etc.

Chapter 40 relates the story of rivalry between Viśvāmitra and Vasiṣṭha, of the water of *Sarasvatī* getting polluted by the curse of the former and of purity restored to it by the water of river *Aruṇā* made to flow into it.

Chapter 46 gives a detailed account of the numerous *Śiva-liṅgas* installed in *Kurukṣetra.*

Chapter 47 gives an account of the heretic activities of king Vena, son of Ikṣvāku, and his being killed by infuriated Ṛṣis and of his son Pṛthu who, by contrast, was a righteous king.

Chapters 52-53 give a detailed account of the marriage of Śiva and Pārvatī and a reference to the amusing interlude of Brahmā's losing his self-control and getting impassioned by the beauty of Pārvatī and the consequent birth of Vālakhilyas.

In chapter 61 subsequent to the narration of a number of interesting episodes of Raktabīja, Ṛtadhvaja, Gālava, Pātālaketu, Madālasā, Viśvāvasu, Andhakāsura, etc. we come across Brahmā's new exposition of 21 hells, each of which comprises one or more moral lapses like calumny, unbelief, deserting one's *dharma*, greediness, etc. All these are collectively named as Puṁnāma Naraka.

Here Sanatkumāra brothers are shown as sons of *dharma* and *ahiṁsā* rather than those of Brahmā whose mental sons (*Mānasa Putras*) they are traditionally known to be.

In chapter 69 demon Andhaka assumes the guise of Śiva to seduce Pārvatī but he fails to get her as Pārvatī soon discovers the fraud and conceals herself in the white flower of *arka* plant. In this chapter Mātali, the charioteer of Indra, is said to have Śamīka as his father.

In chapter 70 the birth of a girl from the perspiration appearing on the forehead of Śiva during his fight with Andhaka is described, who becomes goddess Carcikā, the presiding deity of Mount Hiṅgula in Baluchistan. Andhaka is killed by Śiva and made his Gaṇa and named Bhṛṅgin.

Chapter 73 describes the death of Asura Kālanemi at the hands of Indra and chapter 74 shows *asuras* reorganised under the leadership of Bāṇa who defeats the *Devas* and consequently Bali becomes Indra, Bāṇa becomes Yama, Maya becomes Varuṇa, Rāhu Soma, Ketu Sūrya and Śukra Bṛhaspati. At the request of Bali, Prahlāda expounds the duties of a worthy king, protection of the people being his supreme duty. The *Purāṇa* describes Bali as a perfect model of a king, though an *asura* by race, who established a kingdom of perfect righteousness following the ideals of Bhāgavata *Dharma.* Thereafter we find an account of Prahlāda's *Tīrthayātrā.*

Chapter 82 gives an account of Viṣṇu's weapon *Sudarśana Cakra* which is said to have been given by Śiva, whose twelve spokes are said to represent twelve gods.

Chapters 85-88 contain four *Stotras,* viz. *Gajendramokṣa, Sarasvatī-Stotra,* and two *Pāpapraśamana Stotras*—one recited by Śiva to Viṣṇu and another recited by Agastya to Viṣṇu.

Chapter 90 gives a long list of Viṣṇu Pīṭhas, 127 in number, which are designated as *Mahālayas.*

Chapter 93 renders the finale consisting of a *stotra* in prose recited by Brahmā glorifying the Vāmana form of God Viṣṇu.

—G.P. BHATT

VĀMANA PURĀṆA

CHAPTER ONE

Sportive Hara

[*Oṁ, salutation to* Śrī Gaṇeśa! *Salutation to Goddess* Sarasvatī! *Oṁ, salutation to God* Vāsudeva!]

1. Obeisance to the Lord of gods having the form of Vāmana (dwarf) who captured from Bali the sovereignty over the three worlds and gave it to Indra.

2. *Ṛṣi* Pulastya, the best of the learned, was resting in his hermitage. Nārada inquired of him about the Purāṇa related to Vāmana.

Nārada said:

3. O Brāhmaṇa ! How did Bhagavān Viṣṇu, the almighty, assume the form of Vāmana (*dwarf*) in the bygone age? Please tell me; I am eager to know.

4. How could indeed Prahlāda, the best of *Daityas,* being a devotee of Viṣṇu, fight against gods ? I have a serious doubt in this regard.

5. It is said, O you the foremost amongst the twice-born! that Satī, the beautiful daughter of Dakṣa, was the beloved wife of Śaṅkara.

6-7. Why did she of lovely form abandon her body and take birth in the house of Himavān, the great Lord of mountains ? And again why did the auspicious one become the wife of the Lord of lords? Please clear this doubt of mine. You are, I know, omniscient.

8. O most pious one amongst the twice-born ! Kindly relate to me the greatness of holy places (*tīrthas*) and of gifts and the procedure of the various vows (*vratas*) as well, O twice-born.

9. Having been asked (thus) by Nārada, the most pious sage Pulastya, the foremost of speakers, spoke to Nārada, rich in penance.

Pulastya said:

10. I will relate to you the Vāmana Purāṇa in due sequence, from beginning to end, O most pious sage ! Listen to me with rapt attention.

11. Formerly, seeing the onset of summer season, Haimavatī Devī (the daughter of Himavān) said to Maheśvara, residing on Mandāra mountain—

Devī said:

12. Summer has set in, O lord of gods ! But I do not have a house in which we two can stay and pass the hot summer-wind and blazing sunshine.

13. Having been told (thus) by Bhavānī, Śaṅkara replied: "O lovely lady! I am a shelterless one, you know, and I always roam about in forest, O auspicious one."

Pulastya said:

14. When told thus by Śaṅkara, Satī spent that summer season along with Śaṅkara under the shades of trees, O Nārada !

15. Following the summer, came the wonderful, boisterous rainy season darkening all the quarters with clouds and making (the roads) bereft of people.

16. Observing the advent of such a rainy season, Satī, the daughter of Dakṣa, lovingly said to the Lord of gods—

Satī (Devī) said:

17. O Maheśa ! Strong winds are blowing and thundering clouds break my heart; lightnings are flashing among black clouds and peacocks are giving out shrill cries.

18. Torrents of rain are falling from the sky and herons and cranes are going after clouds. The flowers of *Kadamba, Sarja, Arjuna* and *Ketakī* trees are being shed by wind.

19. Swans abandon the lakes the moment they hear the loud thunder of clouds just as the virtuous ones give up their abodes, though well established, when threatened by the vicious.

20-21. O Śambhu ! These herds of deer are making haste; they are running (hither and thither) and enjoying. They are running about happily in the jungles. Due to the opulence of the clouds, the earth shines with fresh green plants and bushes spread over. So also the lightnings are flashing a lot, indeed, seeing the abundance of blackness (dirt) in the enchanting dark clouds, O Lord !

22-23. The daring ones are moving about in boats and rafts. And the rivers have become instantaneously fast, O Lord ! Charming-with-the-head-marked-by-moon; it is no surprise that women accompanied by base persons approach only those who are not bright. The sky is overcast with dark clouds. The *Sarja* trees (are completely laid) with the flowers. The *Nīpa* trees (are hidden under) buds and the *Śrī* (*Bilva*) trees (are concealed by) fruits, and the rivers (are full of) water.

24. The big lakes (are covered by) lotus leaves and flowers. The rainy season is now difficult to bear with. In such a formidable and awful but wonderful season, I entreat you, O Śaṅkara !

25. Please arrange for a house on this beautiful mountain that makes me quite at ease.

Having heard these words pleasing to the ear, the Three-eyed Lord said thus—

Śaṅkara said:

26. I do not have the money to set a house, O dear one ! You see, I am wearing tiger's skin on my body. I have the Lord of snakes as my upper garment. The serpents Padma and Piṅgala are my ear-ornaments.

27. Snake Kambala is one of my armlets and snake Dhanañjaya is another. So also snake Aśvatara is the bracelet on my left and Takṣaka on the right. Snake Nīla, black as collyrium, is well set as the girdle.

Pulastya said:

28. Having heard these significant but harsh words of Śaṅkara, Mṛḍānī was frightened though (she knew) she heard a falsehood. With downcast eyes and hot sighs of anger and bashfulness, she chastised her Lord for his inability to construct a house.

Devī said:

29. What! Having resorted to you, am I to spend the rainy season like this under a tree? O eternal one ! Please give me a reasonable reply.

Śaṅkara said:

30. You can well pass the rainy season sitting over the clouds in such a way that the rain drops do not fall on your body.

Pulastya said:

31. Then Hara along with the daughter of Dakṣa, climbed over the part of the cloud that rose high. From then onwards, Maheśvara came to be known as *Jīmūtaketu* (cloud-bannered) in the heaven.

CHAPTER TWO

The Birth and Disappearance of Nara

Pulastya said:

1. The three-eyed Lord thus spent the rainy season on the clouds and then set in the enjoyable autumn giving delight to one and all, O sage !

2. Dark clouds disappeared from the sky; herons left the trees; rivers withdrew from the (high) banks; lotuses gave out their scent; crows went out of their nests; Ruru deer shed its horn; and lakes became free from turbidity.

3. The aquatic flowers bloomed; moonlight shone and creepers became lovely with fine flowers. The herds of already happy kine rejoiced and the virtuous felt happy.

4. The lotus in the ponds, the stars in the sky, the water of the lakes, the minds of pious people and the beams of the moon got brighter along with the quarters of the sky.

5. During such a season, Hara taking along Satī who was staying on the backside of the clouds, arrived on the stately mountain Mandāra.

6. Staying on the top of the Mandāra mountain with flattened rock surface, that resplendent Lord Śambhu dallied with Satī.

7. As the autumn marched on and Keśava woke up(from sleep), Dakṣa, the foremost lord of beings, began organising a grandiose sacrifice.

8. He invited the twelve *Ādityas* as well as Indra and other worthy gods including Kaśyapa and made them superintending priests of the sacrifice.

9. He also invited Vasiṣṭha of commended vows, along with Arundhatī, Atri with Anasūyā and Kauśika with Dhṛti.

10-11. O Brāhmaṇa ! Dakṣa invited Gautama with Ahalyā, Bharadvāja with Amāyā and also sage Aṅgiras with Candrā and made these virtuous scholars well-versed in *Vedas* and *Vedāṅgas*, the superintending priests in the sacrificial rite.

12. Having summoned *Dharma* with his wife *Ahiṁsā*, he directed him to guard the door of the sacrificial hall.

13-14. He employed Ariṣṭanemi as the supplier of sacrificial fuel, and, O Brāhmaṇa ! Dakṣa justly appointed Aṅgiras and his wife Candrā to be in charge of preparation of food and drinks and he rightly engaged Bhṛgu to look after the arrangement of *sattra*.

15. That Prajāpati entrusted the administration of funds to the honest Moon-god along with Rohiṇī.

16. He sent for all his daughters and sons-in-law and their children except (his daughter) Satī along with Śaṅkara, (to attend) the sacrifice.

Nārada said:

17. Why is it that Maheśvara, the Lord of wealth, though the seniormost, worthiest, pre-eminent and the foremost one, was not invited by Prajāpati ?

Pulastya said:

18. Though Lord Śiva is the seniormost, worthiest, pre-eminent and foremost one, he was not invited by Dakṣa who considered him as *Kapālin*, or skull-bearer.

Nārada said:

19. Why did the three-eyed Lord, the trident-bearer, the most worthy of the gods, become a skull-bearer ? For what action did Lord Śaṅkara come to be called so ?

Pulastya said:

20. Listen with attention to this story of yore. It was narrated by Brahmā of unmanifest form in the *Ādipurāṇa*.

21. In the (remote) past when there was only water all around, all the movable and immovable things were destroyed; there was neither the Moon nor the Sun nor the stars; wind and fire too had vanished.

22. Nothing could be distinguished nor could anything be ascertained; there was nothing like existence or non-existence; all vegetation was submerged; it was pitch dark all the time.

23. During (that) night (lasting for) a thousand years, that Lord was sleeping (alone). At the end of the night, he assumed *rājasika* form and created the universe.

24. He (of *rājasika* form), a thorough master of *Veda* and *Vedāṅgas*, the awe-inspiring creator of this mobile and immobile universe, shone with five heads.

25. In the same way, another one endowed predominantly with *Tamas*, three-eyed, trident-bearing, having matted hair and wearing a rosary, manifested.

26. Then the great soul created the frightful egoism by which those two gods, Brahmā and Śaṅkara themselves were engrossed.

27. Enveloped by egoism, Rudra told the Grand-sire: "Who are you coming here ? Tell me, by whom were you created?"

28. Brahmā, who was (also) egoistic then answered, "Who are you? You better tell me, who is your father or mother."

29. Thus, in days of yore, there ensued between those two–Brahmā and Śiva–mutual accusation liked by both. At that time, there was your birth.

30. But, as soon as you were born, you soared into the sky, carrying the peerless *vīṇā* and making joyous sounds.

31. Śambhu was defeated by the proud son of (primordial) Brahmā and he stood with his face downcast, dull like the eclipsed Moon.

32. When the lord of the universe was defeated by the honourable Parameṣṭhī, his fifth face told Rudra blind with fury—

33. "I assert, O three-eyed one endowed with *Tamas* ! you shall go about naked riding on a bull and be destroyer of the world."

34. So told by Brahmā, the birthless Śaṅkara desirous of burning him down, stared at him furiously with fearsome eyes.

35. Then the five faces of the three-eyed God also got manifested; they were resplendent and dreadful and were white, red, golden yellow, blue and brown (in colour).

36. Looking at the (new) faces (shining) like the Sun, Brahmā said these words to Rudra: "Bubbles appear on the water that is stirred. Will there be any strength in them?"

37. Hearing it, the enraged great Śaṅkara cut off with the tip of his nail, that head of Brahmā which uttered the censure.

38. That severed head fell on the left hand of Śaṅkara only and the head did never fall away from his palm.

39-40. Then the furious Brahmā of wonderful feat created a mighty and deathless youth, who was intelligent, armoured, decorated with earrings and carrying arrows, who was as brilliant as the Sun, and having four arms carrying a bow, arrows, a spear and a large quiver.

41. He, however, said: "Get away you wicked trident-bearer, I do not slay you. You are tainted by sin. Who does like to kill a sinner ?"

42-43. Śaṅkara told so by that noble soul, then went along with his beloved, to Badarikā hermitage, the abode of Nara and Nārāyaṇa in Himālaya where the excellent holy Sarasvatī river flows.

44. And having gone there, he saw Nārāyāṇa and said: "O Lord ! Please grant me my entreaty. You are very compassionate."

45. Thus asked by Rudra, the son of Brāhmaṇa spoke: "O Maheśvara ! Strike (my) left arm with (your) trident."

46. Having heard the words of Nārāyaṇa, Maheśvara forcibly struck his (Nārāyaṇa's) left arm with the trident.

47. From the scars where the trident had struck, three streams flowed out. One of them resorted to the sky adorned by the stars.

48. The second (stream) fell on to the earth and was received by the great ascetic Atri; from that portion of Śaṅkara, was born Durvāsa.

49-50. The third stream fell on the awesome skull. From it was born a child (who at once grew into) a youth in armour, who was of black complexion, and equipped with bow and arrows in hand, (who) spoke thus thundering like clouds in the rainy season: "Whose head shall I chop off from the neck like a palmyra fruit ?"

51. Recognising him as the one born of Nārāyaṇa's arm, Śaṅkara spoke: "O man ! Vanquish the abusing son of Brahmā as shining as a hundred suns."

52. Addressed thus by Śaṅkara, that hero took the well-known primeval bow, Ajagava, as well as the inexhaustible quiver and he made up his mind for the battle.

53. Afterwards, the mighty ones–Brahmā's son and the arm-born Śarva–had a tough fight for a thousand divine years. Then Brahmā was told by Hara—

Hara said:

54. O Brahmā ! This person of remarkable divine feat has conquered your mighty son hitting him with formidable arrows. Indeed it is a remarkable feat (to which) only the ten directions (bear) witness.

55. Brahmā replied to Śaṅkara: "O Śambhu ! There is no (defeat) here in the life of this unassailable one. But this your man imagines to have defeated my man who is a great soul."

56. So saying to the three-eyed God, Brahmā threw his man into the sun. Then the Lord threw (his) man (also) into the body of Nara, the son of Dharma.

CHAPTER THREE

Dialogue between Hari and Hara

Pulastya said:

1. Then, O Brāhmaṇa ! Rudra was distressed with his senses confused due to the worry caused by the presence of the horrible skull sticking to his palm.

2. The dreadful demoness Brahmahatyā shining like a lump of collyrium and formidable with red hairs, approached Hara.

3. Having seen that repulsive woman approaching him, Hara asked, "Who are you? And for what purpose have you come here ? Tell me that."

4. The dreadful brahmahatyā then told the skull-bearer: "O Three-eyed One ! I, Brahmahatyā, have come to you, admit me."

5. So saying these words, Brahmahatyā entered that Rudra, the trident-bearer, whose body was much tormented.

6. Śarva overpowered by Brahmahatyā came to the hermitage at Badarikā. But there he did not find the sages—Nara and Nārāyaṇa.

7. Not seeing the two sons of Dharma, the worried and sorrowful Śiva proceeded to Yamunā to take a plunge; but she (the river), on the other hand, became dry.

8. Having observed the waters of Yamunā dried up, the Bull-bannered One went to the Plakṣajā (river) to bathe. But she (Plakṣajā) went out of sight.

9. Then roaming aimlessly in the forests of *Puṣkara, Magadha* and *Saindhava,* he (Śiva) was much tired.

10. Īśvara also went to Naimiśāraṇya and Dharmāraṇya and took bath there. The terrible Brahmahatyā, however, did not leave him.

11. Though the Bull-bannered One took ablutions in rivers and sacred pools, and meditated in hermitages and holy temples everywhere, he could not get rid of the sin.

12. The dejected Śaṅkara then went to Kurujāṅgala. Having gone there, he saw the discus-bearer (Viṣṇu) sitting on the bird (Garuḍa).

13. Having seen the lotus-eyed one wielding the conch, discus and mace, Hara joining his hands in obeisance addressed this eulogy.

Hara said:

14. O Lord of gods! salutations to you. O Garuḍa-bannered One ! Salutations to you. O Vāsudeva ! O wielder of conch, discus and mace! Salutations to you.

15. O attributeless and infinite one ! Salutations to you who are the creator beyond doubt. I bow to you who do not depend on knowledge or ignorance but are depended upon by all.

16. Obeisance to you, O one endowed with Rajas ! O eternal one ! O embodiment of Brāhmaṇa ! By you, O Lord! all this movable and immovable universe is created.

17. O one steeped in Sattva ! O Lord of the worlds! O embodiment of Viṣṇu ! O Adhokṣaja ! O protector of people! O mighty one ! O Janārdana ! Obeisance to you.

18. I am indeed born of anger, a part of yourself, O embodiment of Tamas ! I am overpowered by (that Tamas) guṇa, O omnipresent lord of gods ! Obeisance to you.

19. You are this earth, O Lord of the universe ! (you are) waters, ether, fire, wind, intellect, mind and night as well. Salutations to you.

20. You are righteousness; you are sacrifice, penance, truth, non-violence, purity, straightforwardness, forbearance, benevolence, compassion, wealth and celibacy and you are the overlord.

21. You are the four *Vedas* as well as their auxiliaries; you are the one to be known (from the Veda) and you are the master of the (entire) *Veda*; you are the Upaveda; O Lord ! you are everything. Salutations to you.

22. Salutations to you, O endless one ! O wielder of discus. Salutations to you who (assumed) the form of the *Dwarf* and the *Fish.* I know you are the (only) compassionate one in (this) world. O Keśava ! (Kindly) relieve me from the clutches of the sin.

23. Please wipe out the inauspiciousness tugging on to my body which is possessed by Brahmahatyā. I acted in haste. I am (now) tormented and I am undone. Please purify me. You are the benefactor. Obeisance to you !

Pulastya said:

24. Thus eulogized by the great Śaṅkara, Lord Viṣṇu, Cakrapāṇi, spoke those words to destroy Brahmahatyā.

Hari said:

25. O Maheśvara ! Listen to these my words pleasing to the ears, capable of wiping out Brahmahatyā and bestowing favour and enhancing merit.

26. He who is changeless and a manifestation of one of my aspects, ever resides in Prayāga and is well-known in this meritorious universe as one lying-down-in-meditation (yogaśāyin).

27. From his right foot has emerged a laudable stream well-known as Varṇa which washes off sins and is auspicious.

28. From the other foot, another stream widely known as Asī (has flown out). Both the excellent rivers have been honoured by all the people.

29. That land between them is the holy land of *Yogaśāyin,* the most prominent sacred spot in the three worlds, the remover of all sins.

30-31. Such is the auspicious city of Vārāṇasī in which, O Īśa ! Even those who indulge in sensual pleasures attain oneness with you, (the city) in which wanton women again and again laugh at the noble Brahmaṇas who due to the jingling of their (women's) girdles, err in vedic recitation which the teachers correct.

32. Observing the lac-red feet of the ladies walking in the squares of this (city), the Moon wonders whether a hibiscus (flower) is moving out.

33. (In this city) the lofty temples with their long and beautiful banners wafting in the wind obstruct the (path of) the Moon during nights and that of the Sun too during day time.

34. (In this city) the bees enticed by the bright lotus-like face of the women reflected in the marble walls (of the buildings), do not go to any other flower due to confusion.

35. (In this city) no fatigue oppresses the men overcome by amorous play nor the ladies assembled for water sports in private pools, O Śambhu !

36. (In this city) O Śambhu ! None encroaches the house of others except the air; nor do (the men) show the force of their strength against women except, of course, during amorous play.

37. (In this city) tying with ropes is done to bull-elephants (only); stoppage of *dāna* happens in the case of discharge of ichor (only); the people and the elephants have pride and infatuation respectively in the prime of their youth (only).

38. O Lord ! Only the owls and not people, are ever fond of darkness; (only) the group of stars have akulīnatva (not being earth-bound); loss of form (shape) happens in the case of clouds (only).

39. (In this city) sportive women resemble you, O Śaṅkara, in that they are very fond of *Bhūti* (wealth/ash); they embellish their bodies with *Sandal* (camphor/moon); and they are surrounded by *Bhujaṅgas* (paramours/serpents).

40. O Lord of gods ! In my hermitage in such a city, Vārāṇasī, there dwells the venerable Sun called Lola, able to wash off sins.

41. By resorting to that place which is called *Daśāśvamedha* and where Keśava, a part of myself, dwells, O greatest of gods ! You shall be cleansed of the sin.

42. Having been told so by the Garuḍa-bannered one, that bull-bannered one bowed down to him and rushed, like *Garuḍa,* to Vārāṇasī for clearing himself of the stain.

43. Having reached that sacred city, the beautiful place of pilgrimage, he visited Lola and *Daśāśvamedha.* After bathing in the sacred pools, he, free from sin, went to see Keśava.

44-45. Having seen Keśava, Śaṅkara bowed down to him and said thus: "O Hṛṣīkeśa ! By your grace, Brahmahatyā is wiped out. (But) O supreme god ! This skull does not leave my hand. I do not know the reason for this. You please tell me that."

Pulaṣtya said:

46. Having heard the words of Mahādeva, Keśava said thus: "It has a reason, Son ! I will tell you all that.

47. This divine pool covered with lotuses and lilies, that (you see) in front of me, is the best of all holy places and is sacred; it is respected by *Devas* and *Gandharvas.*

48. You take ceremonial ablution in this foremost sacred (pool). Even as you bathe here, the skull will fall away.

49. Then and onwards, O Rudra ! You become well-known as *Skull-bearer* in the world and this sacred pool will come to be called *Kapāla-mocana* or *Skull-reliever.*"

Pulastya said:

50. Told so by Keśava, the supreme deity, Maheśvara took ablution in the *Kapāla-mocana* (pool) in accordance with the Vedic rite.

51. As the Destroyer-of-theThree-Cities bathed in the sacred pool, the skull fell off his palm. That foremost pool came to be known *Kapāla-mocana* then onwards with the blessings of the Lord.

CHAPTER FOUR

The Valour of Hara

Pulastya said:

1. That was how Lord Hara became 'skull-bearer', O divine sage ! For this reason, he was not invited by Dakṣa.

2. In the meanwhile, Jayā, the daughter of Gautama, came to the Mandāra mountain of beautiful valleys, to see Devī.

3. Noticing that Jayā had come alone, Satī asked: "Why did not Vijayā, Jayantī and Aparājitā come (with you)?"

4-8. Having heard the words of Satī, she (Jayā) said: "O supreme goddess ! All of them have gone on invitation to the sacrifice of our grandfather along with our father Gautama as well as our mother Ahalyā. I am eager to go there and have come to see you.

Are you and Lord Maheśvara not going there? Are you not invited by your father? Or will you proceed presently ?

All the sages and their spouses as well as all gods, all aunts (sisters of mother) and Moon with his wife have left for the sacrifice.

All beings, movable and immovable, in all the fourteen worlds have been invited to the sacrifice. Haven't you been invited ?"

Pulastya said:

9. Satī hearing Jayā's words which struck her like a thunderbolt, fell dead then and there overpowered by wrath, O Brahmaṇa !

10. Seeing Satī dead, Jayā was furious and sorrowful. Shedding tears, she wailed bitterly.

11. Having heard that outcry, the Three-eyed God, the trident-bearer, came near Jayā asking, "What goes on there?"

12. When he approached Jayā, he saw Satī Devī fallen on the ground with limbs thrown out like a creeper cut off the plant (support) with an axe.

13. Beholding the fallen Devī, Śaṅkara asked Jayā— "How did Satī fall on the ground like a creeper chopped down?"

14-15. Jayā, hearing Śaṅkara's question, replied thus— "Learning the scorn shown to herself in the context of (Dakṣa's) sacrifice (to which) her sisters along with their husbands and Ādityas as well as Indra and other gods in the three worlds (had been invited), this my aunt broke down with intense mental grief."

Pulastya said:

16. When Rudra heard those harsh words, he was overpowered by anger. Flames of fire were emitted from all parts of Rudra's body.

17. Then due to the fury of the Three-eyed God, O sage! were born lion-faced *Gaṇas* led by Vīrabhadra, who sprang from the hairs (of his body).

18. Surrounded by the *Gaṇas,* (Śaṅkara went) from Mandāra to (the place) called *Himasā;* from there to *Kanakhala;* from there to the place where Dakṣa was performing the sacrifice.

19. Then, O sage ! The leader of the *Gaṇas,* the mighty Vīrabhadra stood wielding a spear in western and northern quarters.

20. Brandishing a mace in hand, the furious Jayā, stood on eastern and southern quarters. In the midst of the great sacrifice, stood the enraged Śarva (Śaṅkara) with trident in hand.

21. Noticing the lion-faced (Vīrabhadra), Indra and other gods, sages and *Gandharvas,* pondered as to what it could be.

22. At that time, the door-keeper dharma with a bow and arrows like venomous snakes confronted Vīrabhadra.

23-24. The *Gaṇa*-leader, seeing dharma rushing on him all of a sudden, took the thunderbolt-like trident in one of his hands; in another, he took the bow; in the third, arrows and in the fourth, a mace and the *Gaṇa*(-leader) attacked dharma.

25-26. The imperishable dharma, noticing the chief of the *Gaṇas* having four arms, stood with eight arms wielding various weapons—a sword, a shield, a mace, a dart (barbed missile), an axe, a goad, a bow and arrows. Carrying these, he stood desirous of killing the *Gaṇa*-leader.

27. The enraged *Gaṇa*-leader too like a cloud during rainy season, showered sharp arrows on the eternal dharma to kill him.

28. O sage ! Those two mighty ones wielding bows and arrows, with their bodies red with the smear of blood, shone like a *Kiṁśuka* (tree).

29. O great seer ! Dharma woefully retired after being vigorously and forcibly defeated with excellent arms by the Leader of *Gaṇas* in the battle. And Vīrabhadra entered into the area of the sacrifice.

30. Seeing the *Gaṇa*-leader, Vīrabhadra, enter the sacrificial area, the gods stood up immediately with their weapons, O sage !

31-34. The eight *Vasus*, the unassailable nine *Grahas*, Indra and others, the twelve *Ādityas*, the eleven *Rudras*, *Viśvedevas*, *Sādhyas*, *Siddhas*, *Gandharvas*, *Pannagas*, *Yakṣas*, *Kiṁpuruṣas*, *Bhūtas*, *Khagas*, *Cakradharas* as well as the various famous kings of the *Vaivasvata* family, those born of the Lunar family, those kings of Bhoja's fame, the sons of Diti, the sons of Danu, and all others who had assembled there—all of them with their weapons raised, encountered the terrible Vīrabhadra.

35. The *Gaṇa* quickly rushed on them with bow and arrows and fiercely attacked them all with a shower of arrows.

36. They discharged a rain of countless missiles on the *Gaṇa*-chief. He too cut them and pierced them (gods and others) with the best missiles.

37. The gods and others, having been hit incessantly with arrows and missiles by the great Vīrabhadra, preferred to flee.

38. The *Gaṇa*-chief went into the middle of the spacious sacrificial hall where he dissuaded the sages from offering oblations.

39. Seeing the lion-faced *Gaṇa,* the great sages were terror-stricken. They gave up the sacrificial rite, and sought refuge in Acyuta (Viṣṇu).

40. That discus-bearer God seeing the noble sages who were afflicted and terrified, said that they had no need to fear and stood up with his excellent weapon.

41. Then bending his Śārṅga bow, he discharged on Vīrabhadra venomous snake-like arrows capable of tearing off the armour.

42. But those efficient arrows of Hari reached his body and without hurting him fell down to the ground like beggars who return disappointed from a godless one.

43. Seeing his never-failing arrows reṇdered futile, Keśava trịed to cover Vīrabhadra with divine missiles.

44. With his spear, mace and arrows, the *Gaṇa*-leader warded off those missiles hurled by Vāsudeva.

45. Finding his missiles ineffective, Mādhava threw the mace at him, which fell to the ground hitten by Vīrabhadra's trident.

46. Hari saw his mace wasted and threw the plough. The *Gaṇa*-chief brushed aside the plough with the mace.

47. The Plough-bearer (Viṣṇu) flung the pestle at Vīrabhadra who evaded the blow of the pestle in the same manner.

48. Seeing the pestle broken and the plough rendered ineffective, the Garuḍa-bannered God hurled the discus at Vīrabhadra.

49. The *Gaṇa*-chief on his part saw the (discus) Sudarśana (blazing) like hundred suns and heading towards him. He gave up his spear and swallowed the discus just as god Viṣṇu (Surendra) in the fish body devoured the (demon) Madhu.

50. When the *Gaṇa*-leader gulped the discus, Murāri with blood-red eyes due to rage, ran towards him (*Gaṇa*-chief) and forcibly felling him down on the ground, crushed him.

51. When he was oppressed on the ground by the force of shoulders and thighs (of Viṣṇu), the discus emerged out of his mouth along with a gush of blood.

52. Then seeing the discus purged out, Hṛṣīkeśa, the killer of Kaiṭabha, seized it and released Vīrabhadra.

53. Being released by Hṛṣīkeśa, Vīrabhadra went to Śaṅkara of matted hair and informed his defeat by Vāsudeva.

54. Then the matted-haired Śaṅkara, the eternal, became furious seeing the *Gaṇa*-chief drenched with blood and heaving like a venomous snake.

55. Then the armed Vīrabhadra was put back in his original place by the enraged Śambhu.

56. Afterwards, ordering Vīrabhadra and Bhadrakālī (to be in their places), Śaṅkara, the trident-bearer, with eyes red due to anger entered the sacrificial hall.

57. As the most prominent god of matted hair, the trident-bearer and destroyer-of-the-three-cities, the Destroyer, went into the sacrificial hall of Dakṣa, there was a great panic among the sages.

CHAPTER FIVE

Śiva as Kāla

Pulastya said:

1. Having seen the Matted-haired God with eyes red due to fury, Hari moved away from that spot and stood hiding in *Kubjāmra*.

2. O sage ! The eight Vasus hastily slipped away at the sight of Hara. And there was (born) the excellent river Sītā known as Sarasvatī.

3. After facing Śaṅkara, the three-eyed and bull-bannered eleven Rudras lost themselves knowing not where to go.

4. The Viśvedevas, Sādhyas, Maruts, Fire-god and Ādityas who were partaking of the sacrificial cake (fled) after encountering (Śaṅkara).

5. The moon along with the group of stars leapt and ascended the sky. He stood in his place indicating night, O great sage !

6. Kaśyapa and other sages stood bowing down with handfuls of flowers, reciting Śatarudrīya, O sage !

7. Dakṣa's wife seeing Rudra stronger than Indra and other leading gods cried piteously again and again.

8. At that time, many gods were put down with slaps by the illustrious Śaṅkara in rage.

9. Some gods and others were killed by kicks, others with the trident and yet others by the fire of his eye, O sage !

10. Then Pūṣan seeing Hara striking down the gods and demons, threw out his arms in anger and ran after Maheśvara.

11. Seeing him advance, the three-eyed lord Śaṅkara seized the two arms of Pūṣan with one of his hands.

12. He was so clasped by Śaṅkara, that a gush of blood spurted out in all directions from the fingers of the Radiant One.

13. Then (Śaṅkara) whirled fast without stop, the Radiant Sun just as a lion does a deer calf.

14. O Nārada ! The arms of the Radiant One thus violently whirled, got reduced in size as the tendons and joints gave way.

15. Maheśvara seeing the body of the Radiant One drenched in blood, left him (there) and went elsewhere.

16. But then Pūṣan laughing and showing his teeth, said again and again to Śaṅkara: "O Skull-bearer ! come, come (here)."

17. At this, with a forceful blow of fist by the enraged Śambhu, the teeth of Pūṣan were felled down.

18. Pūṣan with the uprooted teeth and the mouth full of blood, fell down on the ground unconscious like a mountain struck by thunderbolt.

19. Bhaga, on the other hand, seeing Pūṣan collapse and drenched in blood, stared at the Bull-bannered God with ferocious eyes.

20. The enraged Destroyer-of-the-Triple-Cities, however, hit his eyes with a slap and felled them to ground making all the gods tremble.

21. Following this, all the Ādityas having Indra in front and together with Maruts and Hutāśas dispersed in terror in all the ten directions.

22. As the gods went away, all the prominent *Daityas*, Prahlāda and others, bowed down and stood with folded hands, O sage !

23. Then Śaṅkara looked with angry eyes at the sacrificial hall as well as at all the gods and demons (there) to burn them up.

24. Seeing (such a) Hara, (some) warriors hid themselves, (some) prostrated, (some others) ran away and (yet others) went to the abode of Yama in fear.

25. (Hara) then stared at the sacred fires with his three eyes. Even as they were eyed by the Three-eyed Lord, they were reduced to ashes in an instant.

26. When the sacred fires were destroyed, the sacrifice too falteringly flew away into the sky assuming the divine form of deer, along with *dakṣiṇā*.

27. The great Lord Īśa, having the form of Time, chased it immediately with the Pāśupata arrow fixed in his bent bow.

28. Śarva is called Jaṭādhara, matted-haired lord, because of his aspect (seen) in the sacrificial enclosure (of Dakṣa), and is called kāla, Time, because of his aspect (seen) in the sky.

Nārada said:

29. You said Śambhu appearing in the sky is Time. Kindly expound to me his features, form and all.

Pulastya said:

30. O best of sages ! I will relate to you the formation of the destroyer-of-the-triple-cities who, as Time, pervaded the sky for the welfare of the universe.

31. The constellation Meṣa (Aries) made of the asterisms Aśvinī, Bharaṇī and a quarter of Kṛttikā and ruled by Mars, is the head of time.

32. O Brahmaṇa! The three other quarters of Kṛttikā, the whole of Rohiṇī and a half of Mṛgaśīrṣa constitute the constellation Taurus, the house of Venus; this is the face of Time.

33. The second half of Mṛgaśirsa, the whole of Ārdrā, the three-fourths of Punarvasū form the constellation Gemini, the house of Mercury and this is the pair of shoulders of the skull-bearing God who (showed himself) in the sky.

34. The constellation Cancer constituted by the fourth quarter of Punarvasū, Puṣya and Āśleṣā, the abode of the moon, is the sides of the sacrifice-destroyer.

35. The asterisms Maghā, Purvābhādrapadā, and a quarter of Uttarā constitute the constellation Leo, the house of the Sun. This is the heart of Time, O Brahmaṇa !

36. The other quarters of Uttarā, Hastā and a half of Citrā form the constellation Virgo of which Mercury is the lord. This is the abdomen of Time.

37. The constellation Libra is formed by the other half of Citrā, Svāti and the three quarters of Viśākhā. This is the second house of Venus and is considered the navel.

38. The fourth quarter of Viśākhā, Anūrādhā and Jyeṣṭhā constitute the constellation Scorpio, which is another house of Mars. This is the genital of Time.

39. The constellation sagittarius is constituted of Mūla, Pūrvāṣāḍhā and a quarter of Uttarāṣāḍhā. This is the house of Jupiter and is spoken of as the thighs of Time.

40. The constellation Capricorn formed by the other quarters of Uttarāṣādhā, Śravaṇā and half of Dhaniṣṭhā, is the house of Saturn and is called the knees of Lord Time.

41. The other half of Dhaniṣṭhā, Śatabhiṣak and the three quarters of Proṣṭhapādā constitute the constellation Aquarius which is another house of Saturn. This is considered the shanks of Time.

42. The fourth quarter of Proṣṭhapādā, Uttarā and Revatī constitute Pisces and is another house of Jupiter. This is the feet of Time.

43. Having assumed such a form of Time, the enraged Three-eyed Lord hit the sacrifice with arrows. Wounded thus, (the sacrifice) lost all sense and stayed in the sky surrounded by stars.

Nārada said:

44. O Brahmaṇa ! You told me about the twelve constellations. Please tell me their characteristic features in detail.

Pulastya said:

45. O Nārada ! Listen. I will tell you about the characteristics of the constellations as well as their manners and regions of movements and staying.

46-47. The location of transit of Aries is among stores of grains, and gems etc., and places on earth wholly covered by fresh green grass. It moves always in flowery banks of lakes. True to its name, Meṣa (Ram) it (stays) among the herds of goats and sheep.

48. Taurus (Vṛṣa) moves among those of similar forms-herds of cows and others, its location being cultivated lands.

49-50. Gemini (Mithuna) has the form of a couple; has hold on couches and seats; has lute (and other) instruments in hand; exists in music, dance and (other) arts; and is always interested in sports and pastime of the wealthy. Gemini is a well-known constellation and is the dual form of Śiva.

51. Cancer (Karka) has a form similar to a crab and is spoken of as moving in water as well as cultivated fields, wells, river banks and unpopulated lands.

52. Leo (Siṁha) is lion living in mountains, forests, impassable valleys (and moves about) in hamlets of hunters, caverns and caves.

53. Virgo (Kanyā) is a virgin holding paddy (ear) and a lamp and staying in the feelings (of human beings), moves about in pleasure haunts of women and lives in reedy lands (a bed of reeds).

54. Libra (Tulā) is of the form of a person holding a balance, moving about in markets and shops and living in cities, roads and saloons, O Nārada !

55. Scorpio (Vṛścika) is in the form of a scorpion haunting pits and anthills, living in poison, dung, worms and (under) rocks and others.

56. Sagittarius (Dhanu) appears as an archer having a horse body below hip (centaur), is resplendent, is found in a hero, a master of horse, a courageous one and in missiles; moves in elephants and in chariots.

57. O Brahmaṇa ! Capricorn (Makara) has the shape of a Makara—a deer-faced elephant with shoulders and eyes of bull-moves about in rivers and resides in oceans.

58. Aquarius (Kumbha) appears as a person (with) an empty pot, moving on a road, and drenched in water; frequents gambling halls and exists in liquor shops.

59. Pisces (Mīna) has the shape of a pair of fish mutually conjoined; found in sacred ponds and seas; lives in places of pilgrimage and in the abodes of gods and Brāhmaṇas.

60. O great sage ! I have narrated to you the characteristics of Aries and others. This is an ancient secret and you should not divulge it to anybody.

61. O divine sage ! Thus I have recounted to you how the three-eyed Lord destroyed the sacrifice (of Dakṣa). This story

of yore narrated by me is sacred and most sanctifying, cleanses sins and is auspicious.

CHAPTER SIX

The Burning of Kāma

Pulastya said:

1. Dharma, who has an ever-divine body, is Ṛgvedī and son of Brahmā. His wife, Ahiṁsā, bore four sons.

2. They were: Hari, Kṛṣṇa, Nara and Nārāyaṇa, O sage ! Hari and Kṛṣṇa were ever engaged in yogic practices.

3-4. Having gone to Himālaya, Nara and Nārāyaṇa, the gentle and the most virtuous ancient sages, performed penance invoking the supreme Brāhmaṇa, for the welfare of the universe, in the holy Badarikāśrama on the wide banks of the river Gaṅgā.

5. Agitated by the penance of Nara and Nārāyaṇa, this mobile and immobile universe underwent a great turmoil, O Brahmaṇa !

6. Indra perturbed by the penance of those two (sages), sent the excellent apsarā Rambhā to that great hermitage to distract them.

7. The invincible kāma with his mighty weapons of mango sprout immediately went (there) together with his close associate, Spring.

8. Then spring, Kāma as well as that excellent apsarā came to Badarikāśrama and went on sporting (there) as they liked.

9. At the advent of spring, the leafless kiṁśuka (a bastard teak) trees as radiant as fire, shone adorning the face of the earth.

10. O sage ! It was as if the lion of spring advanced tearing away the elephant of winter with the claws of palāśa (bastard teak) flowers.

11. The spring was sneering as it were with the buds of jasmine and lodhra flowers at winter who felt proud of his prowess: "I made even the elephants tremble due to dew".

12. The forests of blossomed karṇikāra plants appeared like gold ornaments of royal princes.

*13. Behind them the *nīpa* trees appeared like servants, like the servants honoured by the master, like royal princes.

14. The blossomed red *aśoka* groves appeared like the servants of king spring, having bloody wounds received in battles.

15. The swarm of bees turned yellowish in the deep forest, had their own beauty like pious people experiencing horripilation on arrival of good friends.

16. On the banks of rivers, the reeds with bunches of flowers were spectacular as if they wanted to say with their fingers raised: "Which tree does match us ?"

17-21. The Grace of Spring, 'Vasantalakṣmī' arrived in that *Badarikāśrama*. The hands of that beautiful maiden were the red Aśoka: her feet the Kiṁśuka flowers, her hair was the blue Aśoka; her face was the full-blown lotus; O Brāhmaṇa! Her eyes were the blue lotuses and her breasts the *bel* (*Bilva*) fruits; her teeth were the bright jasmine flowers. She having a bunch of flowers as her hands, appeared charming. The *Bandhujīva* flowers were her lower lip. Her nails were the bright fresh sprouts of *Sindhuvāra*. Her voice was that of the cuckoo and her divine dress was the auspicious *kaṅkola*. The herds of peacock were her ornaments. The jinglings of her anklets were the twitterings of cranes. Her waistband was the *Prāgvaṁśa* creeper. Her movement was that of a proud swan, O Brāhmaṇa ! *Putrājīva* was her upper garment. She appeared attractive with the lines of hair (on the belly) in the form of bees.

22. Then Nārāyaṇa having observed the excellence of the hermitage, looked all around and noticed the Bodiless One (*Anaṅga*).

**Ed.* It should be amended as '*narendraputrāṇām*'; '*narendraputrāṇi*' in the printed text does not make sense.

Nārada said:

23. O divine sage ! Who is this Bodiless One in that *Badarikāśrama,* whom Nārāyaṇa, the immortal divinity and the Lord of the universe, saw ?

Pulastya said:

24. That Kandarpa, the son of Harṣa, (usually) called Kāma, was burnt by Śaṅkara, and thus he became Bodiless One.

Nārada said:

25. Why was Kāma reduced to ashes by the great Lord Śambhu? You please tell me.

Pulastya said:

26. O Brahmaṇa ! When Satī, the daughter of Dakṣa, departed to the abode of Yama, the Three-eyed Lord was wandering after having destroyed that sacrfice of Dakṣa.

27. Then the flower-armed Kāma seeing the Bull-bannered God without the wife, struck him with the missile, *unmāda,* madness.

28. Then Hara being hit by the arrow *unmāda,* roamed in forests and lakes as a lunatic.

29. The great lord ever remembering Satī and struck by madness did not have peace of mind like an elephant pierced with an arrow, O divine sage !

30. Then the Lord of gods jumped into the river Yamunā, O sage ! As Śaṅkara dived (into the river), the waters got charred and became black.

31. Since then the waters of Yamunā have been (black) like bees and collyrium. The sacred river flowed like the locks of hair of the earth.

32-33. Then even though Maheśvara roamed about at will among the holy rivers, ponds, streams, lovely banks of rivers, wells and Lotus ponds, charming mountains, forests and hills, he did not at all have peace of mind.

34. O divine sage ! Śaṅkara would sometimes sing, sometimes weep and sometimes think of Dakṣa's lovely daughter of slender body.

35. Thinking of her, Hara would sleep for a while and instantly see a dream. He would say to her in dream thus—

36-41. "O cruel one ! Stop there. Why do you desert me, O innocent one? O defectless young lady ! Having been separated from you, I am being consumed by the fire of love.

Oh my lady ! Are you really angry with me ? O lovely one! please give up your anger. You please speak to me who am bowing down to your feet.

O my beloved ! You are ever being heard, seen, felt, adored and embraced, but why is it that you do not speak to me ?

Who does not indeed have sympathy at the sight of a wailing person, especially a husband ? O young lady ! You are indeed very hard-hearted.

O lady of slender waist ! In the past you had assured me with the words: 'I can not live without you', but this has been belied by you.

O lady of lovely eyes ! You please come, please come; embrace me who am afflicted with love. By no other means can this torment be removed, I swear by truth, O my beloved!"

42. Thus, bemoaning (in his dream) and waking up at once at the end of the dream, he would cry loudly again and again in the forest.

43. Having seen from a distance the Bull-bannered god lamenting and crying, Kāma forcibly bent his bow again and struck him with the arrow called Santāpana (tormentor).

44. Hit by the Santāpana missile, he became all the more afflicted. He was yelling and hissing and agitating the entire universe.

45-46. Again, Kāma struck him with the missile *Vijṛambhaṇa* (Yawner). Then he (Śaṅkara) yawned. Then deeply struck by the arrows of Kāma, yawning and roaming all around, he saw the son of the Lord of Yakṣas, Pāñcālika by name, who was an important person in the world. Having seen the son of Kubera, the Three-eyed Lord moved to his side and said thus: "Dear nephew ! Please do what I tell you today. You are a person of unlimited prowess."

Pāñcālika said:

47. My Lord ! I shall do whatever you say, even if it is the most difficult task for the group of gods. O Śaṁbhu of matchless valour ! Please command me. I am your devoted servant, O Lord !

Īśvara said:

48. Since the loss of Varadāmbikā (*Satī*), my body is being consumed by the fire of love. I have been hit by the arrows causing yawning and madness; I am unable to withstand them; I have no happiness.

49. Indeed there is no person other than yourself, O son! who is capable of withstanding yawning, torment as well as intense madness thrust upon by Kāma. Therefore, please receive them (from me).

Pulastya said:

50. The Yakṣa, so requested by the Bull-bannered god, accepted yawning, etc. The Trident-bearing Lord was immensely pleased at this and said thus—

Hara said:

51. Because you have accepted yawning, etc. which are hard to endure, my son, I am going to bestow a boon on you to felicitate you and it is pleasing to the world (as well).

52. Whoever that sees, touches or devotedly worships you during the month of *Caitra,* that person whether an old man, a boy, a young man or a lady, shall become mad.

53. They will sing, dance and be merry, O Yakṣa ! They will zealously play on (musical) instruments. They get

engrossed in jocular talk in your presence but they shall be endowed with spirituality.

54. You shall be worshipped and be known all over the earth, after my name, as *Pāñcālikeśvara.* By my grace, you shall become the most adored and wish-granter to the people. (Now) you proceed.

* * *

55-56. So said by the omnipresent Śambhu, that Yakṣa went through all the countries at once, and established himself in most of the holy places-to the north of Kālañjara and to the south of Himālaya. He is worshipped by the grace of Rudra. As he (Yakṣa) departed, the Three-eyed Lord too proceeded towards Vindhya mountain.

57. Kāma went there also and saw the Bull-bannered God. After seeing him, Kāma desired to strike. And Hara ran away from that place.

58. Then pursued by Kāma, Hara entered the frightful *Dāruvana,* where the sages were living with their spouses.

59. All those sages, on the other hand, seeing (the lord) cast down their heads. At that time, the lord asked: "Let alms be given to me."

60. All those great sages, however, remained silent. (Hara) then went round the sanctified hermitages, O Nārada !

61-62. Then seeing him (Hara) enter (the hermitage), all the Bhārgava and Ātreya women got agitated and languished, excepting only Arundhatī and Anasūyā. The minds of these two (ladies) were engaged in attending on their husbands and in connected thoughts.

63. All the (other) women there (got) agitated. Wherever Maheśvara went, all the women were afflicted with love and went (after him) with their senses anguished by infatuation.

64. The hermit women, leaving their hermitages vacant, followed him like she-elephants following a tusker in rest.

65. Then all the sages, Bhārgavas and Āṅgiras, enraged at seeing (that), said: "May his Liṅga fall down on the earth." O sage !

66. Accordingly, the *Liṅga* of the lord fell down and rent the earth. The Trident-bearing and brown-coloured god, then disappeared.

67. The fallen *Liṅga* then piercing the earth reached *Rasātala* and also shot upwards into the universe.

68. At this, the earth, the hills, the rivers and the trees, the nether worlds as well as all the moveable and the immoveable dependent on them quaked.

69. Brahmā seeing the earth and other worlds agitated, went to the ocean called *Kṣīroda,* Milky ocean, to meet Mādhava.

70. He saw Hṛṣīkeśa (Viṣṇu) and said devotedly bowing down to him: "O omnipresent Lord ! Wherefore are the worlds agitated ?"

71. Then Hari said: "O Brāhmaṇa ! The *Liṅga* of Śarva was felled by the great sages, and the Earth overcome by its weight rocked."

72. Then hearing that most wonderful event, Brahmā repeatedly said, "O Lord of Gods ! Let's go (there)."

73. Both Brahmā and Keśava, the Lord of the universe, came to the place where that *Liṅga* of Bhava was.

74. Finding the *Liṅga* limitless, the omnipresent Hari, filled with wonder, entered the nether world, riding on the chief of birds.

75. Brahmā going upwards in his aerial car (Swan) surveyed all around but could not see the end of it and he returned struck with wonder.

76. Viṣṇu, the discus-bearer and refuge of the worlds, went down all the seven (*nether*) worlds and came out without reaching the end of it, O great sage !

77. Both the gods, Viṣṇu and Brahmā together, folded their hands and eulogized the *Haraliṅga.*

Hari and Brahmā said:

78. O Trident-bearer ! Salutations to you, salutations O Bull-bannered god ! O rider on the cloud ! O seer ! O Śarva! O three-eyed ! O Śaṅkara !

79. O Maheśvara ! O Maheśāna ! O golden-eyed ! O Vṛṣākapi ! O destroyer of Dakṣa's sacrifice ! O god of the form of Time ! Obeisance to you.

80. You are the beginning of the universe, you are the middle and you are the end of it, O great overlord ! You are omnipresent.

Pulastya said:

81. Thus glorified in that Dāruvana, the best of the speakers, Hara, in his own form, said to them—

Hara said:

82. O Lord of gods, why is it that you are so much extolling me who have disregarded all propriety and was very much afflicted and tormented by *Kāma* ?

The gods said:

83. O Śaṅkara ! You please take back this your fallen *Liṅga.* O lord ! We are glorifying you for this.

Hara said:

84. O supreme gods ! If all the gods worship my *Liṅga,* then only I am withdrawing it and never otherwise.

85. At this, Lord Keśava said: "May it be so." Brahmā himself took hold of that *Liṅga* of yellowish-brown colour.

86. The Lord (Brahmā) made the four Varṇas (fit) for the worship of Hara. For them, he formulated the principal scriptures known for various discourses.

87. First (scripture) is known as *Śaiva;* the other is *Pāśupata,* O sage ! The third is *Kālāsya;* and the fourth, *Kāpālika.*

88. Śakti, the dear son of Vasiṣṭha, was Śiva himself. His disciple was one Gopāyana by name.

89. Bharadvāja of great asceticism, was a great Pāśupata. His disciples were king Somakeśvara and other sages !

90. Āpastamba of great austerities, was (versed in) Kālāsya. His disciple was of the name Krātheśvara, O sage !

91. Dhanada was a person of great vows. His disciple was a heroic person well-known as Arṇodara, a person of *Śūdrajāti* but highly austere.

92. Thus that Lord Brahmā establishing the four *āśramas* for the worship of that (*Liṅga*) of Śiva, went to his abode.

93. When Brahmā went away, Śiva too withdrew that *Liṅga* but established the same in a subtle form in Citravana and went about.

94. Again Kāma with his bow came in front and standing close by tried to torment the wandering Maheśa.

95. Noticing him (Kāma) in front, Hara with eyes inflamed with anger, looked at his body from the tip of tuft of hair to the feet.

96. Being (thus) stared by the Three-eyed God, Kāma, though radiant (himself), was burnt from feet upwards like (a stock of) hay.

97. Finding his feet burning, Kāma dropped down his exquisite bow and it broke into five pieces.

98. The gold-covered and resplendent part held with the fist became the fragrant and brilliant *Campaka* tree.

99. The well-formed middle part adorned by diamond became *Kesarāraṇya*, (known) by the name Vakula, O sage!

100. That finely curved end which was studded with sapphire, became the beautiful trumpet creeper (*Pāṭala*) adorned by a line of bees.

101. The part above the knot and the part held by the fist shining like moonstone became the five-petalled jasmine lustrous like the moon's rays.

102. From the portion above the fist part and below the (curved) ends, which was adorned by coral, arose the various multi-petalled jasmine, O sage !

103. O Nārada ! The multitude of charming and sweet-scented flowers along with jasmine were enjoyed by the god himself.

104. Even as his body was burning, Kāma threw down the fine arrows. (And they) grew into thousands of fruit-bearing trees.

105. By the grace of Hara, the various sweet-scented and delicious mango and other (fruits) became worthy of being relished even by the great gods.

106. Reducing Kāma thus to ashes, that omnipresent and imperishable Lord Rudra, restraining his body, went to Himālaya for austerities to acquire merit.

107. In this way, Kāma was burnt down together with his bow and arrows by the excellent god Śambhu in the past. Then the great archer came to be called *Anaṅga*, the Bodiless One. He was adored by gods and worshipped even by the high-ranking gods.

CHAPTER SEVEN

Prahlāda Fights a Duel

Pulastya said:

1. Then, O Brāhmaṇa ! Seeing the Bodiless One, the omnipresent sage Nārāyaṇa laughed and said: "O Kandarpa (Kāma)! Be seated here."

2. Finding him quite undisturbed, Kāma got surprised. Spring too was at once too much worried, O great sage !

3. Then the Lord saw the apsarās and honoured them with welcome. He then said to spring: "Please come and be seated."

4. Then the Lord took a creeper full of flowers with a smile and first created a damsel of golden body out of his thighs.

5. Kāma, the bodiless one, seeing that lady of perfect beauty and born of the thighs, wondered if she was his own beloved Rati.

6-12. "It is the same voice, the same bewitching eyes, eyebrows, crooked curls, the slender attractive nose and lower lip, the only target of sight (of any one).

Very same are her pair of stout breasts of subdued nipples with little space between them. Her plump breasts look fine like two pious men close together.

Very same is the body of this lady of charming limbs adorned with the three bands. Her belly adorned with a row of hairs appears charming.

The row of hair which reach the slopes of her breasts from the buttocks appears like a line of bees from the (sandy) bank to the lotus pond.

Her wide buttocks wound round by the girdle appear as beautiful as *Mandāra* wound round by the serpent while churning the milk ocean.

With thighs like inverted plantain stems, that most handsome lady with the complexion like that of lotus filament, appears graceful.

Her knees, unnoticeable ankles, and pleasing hairfree shanks as well as her feet with brilliance as that of red lac are spectacular."

13. Musing thus about that lady of blameless eyes, Kāma (himself) became afflicted with love. What to say about any other person, O sage !

14-15. O Nārada ! Even Mādhava (Spring) thought thus seeing the thigh-born damsel (Urvaśī): "Is it the very capital of king Kāma standing before me ?

Verily, the complexion of the Moon must have come here unnoticed by the moon, seeking refuge for fear of torture caused by the scorching rays of the sun at the end of night."

16. That Mādhava (Spring) leaning over the group of apsarās stood musing like an ascetic engaged in meditation.

17. Then observing them, Kāma and others, wonder-stuck, that (sage) of auspicious vows said with a smile—

18. "O Kāma, O Apsarās, O Spring, lead this lady born of my thighs to Heaven and present (her) to Indra."

19. Thus instructed, they, trembling, proceeded to Heaven taking Urvaśī with them. They spoke to the thousand-eyed one (Indra) about the youthful, beautiful maiden.

20. Kāma and others reported to the king of gods the doings of those two knowers of dharma. Then there occurred a great wonder, O great sage !

21. Such (an astonishing) story as this had wide publicity. It spread in the nether world and to all eight quarters on the earth.

22. O sage ! In the days gone by after the terrible Hiraṇyakaśyap was killed, the Dānava called Prahlāda was crowned as the King.

23. When that great Dānava who adored gods and Brāhmaṇas was ruling, the kings performed sacrifices as prescribed.

24. Brāhmaṇas performed austerities, religious duties and pilgrimage. Vaiśyas engaged in the tending of animals and Śūdras engaged in service.

25. The four social classes (*Cāturvarṇa*) had come to stay and (people) duly observed their (respective) *Āśrama* duties. Then the gods got their subsistence, O sage !

26. At that time, a great ascetic by name Cyavana, the best of Bhārgavas, went to river Narmadā for a bath in the holy Nākuleśvara.

27. After visiting the Great Lord (Mahādeva), he stepped into the river for bath. The serpent Kekaralohita caught hold of him who had descended into the river.

28. When caught by the serpent, he mentally invoked Hari. As soon as the Lotus-eyed God was invoked the mighty serpent became poisonless.

29. He was carried down to *Rasātala* by that ferocious snake. The big snake being poisonless released Cyavana.

30. The moment the greatest Bhārgava, Cyavana, was released by the snake, he went around honoured by the Nāga-damsels.

31. Moving about, he then entered the great city of the dānavas. Then Prahlāda waited upon by the *Daitya*-chiefs, saw him.

32. The radiant one offered proper welcome to the son of Bhṛgu (*Bhṛguputro mahātejāḥ–*). After having been greeted and seated, the sage was asked about his welfare.

33-34. That resplendant one replied: "I had come today to bathe in the great holy place and to visit Nākuleśvara of high merits. I went into the river and I was forcibly caught by a snake which brought me to the nether world. And then you were seen."

35. Listening to the words of Cyavana, the *Daitya*-king, a master of speech, spoke righteous words thus —

Prahlāda said:

36. O venerable one ! You please tell me which are the holy places on the earth, which in the mid-air region and which in the nether world (*Rasātala*).

Cyavana said:

37. Naimiṣa is famous on the earth, Puṣkara in the mid-air region and Cakratīrtha in *Rasātala,* O mighty-one !

Pulastya said:

38. O great sage ! Hearing the words of Bhārgava, the *Daitya*-king became desirous of going to Naimiṣa and said this to the *Daityas* —

Prahlāda said:

39. You all get ready; we shall (all) go to *Naimiṣa-tīrtha* for a holy dip and we will see the yellow-robed, lotus-eyed *Acyuta,* Hari.

Pulastya said:

40. So told by the *Dānava*-lord, all those *Daityas* (sons of Diti) and *Dānavas* (sons of Danu) made a great preparation and went out of *Rasātala.*

41. Those mighty *Daityas* and *Dānavas* together reached Naimiṣāraṇya and with pleasure took a dip there.

42. Then that lustrous *Daitya*-lord went for hunting. Moving about there, he saw the holy river Sarasvatī of clear waters.

43. Not far from it he saw a sāla tree of numerous branches covered by arrows and (saw) some more arrows of which tips were joined with each other.

44. Then seeing those odd-shaped arrows entwined like serpents, the *Daitya*-lord was indeed extremely angry.

45. Just at that time, he saw at a distance, two ascetics with standing matted hair and dressed in deer skin, and deeply engaged in austerities.

46. And at their side, there were the divine bows, Śārṅga and *Ajagava,* with auspicious marks and also there were two large inexhaustible quivers.

47. Seeing them both, the *Dānava* then thought they were imposters. Then he spoke these words to those two excellent persons:

48. "Why have you taken up this hypocrisy which destroys righteousness ? Where is penance, where the matted hair and where are these exalted weapons they go ill-together)!"

49. At this Nara answered the *Daitya*: "O *Daitya*-chief ! Why are you bothered ? One who is capable (of doing) will accomplish whatever action one does (i.e. given the capacity, one can accomplish any activity undertaken)".

50. To that the *Daitya*-chief told them: "When I, the Lord of *Daityas,* the promulgator of the bridge of righteousness, am here, what power have you got here ?"

51. Nara replied: "We have amassed power. No one is able to conquer Nara and Nārāyaṇa in a combat."

52. The *Daitya*-Lord was enraged at this and he took a vow: "I shall conquer somehow Nara and Nārāyaṇa in battle."

53. So saying that great lord of *Daityas* keeping his army at the outskirts of the forest, bent his bow and plucking the string, he make a very loud 'twang' sound.

54. Then Nara bending his *Ajagava* bow shot many sharp arrows. The *Daitya* cut them down with peerless arrows of golden feathers.

55. Seeing (his) arrows cut by the matchless *Daitya*-lord in the combat, the enraged Nara bent his great bow, and shot other various types of arrows.

56. Nara hurled one pointed arrow. The *Daitya* hurled two; Nara shot three, the *Daitya* responded with four. Again Nara discharged five and the *Daitya* six.

57. That foremost sage shot the *Daitya* with eight and Nara was shot at by nine arrows. Nara shot back thirty-six arrows and the *Daitya* seventy-two.

58. (Again) Nara discharged one hundred, and the *Daitya* three hundred arrows. (Then) the son of Dharma shot six hundred and the *Daitya*-king one thousand. Then furiously they shot innumerable darts at one another.

59. Then Nara covered the earth, the quarters and the sky with innumerable clusters of arrows. That cover too was immediately broken by the excellent *Daitya* with arrows having golden plume.

60. Then the two heroes, Nara and the Dānava, fought mutually with the best and most terrible missiles and arrows.

61. Then, however, the *Brahmāstra* was fixed on the bow by the *Daitya* who had the best missiles at finger tips. Nara, on the other hand, fixed the fierce *Nārāyaṇāstra* on his excellent weapon (bow).

62. Then the *Daitya*-king hurled the fire-missile and at the same time, the Puruṣottama hurled *Maheśvara-astra* during the fight. Both missiles hit each other and fell down.

63. When the *Brahmāstra* was cowed down, Prahlāda overcome with fury, leapt speedily forward from the excellent chariot with *mace* in hand.

64. Then seeing the *Daitya* coming on with *mace* in hand, Nārāyaṇa, with a view to fight him, made Nara stay behind.

65. O Nārada ! Then the *Daitya* with *mace* in hand ran after Nārāyaṇa, the wielder of *śārṅga* (bow) and arrow, the source of austerities, the well-known sage of yore, of great powers and the protector of the universe.

CHAPTER EIGHT

Boon Granted to Prahlāda

Pulastya said:

1. The *Dānava*-lord seeing Nārāyaṇa coming in front with *Śārṅga* bow in hand, forcibly whirled his mace and struck his head.

2. Then from the eyes of the son of *Dharma* who was thus struck by the *mace*, tears fell like a rain of fire, O Nārada !

3. That mace too with which the head of Nārāyaṇa was hit by the dānava broke into hundred pieces, O Brāhmaṇa ! Like the thunderbolt falling on the peak of a mountain.

4. Then the *Daitya*-lord returned and getting quickly on to the chariot, the hero held the bow and took an arrow from the quiver.

5. Bending speedily his bow, he, whose mind was blind with fury, hurled vulture-feathered arrows on to Sādhya (Nārāyaṇa).

6. (Nārāyaṇa) cut down immediately those darts appearing like crescent-moon even as they were falling (on him) and with other darts struck the *Dānava* too.

7. Then the *Daitya* hit Nārāyaṇa and Nārāyaṇa hit the *Daitya*. Then both of them were pierced at vital parts with arrows going straight.

8. At that time, O sage ! There was in the sky an assemblage of gods desirous of witnessing clearly that fast and wonderful combat.

9. Then the loud kettledrums were sounded in the sky. (The gods) showered matchless rain of flowers over Nārāyaṇa and the *Daitya.*

10. Then as the *Daityas* in the sky were looking on, those two great archers fought to the swelling delight of the onlookers.

11. Both of them shut out the sky with a rain of darts and covered the quarters and the intermediary spaces with a multitude of arrows.

12. Then Nārāyaṇa pulling his bow (-string) pierced Prahlāda in all his vital parts with sharp darts, O sage !

13. The *Daitya*-Lord enraged at that, speedily bent down his bow and pierced the heart, the shoulders and the face of Nārāyaṇa.

14. Then (Nārāyaṇa) with a dart having crescent-moon-like tip and brightness, severed, in the middle, the bow of the *Daitya*-chief who was discharging arrows.

15. The *Daitya* who found his bow broken took another one. After tying the string quickly, he poured out sharp arrows.

16. The excellent *Sādhya* (Nārāyaṇa) however cutting down all those arrows, covered him with arrows and severed his bow with an arrow having a sharp horseshoe-like head.

17. Every time the bow was cut asunder, the *Daitya* would take a new bow which sage Sādhya would at once cut into two.

18. When all the bows were (thus) broken, the *Daitya*-lord took a terrible and large all-steel club (*parigha*).

19. Taking hold of the club, the *Dānava* whirled it. (But) O great sage ! He (Nārāyaṇa) cut asunder (the club) that was being whirled, with an arrow.

20. When the club was broken, the resplendent *Dānava*-lord Prahlāda whirled a *mace* and speedily threw it on to the excellent Nara (Nārāyaṇa).

21. The mighty Sādhya severed that on coming (missile) into ten pieces with ten arrows. And that (mace) having been broken, fell on the earth.

22. When the *mace* was ineffective, he took a noose and quickly hurled it towards the foremost of men (Nārāyaṇa). The son of *Dharma* (in turn) cut that also.

23. As the *noose* was cut, the *Daitya* took a pike (Śakti) and threw (it). The mighty one of great austerity cut that too with a horseshoe-tipped arrow.

24. As all these weapons were broken down, the *Dānava* took hold of another mighty bow and covered with arrows, O Nārada !

25. Then Lord Nārāyaṇa, the teacher of the universe, the tormentor and vanquisher of *Asurās,* hit the *Daitya*-lord on the chest with an arrow.

26. O Brāhmaṇa ! The *Daitya* with his chest pierced by the god of wonderful deeds, sank down inside the chariot and the charioteer took him aside.

27. Before long, the *Daitya*-lord regained consciousness and taking hold of a strong bow, came to fight again.

28. On his return, Nara's elder brother told him: "O *Daitya*-lord, you go (now) and attend to the daily prayer; we shall resume fighting tomorrow morning."

29. So told by Sādhya of wonderful deed, the *Daitya*-chief went to Naimiṣāraṇya and attended to the daily worship.

30. As the god was combating thus, O sage ! Prahlāda recollected and thought at night: "How shall I conquer this imposter in combat ?"

31. In this way, O Nārada ! He fought with Nārāyaṇa for a thousand divine years. Yet the *Daitya* could not win the god.

32. When Nārāyaṇa could not be conquered even after one thousand years, the dānava approached the yellow-robed God and said these words —

33. "O god of gods ! I am unable to conquer now Nārāyaṇa, Hari, Sādhya. Please tell me the reason why."

34. The Yellow-robed God said: "O Prahlāda ! This son of *Dharma,* Sādhya, the best of Brahmanas and a man of

intellect, a great hero, cannot be conquered by you. (He is unconquerable) in combat even by gods or *Asuras*."

35-36. Prahlāda said: "O god ! If this Sādhya is unconquerable by me in combat, then how will it be? My oath will be false. O master of gods ! How can a person like me unable to keep my word, live. Therefore, O Viṣṇu ! I shall dry up my body (here) before you."

Pulastya said:

37. So saying, the lord of *Dānavas*, stood reciting the eternal veda in the presence of the Lord of Gods, after bathing his head.

38. Then the yellow-robed Viṣṇu said these words to the *Daitya*: "You go, you shall win him through devotion and never through fight."

Prahlāda said:

39. (Even) if he is unassailable in all the three worlds, O god of excellent vows ! Because of your grace, it should not be possible (for him) to stand (before me) and all the more so when I am enraged ?

40. O god of gods ! O virtuous one ! All the three worlds have been overcome by me. By your grace, this Indra too has been won over; what to speak of this son of Dharma ?

The yellow-robed god said:

41. O best of *Dānavas* ! He is only myself, engaged in austerities out of sympathy for disseminating righteousness.

42. Therefore, O *Dānava* ! If you wish victory, you worship him. You will defeat him with devotion. So you attend on the son of *Dharma*.

Pulastya said:

43. So said by the great Yellow-robed Lord, the chief *Dānava* called Andhaka and told him these words with pleasure, O sage !

Prahlāda said:

44. O Andhaka ! The *Daityas* and *Dānavas* are to be protected by you. O King ! You please receive the kingdom which I have given up.

(Pulastya said:)

45. The son of Hiraṇyākṣa, so told (by Prahlāda), accepted the kingdom and then Prahlāda went to the holy Badarikāśrama.

46. Seeing gods Nārāyaṇa and Nara, the Lord of *Daityas* prostrated at their feet with folded hands.

47. The resplendent eternal Nārāyaṇa spoke this to him: "O great *Asura* ! Why are you bowing down to me without conquering me ?"

Prahlāda said:

48. O Lord ! Who is capable of overpowering you? Which person can excel you ? You are indeed Nārāyaṇa, the endless, the yellow-robed Janārdana.

49. You are the lotus-eyed god, you are Viṣṇu, the wielder of *Śārṅga* bow. You are the imperishable Overlord. You are the eternal Puruṣottama.

50. The Yogins meditate on you. The wise ones worship you. Those who observe vows repeat your name and the sacrificers offer sacrifices to you.

51. You are Acyuta (destructionless), you are *Hṛṣīkeśa*, you have the discus in hand and you are the support of the earth. You are the *Great Fish*, you are the Horse-headed God, and you are the excellent *Tortoise*.

52. You are the radiant lord who as a *Boar*, was an enemy of Hiraṇyākṣa. And you as the Lion-man destroyed my father.

53. You are Brahmā, the three-eyed god, Indra, Agni, Yama, Varuṇa and Vāyu. O omnipresent master ! O Garuḍa-bannered one! you are the sun, moon and all the moveable and the immoveable objects.

54. All this universe is encompassed by you in thousand-fold, assuming the form of earth, fire, *ākāśa* and water. O Mādhava ! Who can indeed conquer you ?

55. O Hṛṣīkeśa ! O teacher of the universe ! If you are pleased by devotion (you can be defeated), O omnipresent eternal one ! By no other means can any one defeat you.

The Lord said:

56. O *Daitya* of good vows ! I am very much pleased by this your eulogy. I have been conquered by you, O *Daitya* ! through your single-minded devotion.

57. O *Daitya* ! A defeated person has to pay a fine. As a fine, I offer you a boon; you choose one you desire.

Prahlāda said:

58-59. O Nārāyaṇa ! I beg you to grant me a boon. Please grant me that a physical, mental and vocal sin committed by me through fighting with you and with Nara, be destroyed. Please bestow on me this boon, O Lord of the universe !

Nārāyaṇa said:

60. Be it so, O *Daitya*-chief ! May your sin be destroyed. You ask for a second boon. I will grant you that, O *Asura* !

Prahlāda said:

61. O Viṣṇu ! Whatever thought that occurs to me, may all be with reference to you. Let my mind be engaged in your worship and meditation and always be directed towards you, O god !

Nārāyaṇa said:

62. It shall be so, O *Asura* ! You ask for another boon you wish, O brave one ! I will grant you that without a second thought.

Prahlāda said:

63. O Adhokṣaja ! By your grace, I have obtained everything. May I always be devoted to your lotus-feet.

Nārāyaṇa said:

64. Let it be so. And also you shall for ever become destructionless, changeless and be beyond birth and death, by my grace.

65. O best of *Daityas* ! You go and be engaged in your activity. Your mind being immersed in me, there will not be any binding due to *Karma.*

66. Administering these *Daityas*, you look after the kingdom for ever. O *Daitya* ! You attend to the best *Dharma* proper for your birth.

Pulastya said:

67. So told by the Protector of the Universe, Prahlāda said thus: "O universal Guru ! How can I take back the kingdom once abandoned ?"

68. The Lord of universe answered: "You go to your hermitage. Be there preacher of good things to the *Daityas* and *Dānavas.*"

69. Then advised thus by Nārāyaṇa, the contented *Daitya*-leader bowed down to the omnipresent god and went back to his city.

70. He was welcomed and honoured by the *Dānavas* and invited by Andhaka (to take back) the kingdom. But he did not accept it, O Nārada !

71. Renouncing the kingdom, the exalted *Asura* led the *Dānava*-chiefs on good path. Ever meditating and remembering the unknowable Keśava, he remained with a body pure due to *Yoga.*

72. Thus, in days of yore, the best of *Dānavas* was defeated by Nārāyaṇa, the excellent *Puruṣa,* and renouncing the kingdom he lived with his mind fixed on the Lord.

CHAPTER NINE

The Deva-Asura War

Nārada said:

1. Why was the blind Andhaka crowned in the kingdom by Prahlāda though knowing the eternal duties of a king ?

Pulastya said:

2. He got back his eyes even when Hiraṇyākṣa was alive and therefore he was crowned by *Daitya* Prahlāda in his place.

Nārada said:

3. O sage of splendid vows ! What did he do after being crowned in the kingdom ? How did he pull on with the gods and others ? You please tell me quickly.

Pulastya said:

4-5. The best of *Daityas*, Andhaka, the son of Hiraṇyākṣa, worshipped the three-eyed and trident-bearing great Lord with penance and was granted the boon that he would not be defeated or killed by gods, *Siddhas*, sages or *Pannagas*, and could not be burned by fire or get wetted by water.

6. Getting the boon thus, the *Daitya* looked after the kingdom making Śukra his *Purohita*. Thus Andhaka carried on (for some time).

7. Then *Asura* Andhaka began waging war against gods and after invading the earth, he defeated all the kings of men.

8. After defeating the (earthly) kings and appointing them as his allies, he proceeded to the peaks of Meru of wonderful sight.

9. Indra too prepared the army of gods. Arranging for the security of Amarāvatī, he mounted the stately elephant and went (to Meru).

10. Following Indra, the other valorous guardian-deities of the world went out riding on their vehicles and wielding their weapons.

11. The army of gods too went forth with elephants, horses, chariots and so on along with Indra of wonderful deeds.

12. The twelve *Ādityas* were in front; the Three-eyed Lord was in the rear. In the middle were the eight *Vasus, Viśvedevas, Sādhyas, Aśvins, Yakṣas* and *Vidyādharas* along with the groups of *Maruts.* They were all seated on their respective vehicles.

Nārada said:

13. Please tell me now all about the vehicles of Rudra and others. O knower of *Dharma* ! I am very curious (to know).

Pulastya said:

14. Listen, O Nārada ! I will tell you, in brief, about the vehicles of all of them one by one in due order.

15. The vehicle of the King of gods (*Indra*) was the big elephant of white colour, born of the palm of Danu and was of great strength and stamina.

16. O Nārada ! A male buffalo of black colour, called Pauṇḍraka was (the vehicle of) Lord of dharma (*Yama*). This ferocious (animal) was born of Rudra's semen and could run as fast as mind.

17. The vehicle of *Varuṇa* was the porpoise of blackish colour, *Jaladhi* by name, born of the dirt of the ears of Rudra and was of grand movement.

18. The vehicle of *Kubera* was the hill-like excellent man, fierce-looking with eyes round like a cart-wheel and born of the feet of Ambikā.

19. O great sage ! The vehicles of the eleven *Rudras* were the *gandharvas* of great valor, the cruel-looking big snakes, and the white bulls of tremendous speed, born of *Surabhi.*

20. The chariot of Moon was drawn by five hundred swans; O best of sages ! The *Ādityas* had horses, camels and chariots as vehicles.

21. *Vasus* sat on elephants; *Yakṣas* were carried by men. *kinnaras* rode on serpents and *Aśvins* on horses.

22. O Brāhmaṇa ! The fierce-looking *Maruts* were seated on deer; *kavis* (a class of gods) rode on parrots and *Gandharvas* went on foot.

23. Thus the powerful excellent gods went for the battle with enthusiasm arming themselves and riding on their respective vehicles.

Nārada said:

24. O sage ! You told me about the vehicles of gods. In the same way, please do tell me about the vehicles of *Daityas.*

Pulastya said:

25. O best of the twice-born ! Listen about the vehicles of *Dānavas* and others. I will describe them in detail so that you may know.

26. The black-coloured excellent chariot of Andhaka was yoked with the best steeds; it had wheels of a thousand spokes and measured three *Nalvas* (twelve hundred cubits).

27. The auspicious chariot of Prahlāda was covered by gold and silver and was drawn by eight excellent horses shining like the moon.

28. (The vehicle) of Virocana was an elephant; of Kujambha a horse; of Jambha a grand chariot with horses of golden colour.

29. (The vehicle) of Śaṅkukarṇa was a horse; of Hayagrīva an elephant. It is well-known that chariot was (vehicle) of *Maya* and a large serpent (reptile) was that of Dundubhi.

30-31. (The vehicle) of Śambara was an aerial one; of Ayaḥśaṅku was a lion. The strong Bali and Vṛtra were ready wielding a mace and a pestle to attack the army of gods who were on foot.

Then there occurred the fight tumultuous, confused and fierce.

32. O Nārada ! The regions were covered with tawny dust. Neither father could recognise his son, nor a son his father.

33. O sage of splendid vows ! Some killed their own people while others killed the enemies. Speedy chariots overran (other) chariots.

34. Elephant went after elephant in rust, horseman after horseman; even enraged foot soldier chased strong foot soldier.

35-36. They hit each other, each desiring victory over the other. Then, O sage ! During that pitched battle of *Devas* and *Asuras*, there sprang up in the battlefield a frightful river allaying the dust. Blood formed the water. Chariots were the whirlpools. The multitude of soldiers formed the surging flow.

37. (The river was) difficult to be crossed with temples of elephants as the big tortoises, arrows as the fish, sharp-tipped lances as the crocodiles and sabres as the small crocodiles.

38. (The river was) full of moss in the form of intestines; with banners in the form of columns of foams. The river was adorned with herons and vultures as great swans, and eagles as ruddy geese.

39. (The river had) crows for geese; was full of jackals for (aquatic) beasts of prey; it was flocked by fiends for the sages. It was difficult for the ordinary people to cross it.

40. But the brave ones entered it sailing on rafts of chariots; sinking down upto ankles on the battleground and striking each other. The warriors desirous of getting at the wealth of victory, crossed it fast.

41. Then during that great pitched battle between *Devas* and *Asuras*, which was frightening to the timid, the demons

and the *Yakṣas* greatly delighted while hosts of fiends greatly rejoiced.

42. They deeply drank the blood of the soldiers, and embracing (the dead bodies), they ate their flesh. Birds pulled out the marrow, sprang up and roared at each other.

43. Female jackals made howling sounds; the soldiers (fallen) on the ground cried aloud being afflicted with pain; others fell down wounded by weapons; the battle (field) appeared like a cremation ground.

44. As the pitched battle between *Suras* and *Asuras*, terrible with the howlings of female jackals, ensued, it was as it were a gambling play with life itself at stake as seen by the learned.

45. Andhaka, the son of Hiraṇyākṣa, sitting in a chariot drawn by a thousand horses, approached the powerful Indra sitting on the mighty elephant.

46. The strong *Daitya*-lord, Prahlāda by name, riding in a chariot drawn by eight horses, and raising his weapon went to meet Yama who, sitting on the buffalo, was approaching.

47. O great sage! Virocana went against the Lord of waters (*Varuṇa*); Jambha against the strong Kubera; Śatasañcara against Vāyu; and Maya gave fight to Agni.

48. Hayagrīva and other strong sons of Diti and Danu met the gods and had duel with *Agni, Ādityas, Vasus,* and *Nāgas* (*Urageśvara*).

49-50. Confronting in the battle, they shouted at each other: "Oh ! you come", "Oh ! Why are you standing ?", "Are you frightened ?"; They forcibly bent their bows and released thousands of volleys of arrows; they were afflicting (the enemies) with sharp arrows, giving rise to a terrible stream flowing as fast as Mandākinī, and were striking with unfailing missiles.

51. O Nārada ! There appeared a river of blood on the battlefield which nourished well the groups of fiends and demons, which was desired to be crossed by the very alert and tremendously forceful *Suras* and *Asuras* intending (to gain mastery over) the three worlds.

52. The battle drums of *Suras* and *Asuras* were sounding. The groups of sages and *Siddhas* standing in the sky were observing. The *Apsarās* were carrying away from the war-field, those heroes who were killed while fighting face to face (with the enemy).

CHAPTER TEN

The Victory of Andhaka

Pulastya said:

1. Then as the battle striking terror into the timid started, Indra took the great bow and released arrows.

2. Andhaka too bending the resplendent mighty bow, discharged arrows furnished with peacock plumes at Indra.

3. Both of them struck each other with fast moving arrows of very sharp tips, having curved joints and gold feathers.

4. Then the enraged Indra whirled the Vajra in his hand and threw it at the *Daitya* king and Andhaka too saw it.

5. O Nārada ! He (Andhaka) hit it with a multitude of missiles and weapons and that (*Vajra*) reduced them all into ashes like fire (consuming) serpents.

6. Having seen the great power of *Vajra*, the best of the mighty jumped down from his chariot and stood on the ground with only his shoulders as weapon.

7. The *Vajra* reduced to ashes the chariot together with the charioteer, the horses, the flag and the pole and proceeded towards Andhaka.

8. Andhaka then hit hard the *Vajra* falling (on him) with his fist and felled it on the ground, and roared loudly.

9. Seeing him roar, Indra showered arrows on him and he attacked Indra to show his prowess.

10. He struck the elephant on its forehead with his palm and hit it with his knee and broke its tusks.

11. Speedily striking the left side of the elephant, Andhaka felled it which wore out due to continuous blows.

12. Jumping down from the falling elephant, Indra took the *Vajra* in his hand and entered Amarāvatī.

13. As Indra retreated, Andhaka destroyed that large army of gods (striking them) with his feet, fist, palm and so on.

14. O best of the twice-born ! Then the leader of the gods, Yama, whirling his *Daṇḍa* (*staff*) ran after Prahlāda to kill him.

15. The son of Hiraṇyakaśipu quickly bent down his bow and rained a shower of arrows on him who was advancing and shouting again and again.

16. Destroying that unparalleled volley of arrows by hitting them with his staff, the son of Sun hurled his staff terrifying the world.

17. That (staff) which was in the hands of Yama Dharmarāja flew into the air, and was burning like the fire ready to burn the three worlds at the time of dissolution.

18. Seeing the blazing staff which was approaching (Prahlāda), the sons of Diti were shouting: "Alas ! This Prahlāda is indeed killed by Yama."

19. Hearing the wailing, Andhaka, son of Hiraṇyākṣa said: "Be not afraid; who is this vicious god (that is able to kill Prahlāda) when I am there ?"

20. So saying, he stepped forward at once and, O Nārada! He held the staff in his left hand.

21. Holding it, Andhaka whirled it rapidly and then roared aloud like a cloud during rains.

22. Having seen Prahlāda saved from the staff by the *Daitya*-lord, the leaders of the troops of *Daityas* and *Dānavas* gave out shouts of commendation (of praise).

23. O sage ! The Son of sun, Yama seeing him whirling the excellent staff, thought it unbearable and irresistable.

24. O great sage ! As Yama Dharmarāja went underground, the mighty Prahlāda destroyed the army of gods on all sides.

25. Varuṇa riding on the porpoise, pounded the leading *Asuras* with his *mace* after binding them with his *noose*. Virocana attacked him.

26. (Virocana) beat him with iron club as hard as *Vajra*, with pikes, arrows as well as *Vajra*-like clubs.

27. Then attacking him with *mace*, the mighty one (Varuṇa) felled him to the ground and speedily bound his vehicle and the elephant in rut with the noose.

28. (But) the *Dānava*-chief immediately cutoff the *noose* and, having approached Varuṇa, O Nārada ! Held him by the waist.

29. Then the inviolable elephant too with its tusks tossed up the Lord of waters along with his *mace*, and crushed him under its foot.

30. Seeing him thus crushed, Moon of cool rays ran after (the elephant) and struck (it) with arrows tearing (its) body.

31. Being struck with arrows by the cool-rayed god Moon, the majestic elephant ached very much and (because of) being tormented, it further crushed forcibly the Lord of Waters under its feet, time and again.

32. Varuṇa when being trampled, held fast the legs of the majestic elephant with his legs, and, O great sage ! Holding the ground by his hands the strong one lifted his head.

33. Catching the tail of the elephant with his fingers, (*Varuṇa*) tied it with the large snake (*noose*). Then he pulled up Virocana along with his elephant and its driver and threw (them) into the sky.

34. Virocana, thrown up by the Lord of waters, fell on the earth together with his elephant, like Sukeśī's city (which fell down) hurled down from heaven by the Sun as it had obstructed his vehicle with its storeyed houses.

35. Then the Lord of waters ran with his *mace* and noose to kill the (fallen) son of Diti. At that time, those *Daityas* gave out an unprecedented cry like the thunder of clouds–

36-37. "Alas, alas ! The hero Virocana, the guardian of the *Dānava* forces is being killed by Varuṇa. O Prahlāda ! O

Jambha ! O Kujambha and others! you come with Andhaka and save him. Oh ! This noble and strong Lord of waters is shattering the *Daitya* soldiers together with their vehicles; he binds them with his *noose* and strikes with his *mace*, just as Mahendra does the animals in *Aśvamedha* (sacrifice)."

38. Then hearing the shouts given out by the sons of Diti, *Daitya*-leaders led by Jambha, hastened to attack the Lord of waters like moths (attacking) burning fire.

39. The great Lord of waters seeing them come, left the son of Prahlāda there, extended his *noose* and whirling his mace, fell on those enemies, Jambha and others.

40. He struck Jambha with the noose, Tāra with the thunderbolt-like palm, Vṛtra with his leg and Kujambha and Bala with his fist and felled them forcibly.

41. The *Daityas* punched by the excellent god, fled to various quarters abandoning their weapons. Then Andhaka came hastily on to the battleground to fight with the God of waters.

42. Varuṇa bound with the *noose* that *Asura*-lord who was attacking and hit him with the *mace*. That *Daitya*, (however), loosened the noose and snatched the *mace*. He hurled them both back to the God of waters.

43. Seeing the *noose* and the *mace* coming after him, the son of Dākṣāyaṇī hastily entered the ocean and Andhaka shattered the army of gods.

44. Then again, the god of fire wafted by wind burnt down the army of enemies of gods. He was attacked by Maya, the *Viśvakarmā* of *Dānavas*, who had a majestic physique and tremendous prowess.

45. O great seer ! Seeing him attack along with Śambara, Agni together with Vāyu struck Maya with pike and held Śambara by neck.

46. As the armour was torn asunder by the pike, Maya with his body deeply cut fell on the earth while Śambara was ablaze as fire clung to his neck.

47. Then that son of Diti being burnt by Agni, uttered a loud and long shriek like the trumpet of a big elephant suffering with pain when caught by a lion in the forest.

48. Having heard that cry of Śambara, *Daitya*-lord with his eyes red with anger (asked): "Ah, what, what is this ? By whom were the *Dānavas*, Maya and Śambara, defeated ?"

49. Then the *Daitya* soldiers told the lord of *Daityas* "(Śambara) is being burnt by Agni; please go and save him. O (Lord)! Agni has been unassailable at the war-front."

50. Spurred thus by the *Daityas*, that son of Hiraṇyākṣa, holding up an iron club ran after Agni asking him to stop.

51. Hearing the words of Andhaka, Agni, the imperishable one, was enraged and quickly threw up and crushed *Daitya* Śambara on the ground. By then Andhaka approached Agni.

52. With his excellent weapon, (Andhaka) struck the head of Agni. Agni being hit left Śambara there and immediately fell on Andhaka.

53. Andhaka struck again with the iron club the head of Agni who was attacking him. Agni struck by the Lord of *Daityas* ran in fear away from the battlefield.

54. Then valorous Andhaka made the fierce gods–Wind, Moon, Sun, Sādhyas, Vasus, Aśvins and Maruts and whomsoever he attacked with his arrows–to retreat from the battlefield.

55. Then having vanquished the fierce army of gods together with Indra, Rudra, Yama and Soma, Andhaka, honoured by the *Dānava*-chiefs, returned to the earth.

56. Having reached the earth, that wise Andhaka made all kings pay him tributes and after establishing his sway over the entire universe, both moveable and immoveable, entered the excellent city named Aśmaka in the nether world.

57. The assemblage of *Gandharvas*, *Vidyādharas* and *Siddhas* along with *Apsarās* repaired to the nether world and resided there to attend on that great *Asura* who stayed there.

CHAPTER ELEVEN

Puṣkara-Dvīpa

Nārada said:

1. O best of the twice-born ! You told me that the city of Sukeśī was hurled down to earth from Heaven by the Sun; please relate to me the same (in detail).

2. Who was this Sukeśī ? By whom was he blessed and why was he hurled down to earth from the sky by the Sun ?

Pulastya said:

3. O great sage ! Listen carefully to this ancient story which I am going to describe as heard by me earlier.

4. There was a well-known king of the *Rākṣasas* named Vidyutkeśin; his son was Sukeśī pre-eminent in virtue, O sage !

5. Lord Śiva, being pleased with him, gave him a city moving through the sky and made him invincible in battle as well as incapable of being killed.

6. And having obtained the city moving in the sky from Śaṅkara he lived happily along with the *Rākṣasas* following always the path of *Dharma.*

7. Once that *Dānava*-chief went to Magadha forest. There he saw the hermitages of devout sages.

8. Then, having seen the great sages, he fell (at their feet) and saluted them. Accepting the seat (offered by them), he spoke to all those sages—

Sukeśi said:

9. I desire to ask you about a doubt lurking in my heart. You please tell me about it. But I am not commanding (you to do so).

10. O best of the twice-born ! Which is indeed the good thing in the other world and which in this ? By which (action)

is one honoured among the pious ? By which (action) does one attain happiness ?

Pulastya said:

11. Having heard these words of Sukeśi, the great sages replied after deliberating about the good thing on this earth and in the other world.

The sages said:

12. O great *Rākṣasa* ! Please listen. We will tell you what is good and everlasting here and in the other world, O brave one !

13. O *Rākṣasa* ! *Dharma* is the good thing in this and the other world; a person observing *Dharma* shall become worshipful among the pious and happy by that.

Sukeśi said:

14. What are the characteristics of *Dharma* ? What observances make one virtuous and by following which even the gods and others do not suffer ? You please explain to me.

The sages said:

15. According to the *Śruti*, the foremost *Dharma* of the gods is: (attending to) sacrifices and related things, self-study (of the *Veda*), knowledge of the truth and worship of Viṣṇu.

16. The *Dharma* of *Daityas* is spoken of as physical strength, envy, warfare, hospitality, adoration of political science and devotion to Hara.

17. The *Dharma* of the *Siddhas* is set forth thus: achievement of yoga par excellence, self-study (of the *Veda*), knowledge of the ultimate, devotion to Viṣṇu as well as Hara.

18. Intense meditation (on singing), expertise in dance and musical instruments, unswerving devotion to Sarasvatī is the *Dharma* of *Gandharvas*.

19. Mastery of (magical) spells, unmatched worldly wisdom, inclination to endeavour, devotion to Bhavānī is the *Dharma* of *Vidyādharas.*

20. Expertise in the science of music and dance, unflinching devotion to Sun, adeptness in all arts and crafts is known as the *Dharma* of *Kimpuruṣas.*

21. Celibacy, pridelessness, fondness for practice of yoga, moving about everywhere at will is the *Dharma* of fathers (*Pitṛs*).

22. O *Rākṣasa* ! Celibacy, being truthful always, *japa* (silent repeating of sacred names and formulas), knowledge, regulated life, knowledge of *Dharma* is spoken of as the *Dharma* of sages.

23-24. Self-study, celibacy, charity, offering sacrifices, benevolence, fatiguelessness, compassion, non-violence, forbearance, and so on, control of senses, purity, auspiciousness, devotion to Viṣṇu, Śaṅkara, Sun and Devī is known to be the *Dharma* of human beings.

25. Ruling over wealth, enjoyments, self-study, worship of Śiva, egoism, non-aggressiveness is the *Dharma* of *Yakṣas* (Guhyakas).

26. The *Dharma* of *Rākṣasas* is: wishing contact with others' wives, greed for others'wealth, self-study, devotion to Śiva.

27. The *Dharma* of *Piśācas* is: lack of discrimination, ignorance, impurity, untruthfulness, and greed of flesh for ever.

28. O *Rākṣasa* ! These are the twelve types of beings enumerated by Brahmā and their twelve *Dharmas* (observance of) which only leads to Heaven.

Sukeśi said:

29. Of the twelve eternal and immutable *Dharmas* set forth by you, please relate to me again (in detail) the *Dharmas* of human beings.

The sages said:

30. O *Rākṣasa* ! Listen to the *Dharma* of human beings and others who dwell on the earth and the seven *Dvīpas* (continents).

31-32. This earth, fifty crore yojanas wide, rests on water, liike a boat on the water of a river. On that the god of gods and the most pious Brahmā has established an excellent mountain of great height that appears like the pericarp of a lotus. And that god himself created these virtuous beings in the four quarters.

33. The creator (Prajāpati) also created the dwelling places called *Dvīpas.* Among them, we are told, is included Jambū-Dvīpa.

34. It is said to measure one hundred thousand yojanas. Then surrounding it, there is the ocean of saline water twice its width.

35. Twice its width and surrounding it is the Plakṣa-Dvīpa, around which, like a ring, is the ocean of sugarcane juice.

36. It is double (of Plakṣa-Dvīpa in width). Double that in width is the Śālmali-Dvīpa, and the large ocean of wine is double of that in width. Twice larger than it is the Kuśa-Dvīpa.

37. The ocean of *Ghṛta* (clarified butter) is spoken of as twice wider than Kuśa-Dvīpa. Twice wider than the ocean of *Ghṛta* is the Krauñca-Dvīpa, and the ocean of curds is twice wider than the former.

38. The Śaka-Dvīpa is twice wider than the curd-ocean and the excellent Milk ocean is double of Śaka in width and here lies Hari on the Śeṣa couch.

39. Next to it is the Puṣkara-Dvīpa surrounded by the ocean of fresh water. Each of these is said to be the twice wider than the preceding one.

40-42. O *Rākṣasa*-chief ! These (*Dvīpas*) from Jambū-Dvīpa to the end of the Milk ocean are known to spread to forty crore ninety lakh yojanas. O *Rākṣasa* ! The width of Puṣkara-

Dvīpa is four crore fifty two lakh yojanas. At the end, there is the great ocean (of fresh water). It is covered all around by the egg-shell (of Brahmā) for one lakh yojanas.

43. These seven *Dvīpas* have their own *Dharmas* and conduct. We will relate them all to you. Listen, O *Rākṣasa* !

44. O brave one ! Those people who live in *Plakṣa* and other *Dvīpas* upto *Śaka* are ageless and there is no change of any sort due to *Yugas.*

45. They enjoy like gods and their *Dharma* is stated to be divine. At the end of the cycle (*Kalpa*), they are said to undergo dissolution, O warrior !

46. Those people who dwell in the Puṣkara-Dvīpa that appears fierce, follow the *Dharma* of goblins (*Piśācas*) and they perish at the end of their action.

Sukeśi said:

47. Why is it that the Puṣkara-Dvīpa was described by you as fierce, devoid of purity and terrible and as destroying the fruits of action ?

The sages said:

48. O *Rākṣasa* ! The Raurava and other cruel hells are there in that Dvīpa. Therefore, Puṣkara is fierce.

Sukeśi said:

49. O sages ! How many are these terrible hells ? What are their measurements by distance? What are their nature ?

The sages said:

50. O *Rākṣasa*-chief ! Listen to the area and description of all Raurava and other hells; their number being twenty-one.

51. The first hell is said to be Raurava which has an area of two thousand yojanas, all spread with burning coal.

52. The second hell spoken of is Mahāraurava twice as big as the first; its ground is made of molten copper which is ever heated underneath by fire.

53. The next one is Tāmisra, known to be (twice) wider than the previous one, the fourth one 'Andhatāmisra' is twice wider than the earlier one.

54. Then Kālasūtra is considered as the fifth; the sixth is Apratiṣṭhita and the seventh is Ghaṭīyantra (bucket-wheel).

55. The eighth hell Asipatravana (forest of swords) measures seventy-two thousand yojanas and is the foremost hell.

56. The ninth one is Taptakumbha (melting-pot) and Kūṭaśālmalī is the tenth. The next Karapatra (saw) is followed by Śvāṇabhojana (dog-eating).

57. Sandaṁśa (pincers), Lohapiṇḍa (iron ball), Karambhasikata (hot-sand), then the terrible Kṣāranadī (brine river), and Kṛmibhojana (worm-eating). The eighteenth is said to be the terrible Vaitaraṇī.

58. The next being Śoṇitapūyabhojana, then Kṣurāgradhāra and at the end Saṁśoṣaṇa. O Sukeśin ! You have been told about these hells.

CHAPTER TWELVE

Fruits of Karma

Sukeśi said:

1. For which action do (people) go to these hells and how ? O most venerable Brāhmanas ! Please tell me about this. I am very curious.

The sages said:

2. O Śālakaṭaṅkaṭa ! Listen to me. I will tell you those karmas for which (people) go to the respective hells and are subjected to various kinds of pains as the fruit thereof.

3-4. Those who always despise the gods, the *Vedas*, the twice-born and so on, those sinners who do not honour the contents of *Purāṇas* and *Itihāsas*, those who abuse their teacher, those who obstruct sacrifices, those who prevent donors from making gifts, fall into them (the hells) indeed.

5-6. Those vile ones who bring about estrangement between friends, married couples, brothers, between master and servants, father and son, sacrifices (and the priest), teacher (and the taught) and those vile ones who (orally) give their daughter (in marriage) to one but (actually) get her married to another—all these will be sheared into two with a saw by the servants of Yama.

7. Those who torment others, those who steal sandal, fragrant grass, chowries and fans are doomed to the hell Karambhasikatā.

8. Person who being invited to eat in a ceremony in connection with a deity or the Fathers (*Pitṛs*), eats elsewhere, is cut into two by large birds with sharp beaks.

9. Birds perch on and inflict pain with their beaks on a person who pierces the vital parts of the pious and hurts them with harsh words.

10. Crows with beaks as hard as diamonds pull out the tongue of the thoughtless one who maligns the pious.

11. Those haughty ones who despise their father, mother or teacher, get immersed face downwards in pus, excreta and urine in the Apratiṣṭha hell.

12-13. Those wicked ones who eat food before it is partaken by deities, invitees, servants, animals, guests, children, parents and Firegod, shall eat foul viscous blood and pus and are reborn having hill-like bodies afflicted with hunger but with needle-like (thin) mouths.

14. Those who serve food differently to the persons sitting in one and the same row, go to Viḍbhojana hell, O chief *Rākṣasa* !

15. Those travellers who eat food without sharing it with a fellow-traveller known to be in need, go to the Śleṣmabhojana hell.

16. The hands of those who, being defiled, wantonly touch a cow, a Brāhmaṇa or fire, are thrown into awful Taptakumbha (hot-pot hell).

17. The fire in eyes of those who, being defiled, wantonly look at the sun, moon and stars, is blown out by the Servants of Yama.

18-19. The feet of those who, with their foot, touch the wife of a friend, own mother, elder brother, father, sister or any other woman in the house or any other respectable and elderly person, are tied with iron shackles heated in fire, and they are thrown into the horrible Raurava hell with fire burning upto their knees.

20. Dreadfully hot iron balls shall be thrown into the mouths of those who partake of rice cooked in milk or rice cooked with sesamum and meat, without offering the same to deities.

21-22. Red-hot iron spikes will be thrust again and again by the servants of Yama, into the ears of those wretched people who time and again listen to censorious remarks made against teachers, deities, Brāhmaṇas and the *Vedas* by people inclined to committing sins.

23-24. The most terrible servants of Yama peel away with very sharp scissors, the skin from the bodies of those who ruin and destroy rest-houses, temples, parks, dwellings of Brāhmaṇas, assembly-halls, schools (monasteries), ponds, wells and tanks.

25. Crows pull out the entrails from the anus of those who urinate facing a cow, a Brāhmaṇa, sun or fire.

26. A man who, bent on looking after himself, abandons his children, servants, wife and other poor (dependent)

relatives, during famine or state of fright, shall be reborn as a dog.

27. Those who forsake a person seeking refuge and who are keepers of prisoners shall fall into a crippled posture (*Yantrapīṭha*) after being beaten by the servants of Yama.

28. Sinners who molest Brāhmaṇas and others during a sacrificial performance, are pounded on a stone and are dried up by fire.

29. Sinners who with hold a deposit shall be tied with fetters; they, emaciated with hunger and with dried lips and palate, shall be thrown into Vṛścikāśana hell.

30. Sinners who indulge in sexual intercourse on holy days, and who are attached to wives of others, are made to embrace red-hot club with sharp thorns (*Kūṭaśālmalī*).

31. Such of the wicked ones of the twice-born as study under (a different) teacher after despising (an earlier) teacher, as well as that (new) teacher shall carry a stone on their heads.

32. Those who urinate or cast phlegm or pass excreta in water (of a river or a tank) shall be thrown into the foul-smelling Viṇmūtra (hell) full of pus.

33. Those ignoramus who mutually partake the offering of food on ceremonies, shall eat the flesh of each other.

34. Those who forsake *Veda*, the fire, the teacher as also the parents shall be hurled down from the peak of a mountain by the servants of Yama.

35. Those who marry widows, or have sexual connection with unmarried girls and cause abortion to them, shall eat worms and ants.

36. He who receives *Dakṣiṇā* from a *Caṇḍāla* or a person of low birth, for a sacrifice performed for him, as well as the person who causes the performance, shall be born as insects inside stone.

37. O *Rākṣasa* ! Backbiters and those fools who live by service to others, will be thrown into Vṛkabhakṣa hell.

38-42. A gold thief, a murderer of a Brāhmaṇa, a drunkard, one having sexual relation with the wife of teacher, one who takes away cows and land (unlawfully) and a killer of cows, women and children as well as those twice-born persons who are the sellers of cows, similarly those twice-born ones that trade in *Soma* (juice) and those who sell the *Veda*, and also those that feign to be truthful (cheats), those that are impure, those that have given up the nitya (regular) and naimittika (occasional) acts, those that tender false evidence: all these remain in the Mahāraurava hell for ten thousand years. They continue to remain in Tāmisra hell for the same duration. Further, they spend a similar period of time in Andha tāmisra and Asipatravana hells, as well as in Taptakumbha hell. (Such is) the great fall for those who commit these sins.

43. An ungrateful person condemned by the people will dwell in these Raurava and other horrible hells in due order, as described to you.

44. Just as Janārdana (Viṣṇu) is the most distinguished of the gods, the Himālaya among the mountains, Sudarśana-disc among weapons, Garuḍa, the son of Vinatā among birds, Ananta among large serpents, the earth among the great elements;

45. just as the river Gaṅgā is the foremost of the rivers, lotus among aquatic flowers, a devotee of the feet of Hara among the chief enemies of gods, *Kurujāṅgala* among holy places, *Pṛthūdaka* among sacred ponds;

46. just as *Uttaramānasa* (is the foremost) among lakes, *Nandana* of the sacred groves, the dwelling of Brahmā among the worlds, (speaking) truth among the acts enjoined as *Dharma*;

47. just as among sacrifices Aśvamedha excels, among those (who give joy by) touch, a son; among ascetics, Agastya, among Āgamas, the *Veda* (*Śruti*) excels;

48. just as the *Matsya-purāṇa* excels among the *Purāṇas*, the *Svāyambhuva-saṁhitā* among the *Saṁhitās*, *Manusmṛti* among *Smṛtis*, *Darśa* (new-moon day) among the *Tithis* (auspicious days) and Indra among the heavenly beings;

49. Just as the sun is the foremost of the effulgent ones, the moon among the stars, ocean among reservoirs (of water), you among the chief *Rākṣasas, Nāga* among fetters (*Pāśa*), (*yogic*) posture among the rigid ones;

50. just as paddy (is best) among corns, Brāhmaṇa among human beings, cow among quadrupeds, lion (among wild beasts), jasmine among flowers, Kāñcī among cities, Rambhā among women, householder (gṛhastha) (stage) among the *Āśramas*;

51. just as Kuśasthalī is the best of towns, Madhyadeśa of all the states, Mango among fruits, *Aśoka* among buds, *Terminalia bellerica* (*Pathyā*) among medicinal plants;

52. just as bulbous root (of *garlic*) is the best of the roots, indigestion is foremost among illnesses, milk among white objects, cotton cloth among fabrics; O great *Rākṣasa* !

53. just as knowledge of arithmetic is first among skills, magic among proficiencies, Kācamācī among vegetables, salt among the flavours;

54. just as palm is the best of tall (trees), Pampā among lotus ponds, the bear-king among wild beings, banyan among trees, *Hara* among the wise;

55-57. just as the daughter of Himavān is the foremost of chaste women, *Kapilā* (black cow) among cows, blue-coloured one among bulls, and in the same way just as Vaitariṇī river is the foremost of all the unbearable, impassable dreadful (rivers), O King of *Rākṣasas* ! So the ungrateful (stands first) among sinners. O King of *Rākṣasas*! for all sinners, (even) for the killer of a Brāhmaṇa or of a cow, there is an atonement found, but not for this evil-doer. For an ungrateful person who sets at naught all that was done by a friend, no expiation can be found even in ten million years.

CHAPTER THIRTEEN

Description of the Universe

Sukeśi said:

1. O great sages ! The horrible features of Puṣkara-Dvīpa were described by you. Now please describe the features of Jambū-Dvīpā.

The sages said:

2. Listen to the description of the features of Jambū-Dvīpa. It is very extensive and has nine divisions; it bestows the fruits of heaven and emancipation.

3. In the middle is the *Ilāvrta-varṣa,* in east is the wondrous Bhadrāsya and in south-east is Hiraṇmān, O *Rākṣasa*-chief !

4. Bhārata is said to be in south and Hari in south-west. In west is Ketumāla and in north-west, Campaka.

5. In the north is Kuru's varṣa surrounded by heavenly trees (Kalpa-vṛkṣa). In north-east is the charming Kimpuruṣa-varṣa.

6. O Śālakaṭaṅkaṭa ! These are the nine holy and pleasant continents (*Varṣas*). Ilāvṛta and others are eight besides Bhārata-varṣa.

7. In those (eight *Varṣas*), there is no system of Yugas (eons), nor is there the fear of old age or of death. For them, attainment of faculties is natural, full of happiness and without any effort.

8. There is no adversity in them nor do they have (the distinction of) best, worst and medium.

O *Rākṣasa* ! This Bhārata-varṣa consists of nine *Dvīpas.*

9-11. All these (nine Dvīpas) are separated by oceans and are mutually unapproachable. They are Indra-Dvīpa, Kaśerūṇā, Tāmraparṇa, Gabhastimān, Nāga-Dvīpa, Kaṭāha, Siṁhala, and Vāruṇa. The ninth Dvīpa called Kumāra is surrounded by ocean and this Dvīpa is known to be lying in north-south.

In the eastern border are *Kirātas* and in the western border, *Yavanas.*

12. O brave one ! In the south, there are Āndhras and in the north Turuṣkas. Brāhmaṇas, Kṣatriyas, Vaiśyas and Śūdras live in the middle part.

13-15. These are sanctified by sacrifices, warfare and trading and other activities. Their interaction, attainment of heaven and emancipation as well as of merit and demerit are determined by these actions.

Mahendra, Malaya, Sahya, Śakti, Akṣa, Vindhya and Pāriyātra are the seven major mountains here. And also there are other one hundred thousand mountains in between.

16-19. They are extensive, high, charming, huge and have pleasant slopes. They are: Kolāhala, Vaibhrāja, Mandāra, Durdhara, Vātadhūma, Vaidyuta, Maināka, Sarasa, Tuṅgaprastha, Nāgagiri, Govardhanācala, Ujjayanta, Puṣpagiri, Arbuda, Raivata, Ṛṣyamūka, Gomanta, Citrakūṭa, Kṛtasmara, (Śrī)-parvata, Kokaṇaka, and there are other mountains, hundreds in number. The Mleccha and Ārya districts are partly mixed up in them.

20-33. Listen to the rivers by which they are watered: Sarasvatī, Pañcarūpā, Kālindī, Hiraṇvatī, Śatadrū, Candrikā, Nīlā, Vitastā, Irāvatī, Kuhū, Madhurā, Hārarāvī, Uśīrā, Dhātakī, Rasā, Gomatī, Dhūtapāpā, Bāhudā, Dṛṣadvatī, Nissvarā, Gaṇḍakī, Citrā, Kauśikī, Vadhūsarā, Sarayū, and Lauhityā — all these rise from the slopes of Himālaya.

Vedasmṛti, Vedasinī, Vṛtraghnī, Sindhu, Parṇāsā, Nandinī, Pāvanī, Mahī, Śarā, Carmaṇvatī, Lūpī, Vidiśā, Veṇumatī, Citrā, Oghavatī, Ramyā — all these rise from Pāriyātra.

Soṇa, Mahānadī, Narmadā, Surasā, Kriyā, Mandākinī, Daśārṇā, Citrakūṭā, Devikā, Citrotpalā, Tamasā, Karatoyā, Piśācikā, and others like Pippalaśreṇī, Vipāśā, Vañjulāvatī, Satsanajā, Śuktimatī, Cakriṇī, Tridivā, Vasu as well as

Valguvāhinī — all these rise from the slopes of Ṛkṣa mountain.

Śivā, Payoṣṇī, Nirvindhyā, Tāpī, Niṣadhāvatī, Veṇā, Vaitariṇī, Sinībāhu, Kumudvatī, Toyā, Revā, Mahāgaurī, Durgandhā and Vāśilā — these auspicious rivers of holy waters rise from the slopes of Vindhya mountain.

Godāvarī, Bhīmarathī, Kṛṣṇā, Venyā, Saridvatī, Viṣamadrī (Tuṅgabhadrā), Suprayogā, Vāhyā, Kāverī, Dugdhodā (Pālār), Nalinī, Vārisenā, and Kalasvanā — these great rivers emerge from the slopes of Sahya mountain.

Kṛtamālā, Tāmraparṇī, Vañjulā, Utpalāvatī, Śunī, and Sudāmā — these take their birth from Śuktimat mountain.

All these rivers with flowing waters are holy and destroy sin.

34. These are the mothers of the world and all these are wives of the ocean (i.e. all these flow to the ocean) O *Rākṣasa*! there are others thousands of smaller rivers.

35. Some rivers flow all through the year and some flow during rainy season. Those fortunate ones who are born in the mid-region freely drink the waters of these rivers.

36-46. The people living in the mid-region are: Kuśūdras, Kilas, Kuṇḍalas, Pañcālakas, Kauśikas, Vṛkas, Śakas, Barbaras, Kauravas, Kaliṅgas, Vaṅgas, Aṅgas, and Marmakas.

Ābhīras, Śādhyadhānakas, Bāhlīkas, Vāṭadhānas, Abhīras, Kālatoyadas, Aparāntas, Śūdras, Pallavas, Gakhaṭekas, Gāndhāras, Yavanas, Sindhus, Sauvīras, Bhadrakas, Śātadravas, Lalitthas, Pārāvatas, Mūṣakas, Māṭharas, Udakadhāras, Kaikeyas, Daṁśanas, Kṣatriyas, Prati-vaiśyas, and Śūdra families, Kāmbojas, Daradas, Barbaras, Aṅgalokikas, Veṇas, Tuṣāras, and various communities living outside the inhabited territory (Bāhyatodaras), Ātreyas, Bhāradvājas, Prasthalas, Daśerakas, Lampakas, Stāvakas, Ārāmas, Cūḍikas, Taṅgaṇas, Alasas, Alibhadras, tribes of Kirātas, Tāmasas, Karmamārgas, Supārśvas, *Gaṇa*kas, Kulūtas, Kuhikas, Cūrṇas, Tūrṇapādas, Kukkuṭas, Māṇḍavyas, Pāṇavīyas — these are the dwellers of the northern region.

Aṅgas, Vaṅgas, Madguravas, Svantargiris, Bahirgiris, Pravaṅgas, Vāṅgeyas, Māṁsādas, Baladantikas, Brahmottaras, Prāvijayas, Bhārgavas, Āṅgeyas, Marṣakas, Prāgjyotiṣas, Pṛṣadhras, Videhas, Tāmraliptakas, Mālās, Magadhas and Mānandas — these are the janapadas (peoples) of the east.

47-50. O Rākṣasa ! Puṇḍras, Keralas, Cauḍas, Kulyas, Jānukas, Mūṣikādas, Kumārādas, Mahāśakas, Mahārāṣṭras, Māhiṣikas, entire Kaliṅgas, Ābhīras, Vaisakyas, Āraṇyas, Śabaras, Pulindas, Vindhyas, Śaileyas, Vaidarbhas, Daṇḍakas, Paurikas, Sārikas, Aśmakas, Bhogavardhanas, Naimikas, Kundalas, Āndhras, Uḷidas (or Udbhidas), and Nalakārakas—these are the southern peoples (Jānapadas), O Śālakaṭaṅkaṭa.

51-53. Śūrpārakas, Vāridhānas, Durgas, Cālikaṭas, Pulīyas, Asinīlas, Tāpasas, Tāmasas, Kāraskaras, Bhaminas, Nāsīkāntas, Sunarmadas, Dārukacchas, Sumāheyas, Sārasvatas, Vātsīyas, Surāṣṭras, Āvantyas, and Arbudas — these people dwell in the western region.

54-56. Kārūṣas, Ekalavyas, Mekalas, Utkalas, Uttamarṇas, Daśārṇas, Goptas, Kiṁkaravas, Tośalas, Kośalas, Traipuras, Khelliśas, Turagas, Tumbaras, Vahelas, Naiṣadhas, Anūpas, Tuṇḍikeras, Vītihotras, Avantis — these are known to be the people at the foot of Vindhya mountain.

57-58. We will now speak about the important people of the mountainous regions. Nirāhāras, Haṁsamārgas, Kupathas, Taṅgaṇas, Khaśas, Kuthaprāvaraṇas, Ūrṇāpluṣṭas, Suhūhukas, Trigartas, Kirātas, Tomaras, Śaśikhādrikaṣ.

59. O King of *Rākṣasas* ! These details of Kumāra-Dvīpa were narrated to you. Now listen to the local customs of these countries being described accurately.

CHAPTER FOURTEEN

Sukeśi Instructed

The sages said:

1-2. O *Rākṣasa* ! Non-violence, truth, non-stealing, charity, forbearance, self-restraint, mental repose, non-niggardliness, purity, perseverence—these, O great *Rākṣasa* ! Are the ten constituents of Dharma which is common to people of all *Varṇas.* In case of Brāhmaṇas, however, the scheme of four *Āśramas* or stages of life, is also enjoined.

Sukeśi said:

3. O sage rich in penance ! Please describe to me in detail the four life-stages of Brāhmaṇas. I have no satiation in listening to you.

The sages said:

4. After duly undergoing initiation ceremony, a *Brahmacārī* should live with the teacher. The duties he should attend to them will be described to you, listen.

5. (They are:) Attending to his studies, tending the sacred fire, ablution, and begging for his food; the begged food shall be eaten after informing the teacher and being permitted by him.

6. The student shall help the teacher in his activities and show respect to him; the student should be ready to be taught whenever called to do so; he shall be devoted to the teacher without thinking of anything else.

7-8. After learning directly from the teacher one, two or all the *Vedas,* and after being permitted by him, the student should pay the teacher *Dakṣiṇā* (fee) as indicated by him. Then he should enter the stage of householder if he chooses to become a householder or if he so desires, he may as well take up the stage of hermit or the fourth stage (of *monk*).

9-10. Or else, the twice-born may stay in the house of the teacher only. He shall continue to be in the *Brahmacārī* stage and engage himself in selfless service to the son or a disciple of his teacher but not to his daughter, in case the teacher passes away. O Śālakaṭaṅkaṭa ! Such a twice-born will thus conquer death.

11. He that returns therefrom desirous of setting up a household, shall marry a girl who is not born in a family having the same *Ṛṣis* (in the Gotra-Pravara as his own), O *Rākṣasa* !

12. The twice-born shall engage himself in worthy conduct and shall propitiate the Pitṛs (Fathers), the deities and the guests as well, with the monastery he earns through his assigned work.

Sukeśi said:

13. O sages of worthy vows ! Mention was made of 'worthy conduct' by you to me; I would like to know the characteristics of the same; you please describe them to me.

The sages said:

14. We will describe, out of regard for you, the characteristics of 'worthy conduct' which was mentioned by us to you; listen to it, O Rākṣasa !

15. A householder should always take care to do (proper) conduct. There is no happiness here or in the other world for a person who has no (good) conduct.

16. The sacrifices, charities or austerities (performed) do not beget prosperity for a person who violate rules on good conduct.

17. A person of bad conduct can be happy neither here nor in the other world. (Therefore) one must strive to maintain good conduct. (Good) conduct destroys inauspiciousness.

18. O Rākṣasa ! We will now tell you the true nature of good conduct. Listen to it with attentive mind if you desire prosperity.

19. Good conduct is a tree, the root of which is Dharma (righteousness); its branch is *Artha* (wealth); its flower is *Kāma* (desire/love), and its fruit is *Mokṣa* (emancipation). O Sukeśin ! He who attends on this (tree), will enjoy (the fruits of) merit.

20. One should wake up early in *Brāhma Muhūrta* and remember the great deities and the exalted sages. The morning prayer to which the Three-eyed Lord of gods gave expression, should be recited.

Sukeśi said:

21. Which is that morning prayer that was given expression to by the great Śaṅkara and by reciting which a mortal being gets rid of the clutches of sin ?

The sages said:

22. O Rākṣasa-chief ! Listen to the morning prayer which Hara recited and by hearing, recalling or reciting which one will get rid of all sins.

23. "May all these—Brahmā, the Destroyer of Mura (*Viṣṇu*), the Destroyer of the three cities (*Śiva*), Sun, Moon, the Son of Earth (Mars), Buddha (Mercury), Guru (Jupiter), Śukra (Venus)as well as the Son of Sun (Śani, Saturn)—make my morning auspicious !

24. "May all these—Bhṛgu, Vasiṣṭha, Kratu, Aṅgiras, sage Pulastya, Pulaha, Gautama, Raibhya, Marīci, Cyavana and Ṛbhu-make my morning auspicious !

25. "Sanatkumāra, Sanaka, Sanandana, Sanātana, Āsurī and Piṅgala, the seven notes (svaras), the seven nether regions (Rasātalas)—may all these make my morning auspicious !

26. "Earth with its smell, waters with their flavour, wind with its touch, fire with its brightness, *Ākāśa* with its sound-may these along with Mahat grant me a beautiful morning.

27. "The seven seas, the seven mountain chains, the seven sages, the seven *Dvīpas,* and the seven Lokas—Bhū and others—may these grant me a beautiful morning."

28. Whoever that recites or recalls or hears (recited by others) with devotion this most ennobling (prayer), the bad dreams of such a person shall indeed be destroyed and will have an auspicious morning due to the blessings of the Lord, O sinless one !

29. Afterwards, rising and leaving the bed, one should ponder over *Dharma* and *Artha* (aspects of that day). Then the person should get up repeating the name 'Hari' and should proceed to attend to evacuation (of stools, etc.).

30. Excreta should not be evacuated on a path (leading) to deities (i.e. temples), cows, Brāhmaṇas and fire, or on a highway, at a cross-road, or in a cow-pen, or facing east or west direction.

31. Then mud should be used for cleaning. The anus should be cleaned thrice with mud, the palm ten times, both the feet seven times, and the genital once.

32. O *Rākṣasa* ! Mud for cleaning should not be taken from a pool of water, nor from the hole of a rat nor from that left after use by others. A person knowing good conduct should always use the mud of an anthill for cleaning.

33. Having cleansed the feet, the person who knows the way should sit on the ground facing north or east. He should first wipe the face twice (with water) and sip foamless water thrice.

34. Then he should touch the organs of sense and the head with the hand and should offer morning prayer. Then in due course, he should dress his hair, brush the teeth and look into a mirror.

35. Afterwards, he should have head-bath or bath for (other) limbs only; should offer water libation to the Fathers along with gods, and perform *Homa.* Then going out (on one's business) after touching auspicious objects, is commended.

36-37. *Dūrvā* grass, curds, ghee, a water-pot, a cow with a calf, a bull, gold, earth, cowdung, *Svastika, Akṣata* (unbroken rice grains), parched rice, honey, Brāhmaṇa virgins, white and fragrant flowers, fire, red sandal, the orb (rays) of the

Sun, the *Peepal* tree—all these auspicious objects are to be touched and then should one engage oneself in the activity proper for one's *Jāti*.

38-39. A person should not give up the *Dharma* of his family as ordained in his country nor the chief duty of his own clan. He should strive to earn wealth from that only. He should not speak evil things. He should not utter statements which are not true, those which are harsh, those which go against *Veda* or *Śāstra* or those by uttering which one becomes censurable by pious people. He should not transgress *Dharma*, nor should he associate himself with the wicked.

40. O hero ! A person should avoid sexual intercourse during both the twilights, and during the day, and in water or with any animal or with others' wives, or with a menstruating woman.

41. A householder should not wander without a purpose, should not gift without propriety, should not wantonly kill an animal; nor should he marry illegally.

42. Purposeless wandering comes in the way of one's daily routine; improper charity causes loss of wealth; wanton killing of animals is sinful leading to hell.

43. Loss of progeny is not commendable. Intermixture of *Varṇas* through intercaste marriage is fearful. One should be afraid of unfruitful marriage.

44. The best ones should not think of the property of others, nor of the wives of others. Others' wealth leads to hell and others' wives to death.

45. One should not look at another's wife who happens to be naked. One should not talk to thieves. One should avoid seeing, touching or talking to a woman having menstruation.

46. One should not share a seat with one's sister, or with the wife of another, or one's step mother or (even) one's own daughter.

47. A person at no time should bathe nor sleep naked. So also it is not commendable to roam about that way (i.e.

nude), even for the one who considers the quarters as the clothes.

48. For the sake of cleanliness a person should throw away beds, seats, utensils and so on which are torn or mutilated.

One should not take oil-bath on *Nandā* days (first, sixth or eleventh day of a lunar fortnight). Shaving should be avoided on *Riktā* days (fourth, ninth and fourteenth day of lunar fortnight) and meat should not be eaten on *Jayā* days (third, eighth and thirteenth day of a lunar fortnight).

49. On the *Pūrṇā* days (fifth, tenth and fifteenth day of a lunar fortnight) there should be no sexual intercourse. But all this is allowed on *Bhadrā* days (fourth, seventh and twelfth days of a lunar fortnight).

So also oil-bath should not be taken on Sundays and Tuesdays. Shaving should be avoided on Fridays and meat on Saturdays.

50. Sexual intercourse should be avoided on Wednesdays. On other days (i.e. Mondays and Thursdays) any of these could be attended to.

Oil-bath should be avoided on *Ćitrā*, *Hastā* and *Śravaṇa*; shaving on *Viśākhā* and *Abhijit.*

51. Meat should not be eaten on *Mūla*, *Mṛgaśirā* and both the *Bhādrapadas*; sexual intercourse to be avoided on *Maghā*, *Kṛttikā* and *Uttarā.*

O lord of *Rākṣasa*! One should always avoid keeping head towards north or west while sleeping.

52. One should not dine facing south nor facing west. When one comes across a temple, a sacred tree, a square, a scholarly teacher, one should move keeping them to one's right.

53-54. A wise man should be careful not to make use of garlands, food, drinks or clothes used by others.

Head-bath should be taken daily. One should not bathe in the dead of night except when there occurs an eclipse, death of a kinsman or moon's entry into the asterism of one's birth.

One should not touch a person anointed (with oil) and the hair should not be shaken after bath.

55. O King of *Rākṣasas* ! After bath the body should not be wiped with a cloth in hand.

One should always reside in countries of plenty, governed by good kings and where the people are well knit together (i.e. very cooperative).

56. One should always dwell in a place where the people are free from anger, law-abiding and bereft of jealousy, where there are farmers, where (are grown) various kinds of plants, where a physician is easily available and where there are wealthy men and good persons learned in Vedic lore.

57. An intelligent person should not reside in those countries where an inefficient king is always inclined to inflict punishments and the people are averse to celebrating festivals but are always engaged in mutual rivalry, O King of *Rākṣasas* !

58. O great hero ! We will now tell you about the food that is prohibited for eating and about that recommended to be eaten by (righteous) people who are devoted to *Dharma*.

59-60. Cooked food mixed with fats (oil, ghee, etc.) though stale and kept for long time, is worthy to be eaten; fine rice though without fat, milk products, rabbit, porcupine, alligator, hedgehog, fish and tortoise; so also pulses and such others are fit to be eaten. So has said Manu.

61-62. Precious stones, cloth, coral and pearls, things made of stone and wood, grass, roots and also herbs, winnowing basket, corn, straw and used clothes, all types of bark-all these can be purified with water.

63. Things that are greasy are cleansed with hot (water) and wool is cleansed with the dough of sesamum. Cotton clothes are cleansed by water outside (the house).

64. Ivory, bones and horns are instantaneously pure. Earthenware is purified by baking them again.

65. The food begged, the hand of an artisan, the mouth of a courtesan, an article brought by the highway, an

unidentified object, anything executed by the servants—are pure.

66. That which is highly spoken of, that which is longstanding, that which is intervened by many, light objects, the deeds done by young children and old persons, the mouth of a young child are pure.

67. A store of grain, a furnace-room (of a blacksmith), women with suckling babies, drops (of saliva) of foremost of the twice-born while speaking, drops of boiling water are pure.

68. An open ground is cleansed by scraping, scorching, sweeping, or by making a cow walk on it. The (floor of a) building is cleansed by smearing (cowdung), scratching (away the defiled part), sprinkling (with water), mopping (with water) or by worship (of the deity of residence).

69. If food is defiled by hair or insects, if it is sniffed by a cow, or defiled by flies, then earth, water, ash and salt are to be sprinkled over it, to cleanse it.

70. Utensils of copper are cleansed with acids (tamarind), tin and lead articles with salt, bronze with ash and water; cleaning of liquids is by straining.

71. An article defiled by some impurity (like excreta), becomes pure by cleaning off the (foul) smell with mud and water. Other articles (defiled similarly) are cleaned by removing the (bad) smell with the same materials (mud and water).

72. A calf (or a baby) is pure while sucking its mother, a bird while felling a fruit, an ass while carrying a load, and a dog while catching a deer.

73. Road, earth, water, cows, grass on the way as well as structures of baked bricks are cleansed by wind only.

74. If cooked food measuring more than a *Droṇa*, gets into contact with some contamination, then the top-layer (i.e. the defiled portion) is to be removed and thrown out and the rest to be sprinkled (with water).

75. If contaminated food is partaken, one should fast for three nights. In case it (contamination)was not known

(earlier) or was known beforehand, there is no purification prescribed.

76. One should take ablution for purification after coming into contact with a woman in her courses, a woman just bathed after her courses, a nude woman, a woman who has just delivered (a baby), persons of lowest caste as well as with those who carried the bier.

77. Having touched greasy (i.e. with fat) bones, one should bathe with the clothes on; and if it is not greasy, one (becomes pure) by touching a cow and looking at the sun.

78. One should not cross a human being, blood or material used to clean the body. Remnants, excreta, urine and water in which feet have been washed are to be thrown out of house.

79. One should not bathe in water belonging to another without throwing out five handfuls of water. One should (make it a point to) bathe in ponds dug by gods (i.e. natural) and rivers.

80. A wise man should not stay in parks and such places at improper hours. One should not talk to a person despised by the public nor to a lady who has lost her husband.

81. Having touched or conversed with those who speak ill of deities, parents, holy Śāstras, minor and major sacrifices and so on, one becomes pure by looking at the sun.

82. Food offered by a *Sūtika* (defiled), a *Ṣaṇḍa* (eunuch), a *Mārjāra* (cat), an *Ākhu* (rat), a *Kukkuṭa* (cock), a *Patita* (fallen one), a *Apaviddha* (despised one), a *Nagna* (nude one), a *Cāṇḍāla* and the people of the lower order is not fit to be eaten.

Sukeśi said:

83. I would like to know the characteristic features of these *Sūtika* and others said by you as those whose food should not be accepted.

The sages said:

84. That Brāhmaṇa (man) or Brāhmaṇī (woman) who becomes remnant (i.e. survivor) is called *Sūtika* and the food offered by (either of) them is despised.

85. He who does not offer *Homa* at proper times, nor performs ablution nor gives any charity, and has given up the worship of *Pitṛs* and gods is described as *Ṣaṇḍa* (eunuch).

86. He who pretends to perform *Japa,* austerities and to recite (scriptures), and does not (really) strive for the other world, is declared a *Mārjāra* (cat), a hypocrite.

87. He who, inspite of having plenty, does not enjoy, nor gives any charity, nor offers any sacrifice, is spoken of as a *Ākhu* (rat), a miser; after eating his food, one can hardly get purified.

88. That member of an assembly, who resorts to partisanship towards the (other) members of the assembly is called a *Kukkuṭta* (cock) by gods. His food too is prohibited.

89. He who takes over the *Dharma* of others giving up his own even at times of non-adversity, is declared *Patita* (fallen) by the learned.

90. A person who abandons the deities, who deserts the parents, who disregards the teacher as well as the killer of a cow, a Brāhmaṇa or a woman, is considered *Apaviddha.*

91. Those in whose family (though in the tradition) there is no (study of the) *Veda,* nor of a *Śāstra* nor (the observance of) any vow, are called the *Nagna* (nude) by the pious; the food served by them is prohibited.

92. A person who does not give (anything) to those who are oppressed by desire and one who thwarts the benevolent and one who abandons those seeking refuge is *Caṇḍāla* (a lowly person).

93. After partaking the food served by one who has been abandoned by the relatives and pious Brāhmaṇas, as well as the food served by a pimp, one should perform *Cāndrāyaṇavrata.*

94. After eating the food served by one who has given up both *Nitya-karmas* and *Naimittika-karmas,* a person becomes purified by fasting for three nights.

95. *Nitya* (routine) *karmas* are not performed only (due to the pollution) because of birth or death (in the family); but *Naimittika* (occasional) *karmas* are not to be given up at any time.

96. *Bhagavān* Bhṛgu is of the opinion that a father shall bathe with his clothes on at the birth of his son while at the death of a person all the relatives (of the dead) (are to bathe with the clothes on).

97. Having cremated the dead body outside (the village, etc.) paternal relations shall offer water libation to the deceased. The bones are to be collected on the very day (of cremation) or on the fourth or the seventh day (therefrom).

98. Only after the collection of bones, paternal relation are fit to mix with others. *Sapiṇḍas* (close relatives on the paternal side), however, are to offer water libation during the period of pollution.

99-100. In the case of death caused by poisoning, hanging (also strangling), or by any weapon, drowning, setting fire, falling (from a height), or of a child, a wandering mendicant, or of a person in a far-off place, purification is immediate. And that (purification) is of four kinds, O hero !

In the case of abortion, (purification) is on that day only and one need not undergo (the pollution) for the period mentioned earlier.

101. For Brāhmaṇas the pollution lasts for one day and one night, for Kṣatriyās it is three full days, for Vaiśyas, six nights and for Śūdras, twelve days.

102. People of all the *varṇās* should perform the ceremonies at the time prescribed for each of them in order: after ten, twelve, fifteen and thirty days.

103. *Ekoddiṣṭa śrāddha* as well as *Sapiṇḍīkaraṇa śrāddha* for the deceased should be performed within one year (of death).

104. Then after the deceased attains *Pitṛtva* (i.e. becomes one with the *Pitṛs*), the deceased is to be satiated on the New-Moon and Full-Moon days and such other days as directed in the *Śruti.*

105. One must carry out, with the *Pitṛs* in view, gifting of land and so on, by which they go pleased, O *Rākṣasa* !

106. All such objects as were most liked by and anything in the house that was dearer to the deceased are to be gifted to one who is qualified, desiring the same to become inexhaustible.

107. The three *Vedas* are to be recited every day without fail by a learned man; money should be earned through rightful means and sacrifices are to be performed in accordance with one's capacity.

108. O *Rākṣasa* ! That activity which one does not hesitate to do and that which need not be hidden from the public, shall be attended to without any fear.

109. By functioning thus in this world, a householder achieves *Dharma, Artha* and *Kāma,* and happiness here and hereafter.

110. Thus the best stage of the householder have been described in brief. We will now speak of the *Dharmas* of *Vānaprastha* (forest-dweller) stage. Please listen.

111. After seeing the grand children and (noticing) the stooping of the body, a wise man should go over to the stage of *Vānaprastha* (forest-dweller) which brings about purity of self.

112-113. The way of *Vānaprastha* is this: (living) on the forest produce; self-realisation through austerities; sleeping on the ground; celibacy; worshipping gods, *Pitṛs* and guests; offering oblations; bathing thrice; growing hair and wearing bark garments; making use of oils (i.e. oily substances) available in the forest.

114-116. Giving up attachment to everything; celibacy; humility; control of senses; not residing in any place for a long time; not initiating any activity; having food by begging; not being easily irritable; desiring to seek knowledge of the self and self-realisation. These are the *Dharmas* of the fourth stage of life and they have been described by us.

O *Rākṣasa* ! Listen to other *Dharmas* of the *Varṇas* in general.

117. The three stages of householder, student and forest-dweller are also prescribed for a Kṣatriya and the conduct is as prescribed in the case of a Brāhmaṇa.

118. For a Vaiśya two stages are prescribed — those of householder and forest-dweller. A Śūdra has only one stage, that of householder, O *Rākṣasa* !.

119. No one should transgress the particular *Dharmas* prescribed for one's own *Varṇa*. God Bhāskara (Sun) gets angry with a twice-born who violates the *Veda* by abandoning one's own *Dharma* and resorting to the *Dharma* of others.

120. O *Rākṣasa* ! the wrathful God Sun destroys the family of such a person and augments his bodily ailments.

121. Therefore, no one shall give up one's *Dharma* and shall not (thereby) destroy one's family. For God Sun gets angry with him who abandons his own *Dharma*.

Pulastya said:

122. Thus said by the sage(s), Sukeśi having bowed down to the venerable sages, the very abodes of Brahmaṇa, flew up and went (back) to his city, pondering over the *Dharma* again and again.

CHAPTER FIFTEEN

The Birth of Lolārka

Pulastya said:

1. O divine sage ! Sukeśi after going to his excellent city, called all the *Rākṣasas* and spoke to them these righteous words—

Sukeśi said:

2-3. Non-violence, truthfulness, non-stealing, cleanliness, control of senses, charity, compassion, perseverance, celibacy, humility, speech which is always auspicious, and truthful and sweet, love of good actions, observance of good manners—all these lead to the other world.

4. Thus did the sages tell me the foremost *Dharma* coming down from ages. And I order you to follow it without any exception."

Pulastya said:

5. Then at the behest of Sukeśi, all the *Rākṣasas* gladly followed the *Dharma* upto thirteen parts.

6. Then the *Rākṣasas* endowed with good manners, indeed became most prosperous with children, grandchildren and material benefits.

7. Due to the powerful influence of the noble *Rākṣasas*, neither the sun nor the stars nor the moon could dare to move (across the sky).

8. Then, O Brāhmaṇa ! That city of the *Rākṣasas* (shone) in the worlds like the sun during the day and moon during the night.

9. Thus the movement of the sun across the sky could not be observed. The excellent city was taken for the moon because of its brightness.

10. The lotuses in the lotus ponds which refrained from blooming (during actual day time) thinking it to be night, opened during (actual) night desiring to bestow dignity, taking the city to be the sun.

11. The owls went out (during the day) thinking it to be night; the crows taking it to be the day (moved out and) killed the owls.

12. The Snātakas engaged in ablution (and recitation), stood in neck-deep waters of rivers, mistaking the night for day.

13. At the appearance of the city, the ruddy geese (*Cakravāka* birds) were not separated (at the end of the day) thinking that it was (still) day and they said this aloud.

14. Surely, some ruddy goose being separated from his mate, has given up his life sobbing on the lonely bank of a river.

15. At that, the *Sun* full of compassion, is heating up all the world with his hot rays and is not at all setting.

16. Others said: Surely some *Cakra* cock was dead and the hen afflicted with the grief of her mate, then performed penance.

17. The Sun god propitiated by that penance, has conquered the Moon and does not set indeed.

18. O great sage ! Those who were engaged in sacrifices, along with the Ṛtviks, kept the functions on in the sacrificial halls even during the night.

19. The devout Bhāgavatas worshipped Viṣṇu with devotion and others worshipped Brahmā and (yet) others Śiva (*Hara*) mistaking the Moon for the Sun (or vice versa).

20. The lovers felt that the Moon had done the right thing as the night was made enjoyable due to continuous moonlight.

21-22. Others said: The master of the universe, the great *Yogī*, the Discus-bearer along with Lakṣmī, was worshipped by us with fine flowers of great fragrance without hypocrasy, (on) the wish-granting second day called *Aśūnyaśayanā*, during the four months, *Bhādrapada* (*Nabhasya*) and others.

23. The Lord, pleased by that, has bestowed this excellent couch which is never disassociated from the best enjoyment and whose crest-garland (or glory) has not faded.

24-25. Others said: Observing the emaciation of the Moon, surely goddess Rohiṇī herself performed severe penance as per Vedic injunction, desirous of appeasing Rudra, on the meritorious eighth day called *Akṣaya*. And the pleased Śambhu conferred the boon on her spontaneously.

26. (Yet) others said: Lord Hari was certainly propitiated by the Moon with an unbroken (*Akhaṇḍa*) vow. Because of that, the Moon has never diminished in the sky.

27. (Some) others said: The Moon has worshipped the feet of Viṣṇu of infinite effulgence, who protected Dhruva.

28. Because of that the bright Moon, setting at nought the Sun, has given us joy and is shining like the Sun during the day.

29. That the Sun overpowered by the Moon is not shining as before is amply demonstrated by several other factors.

30. Since the charming groups of lotuses full of swarms of humming bees, are found blossomed, certainly the Sun has risen.

31. Even as these other lilies have brightly blossomed, it is known for certain that the mighty Moon has risen.

32. O Nārada ! (Having heard) the people uttering such words, the Sun thought, "How come the people are talking good and bad (about me)?"

33-34. The Lord thinking thus, went into meditation and came to know that the entire universe of three worlds had been enveloped by the *Rākṣasas*. The Master of *Yoga* reflected about the unbearability of the power and prosperity of the *Rākṣasa*.

35. Then he came to know that all of them were pure, deeply fond of good behaviour, engaged in the worship of gods and Brāhmaṇas, and endowed with *Dharma*.

36. At that the Sun, the destroyer of *Rākṣasas*, the lion to the elephant of darkness, having claws of hot rays, thought of their destruction.

37. Soon the Lord of Day understood the lapse of the *Rākṣasas*, namely, swerving from one's own *Dharma*—that destroys all *Dharmas*.

38. Anon the Sun, the destroyer of foes, was overpowered by anger. That city of the *Rākṣasas* got terrified and by the very thought (of the Sun), it got annihilated.

39. Then, that city when looked at by the Sun with eyes bulging with anger, got dislodged from the sky and fell down like a planet of exhausted merit.

40. Śālakaṭaṅkaṭa (Sukeśi) noticing all this (happening) thus, burst out loudly: "Salutations to Hara; (salutations to) Śarva."

41. Hearing that lament all the celestial bards moving about in the sky cried: "Alas ! Alas ! Here falls down a devotee of Hara."

42. The eternal and omnipresent Lord Śarva heard that cry of the celestial bards. Having heard it, he pondered: "By whom is he being felled to the earth?"

43. He came to know that that city of the *Rākṣasa* was felled by the Thousand-rayed leader of the gods. Then the Three-eyed Lord became furious.

44. The furious Lord Śambhu saw the Sun. By the mere sight of the Three-eyed Lord, (the Sun) fell down from the sky.

45. Dislodged from the sky, the Sun fell down of his own accord into the region occupied by *Vāyu* (wind), like a stone ejected by a machine.

46. Falling through the mid-region of the air, the Sun with his body shining like the flower of *Kiṁśuka* (bastard teak), was surrounded by *Kinnaras* and celestial bards.

47. The Sun enveloped by rays and falling from the sky appeared like the half-ripened palm fruit surrounded by monkeys and falling from tree.

48. "If you wish your welfare, you drop yourself in the (sacred) region of Hari" (so said the sages). Then the Sun even as he was falling down, asked the sages rich-in-penance—

49. "Which is that holy region of Hari ? You please tell me quickly." The sages told that Sun: "Listen about the region of great benefits.

50. (This land) is now (holy to) Vāsudeva and in future (it will be holy) to Śiva. (It extends) from Yogiśāyī to Keśava. This holy place by name Vārāṇasī is sacred to Hari."

51. Hearing it, Lord Sun scorched by the eye of Śiva, landed in the area between the rivers *Varaṇā* and *Asī*.

52. Then the Sun being burnt dived into the river *Asī* and rolled about. (Then) he reached *Varaṇā* (river) and immersed himself freely.

53. Again he went to *Asī* and back to *Varaṇā*. (The Sun) afflicted with the fire of the Three-eyed Lord, restlessly tossed himself like a revolving firebrand.

54-55. O Brāhmaṇa ! At that juncture, the sages, *Yakṣas, Rākṣasas, Nāgas, Vidyādharas,* birds, *Apsarās* and all the *Bhūtas, Pretas,* etc., that were in the chariot of the Sun—all those went to the abode of Brahmā to inform him, O sage!

56. Then Brahmā, the Lord of gods, along with the gods, hastened for the sake of the Sun to the *Mandāra* (mountain), the charming abode of Maheśvara.

57. Having gone there, they saw the Trident-wielding Lord of gods, Śaṅkara. Having propitiated him, they brought him to Vārāṇasī for the sake of the Sun.

58. Then, Śaṅkara took the Sun in his hand, named him Lola and again put him in the chariot.

59. As the Sun was put back into the sky, Brahmā approached Sukeśin and fixed him again in the sky along with his city and relatives.

60. Śaṅkara embraced Sukeśī who was also made to ascend. (Then) (Śaṅkara) went to his abode *Vairāja* after bowing down to Lord Keśava.

61. Thus in the past, O Nārada ! The city of Sukeśi was hurled down to earth by the Sun-god. And the Sun-god was thrown down to earth and burnt by the eye of Śiva.

62. The Sun was again raised to the sky from the earth for shining brightly by Bhava and the Lord of *Rākṣasas* along with his city and relatives was raised to the sky by Brahmā.

Note: *'Sukeśiḥ'* and *'Sukeśin'*: both the names occur in this and previous chapters.

CHAPTER SIXTEEN

Aśūnyā-Śayanā-Dvitīyā and Kālāṣṭamī

Nārada said:

1. Please tell me about (the vows) which the lovers spoke as having been observed by Moon to propitiate gods Hari and Hara.

Pulastya said:

2. O Nārada ! Listen to the description of the meritorious vows to be observed in order to please the all-knowing Śiva and Viṣṇu as set forth by the lovers.

3. When the Sun reaches *Āṣāḍha* after the completion of *Uttarāyaṇa* (summer solstice), then the Lord of gods, the Consort of Lakṣmī, sleeps on the (couch of) hoods of Śeṣa.

4. When the Lord goes to sleep, *Gandharvas, Yakṣas,* and the Mothers of gods go to sleep in due order.

Nārada said:

5. Please tell me about the auspicious mode of sleeping of the gods and others following that of Janārdana (Viṣṇu) in due order.

Pulastya said:

6. O sage ! When the Sun is in Gemini constellation, on the eleventh day of the bright fortnight, the Lord of the universe prepares the bed.

7. Making the bed of hoods of *Śeṣa* serpent, he worships Keśava. Wearing *Pavitra* (a ring of *kuśa* grass worn on the fourth finger — MW), he properly honours the twice-born ones.

8. On the twelfth day, he, clad in yellow (silk) garments, being devout and purified, gains permission of the Brāhmaṇas and goes to sleep with comfort.

9. Then on the thirteenth day, *Kāma* sleeps on the auspicious bed made of sweet-smelling *Kadamba* flowers.

10. Then on the fourteenth day, *Yakṣas* (sleep) on the cool and comforting bed made of golden lotuses spread with comforting pillows.

11. On the Full-Moon day, the Spouse of Umā (Śiva) sleeps on the bed of tiger skin, covering his matted hair with another piece of skin.

12. By then the Sun enters Cancer constellation; it is *Dakṣiṇāyana* (winter solstice), and it is the night of the heavenly beings.

13. O sinless one ! On the first day (of the dark fortnight), Brahmā sleeps on the bed of blue lotuses, steering the universe on the excellent path.

14. On the second day, Viśvakarmā, on the third day, the Daughter of Mountain (Pārvatī); on the fourth day Vināyaka and Dharmarāja (*Yama*) (sleeps) on the fifth day.

15. Skanda sleeps on the sixth day, God Sun on the seventh day, Kātyāyanī on the eighth day, Lakṣmī on the ninth day.

16. O Brāhmaṇa ! The chief snakes who live on wind sleep on the tenth day; Sādhyas on the eleventh day (of dark fortnight).

17. O sage ! The order (of gods) sleeping in the months beginning with *Śrāvaṇa* was spoken to you. As the gods sleep, rainy season arrives.

18. O best of sages ! The male cranes along with females reach the top of lofty trees; the crows too build nests.

19-21. The female crows languid due to pregnancy, retire in this season.

The day on which Prajāpati Viśvakarmā retires to sleep, is the second day which is auspicious and holy and is called (*Aśūnya*) *Śayanā.* On that day, one should worship four-armed Viṣṇu (with *Śrīvatsa* on the chest), reclining on a couch along with his consort Lakṣmī, with scents (sandalpaste) and flowers, O sage ! Then a knowing devotee should keep fruits on the couch for the Lord. Having offered wholesome fruits, Viṣṇu should be prayed to—

22-23. "O Lord of three strides ! O infinite one ! O lord immanent in the universe ! Just as you are not separated from Lakṣmī, so please our beds be never vacant with your favour.

O Lord of gods ! O one of unlimited prowess ! O Viṣṇu ! by that very truth by virtue of which you have found a bed never bereft of Lakṣmī, please there not be loss of family-life to me."

24. So putting forth (the prayer), propitiating the god of gods again and again, O divine sage ! The devotee should eat food without oil and salt at night.

25. Next day, the wise (devotee) should offer fruits to a venerable twice-born. With the offering one should pray, "May the Consort of Lakṣmī be pleased."

26. One should observe the four-month vow in this way, till the Sun is found to be in the constellation *Scorpio.*

27. Then the gods get awakened in the sequential order, O sage ! When (the Sun is) in the constellation *Sagittarius,* Viṣṇu gets awakened first and then *Kāma.*

28. On the second day then, one should gift an idol of Lakṣmīdhara (Viṣṇu) and a bed with bedspreads, in accordance with one's financial capacity.

29. This is the first vow which I have described to you, O great sage ! By observing which no one experiences (the pangs of) separation.

30. Similarly, the auspicious eighth day of the dark fortnight of *Bhādrapada* conjoined with *Mārgaśirā* asterism is known as *Kālāṣṭamī.*

31. On that day, Śaṅkara rests in all *Liṅgas.* If one stays near a *Liṅga* (on that day), the worship, then is considered inexhaustible.

32. On that day, a man of learning should bathe with cow's urine and water. After the ablution, the Three-eyed Lord is to be worshipped with flowers of *Dhattūra* (white thorn apple).

33. He should offer incense with the resin of saffron. The food to be offered is honey and clarified butter. Then

praying 'May the Lord with three-eyes be pleased with me', he should be gifted *Dakṣiṇā.*

34. O best of the twice-born ! Brāhmaṇa should be offered food (of honey and ghee) as well as gold. In the same way, one should observe fast with all the senses under control, during the *Āśvina* month.

35. On the ninth day, one should bathe with cow-dung and perform worship with lotuses, offer incense of the resin of *Sarja* (*Sal*) tree, and honey and sweets for food.

36. After fasting on the eighth day, one should have ablution on the ninth day. *Dakṣiṇā* should be gifted with sesamum, saying 'May Golden-eyed Lord be pleased with me'.

37. During the month of *Kārttika*, ablution is with milk; worship is with *Karavīra* flowers; incense is of resin of *Śrīvāsa* and the food-offering is honey and rice baked in milk.

38. Silver along with the food-offering is to be gifted to a Brāhmaṇa and should politely pray, "May Lord Sthāṇu be pleased with me."

39. After fasting on the eighth day ablution is to be taken on the ninth day.

During the *Mārgaśirā* month, ablution is with curds and worship is of Rudra.

40. Incense is of the resin of *Śrī* (*Bilva*) tree; food-offering is rice with honey; *Dakṣiṇā* of red paddy with the food-offering is spoken of.

41. The learned one should say, "Salutations! May Śarva be pleased."

Ablution during *Puṣya* month is with ghee and worship is with the auspicious *Tagara* flowers.

42. Incense is the resin of *Madhuka* tree and the food-offering is honey with rice flour. *Dakṣiṇā* is to be given with green-gram to propitiate the Lord of the universe.

43. One should say, "Salutations to the Three-eyed God of gods"

During *Māgha* month, ablution is with waters of *Darbha* grass; worship of Śiva is with *lilies.*

44. Incense is of the resin of *Kadamba* tree and food-offering is rice cooked with sesamum. Gold with the food-offering cooked in milk is to be given (as *Dakṣiṇā*).

45. One should pray, "May the Great Lord, the Consort of Umā, be pleased with me." Thus the vow set forth is completed after six months. On the completion of the vow, the Three-eyed God is to be bathed (*abhiṣeka*) in due order.

46. The Lord is to be worshipped, smearing (the idol) with jaggery mixed with *Gorocana* (yellow pigment). (The Lord should be prayed:) "Be pleased, I am in misery and you are the master. Please effect proper destruction of my agony."

47. Then on the eighth day of dark fortnight of *Phālguna* month, people with vow of control of senses should observe the prescribed fast, O best of the twice-born..

48. Then the next day, having bathed (the Lord) with the five products of cow, one should worship with jasmine flowers and with incense of red sandal.

49-50. The food-offering is rice mixed with jaggery along with ghee in a copper pot. O sage ! The food should be offered to the twice-born ones together with *Dakṣiṇā.* A pair of clothing is also to be given and Rudra to be propitiated by uttering his name.

In the month of *Caitra,* bathing is with the waters of fig and worship is with white thorn-apple flowers.

51. A wise man should offer the incense of *Mahiṣa guggulu* mixed with ghee. The food-offering is the pleasing ghee with deep fried sweets (modaka).

52-53. The *Dakṣiṇā* along with food offering is spoken of as deer skin (and to be given) saying: "Salutation to you, O Nāgeśvara !" O Nārada ! Devanātha should be propitiated with faith.

In the month of Vaiśākha, bathing with waters of fragrant flowers is prescribed.

54. Worship of the omnipresent Śaṅkara is to be done with mango blossoms. The incense is the gum of *Sarja* (*Sal*) tree. The food-offering is ghee with fruits.

55-56. A scholar should be repeated the name of *Śiva-Śālaghna.* Water-pots with the food as well as clothes and rice and other things should be offered to the Brāhmaṇas, fixing the attention on and having deep devotion to the Lord.

In the month of *Jyeṣṭha,* bathing is to be done with myrobalan fruits, and worship is to be done with white thorn-apple flowers.

57. The Lord with ferocious eyes, having emblem of the bull and bestowing prosperity should be worshipped. The food-offering to the god is fried flour with ghee and mixed with curds.

58-60. A devotee should be given in charity a pair of foot-wear and an umbrella. To propitiate the Lord of the universe, one must utter this with devotion: "O blotter of Bhaga's eyes! O feller of Pūṣan's teeth ! Salutations to you."

In the month of *Āṣāḍha,* bathing with *Bilva* fruits and worship with white thorn-apple flowers is prescribed. Incense to be offered is with the gum of *Sallika.* The food-offering is cakes with ghee and the *Dakṣiṇā* is barley with ghee.

61-64. This must be uttered loudly: "O Destroyer of Dakṣa's sacrifice ! Salutations to you."

In the month of *Śrāvaṇa,* one must bathe with *Bhṛṅgarāja* and worship with the leaves and fruits of *Bilva* tree. Incense of *Agaru* (*agallochum*) is to be offered; food-offering being sweets (*modaka*) with ghee and curds and rice, sesamum flower with jaggery, dishes made of black-gram with deep fried *śaṣkuli* snacks.

Dakṣiṇā–a white bull, an auspicious black cow, gold and red cloth–is to be offered to a Brāhmaṇa. And the wise ones should repeat the name of Śiva; the bearer-of-Gaṅgā.

65-66. It is good to end fast after these other six months. Having thus worshipped the Bull-bannered Lord for a whole year, one attains imperishable world as assured by Maheśvara.

O divine sage ! this meritorious and auspicious vow destroying all sins, was revealed by Śaṅkara himself and it is as it has been revealed and not otherwise.

CHAPTER SEVENTEEN

Birth of Mahiṣāsura

Pulastya said:

1. O Brāhmana ! When in the month of *Āśvayuja* (*Āśvina*), the lotus of the Prajāpati (Brahmā) emerged out of the navel (of Viṣṇu), then there came into existence, the divine gardens.

2. (There appeared) from the tip of the hand of *Kāma*, the *Kadamba* (tree) charming to the eyes; hence his pleasure swells by the *Kadamba.*

3. The banyan tree, O Nārada ! Came into existence because of Maṇibhadra, the chief of *Yakṣas*; and he is always delighted in that.

4. The auspicious *Dhattūra* (white thornapple) plant grew from the chest of Śiva (*Maheśvara*) and, is an object of pleasure to that Śerva (Śiva).

5. From the middle of the body of Brahmā the thorny *Khadira* tree shining like emerald was born and it became dearer to the Creator.

6. From the hand of Pārvatī, grew the jasmine bush. The temples (forehead) of *Gaṇeśa* is adorned by *Sindhuvāra.*

7. From the right side of Yama was born *Palāśa* (bastard teak tree) and from his left side, the dreadful black *Udumbara* (fig tree), the agitating and imperishable one.

8. From Skanda was born *Bandhujīva* (red hibiscus); from the sun, the *Pipal* tree; from Kātyāyinī grew *Śamī* and from Lakṣmī's hand, the *Bilva* tree.

9. O Brāhmaṇa ! From the mouth of the serpents came into being the clump of reeds, and from the back of the large tail of Vāsuki, both white and black *Dūrva* grass.

10. *Harita Candana* (yellow sandal tree) grew from the chest of Sādhyas. These trees born of the particular gods are their favourites.

11-12. (During this beautiful and happy *Āśvīna* month), on the fine auspicious eleventh day of the bright half, one should worship Viṣṇu before the onset of autumn, with leaves, flowers, fruits, scents, colours, juices, and principal herbs. By that one grows strong and powerful.

13-15. One should offer for worship of Keśava: ghee, sesamum, barley, gold, silver, etc.; gems, pearls, corals, and various kinds of cloth; and those food-offerings whole of which could be partaken and having sweet, pungent, sour, astringent, salt and bitter tastes. These (when offered to Keśava) become plentiful before the completion of the year.

16. O divine sage having fasted (that day), one with self-control, should bathe the next day (as prescribed) and in the same manner, one should take bath for a whole year (on the days of vow).

17. White mustard or sesamum is prescribed to be used for the cleaning the body. (The idol of) Viṣṇu (*Padmanābha*) should be bathed with ghee.

18. Oblations are to be offered with the same (material) and charity should be performed in accordance with one's capacity, O twice-born ! Then one should adorn Keśava from foot to head with flowers.

19. Different fragrant substances should be used for incense, so that the whole year may have a distinction. The master of the universe should be worshipped with gold, gems and cloths.

20-24. The food-offerings should be: red sugar-candy, semi-liquid dishes and sacrificial offerings. Then, O best of sages ! Worshipping Padmanābha (Lotus-navelled Lord), the Lord of gods and the master of the unverse, one should pray with this *Mantra*, O sage of good vows ! "O Lotus-navelled god ! O consort of Lakṣmī ! O effulgent one ! Salutations to you. O Keśava ! May *Dharma, Artha, Kāma* and *Mokṣa* be mine in their entirety even as you are the whole from all counts, O Lord having lotus-petal like eyes. By that very truth, O Keśava ! May *Dharma* and others be mine in full." Thus a self-controlled person should observe that vow in all its details keeping fast during one full year without break. On the completion of this, the deities are certainly pleased.

25. *Dharma, Artha, Kāma* and *Mokṣa* and others become inexhaustible indeed. Thus I have described the vows which were referred to by the solicitory ones.

26-38. I shall now dwell on this auspicious *Viṣṇu-pañjara* (magical prayer): "O lord of gods ! Salutations, salutations to you. With the discus *Sudarśana* in your hand, protect me in the east. O Viṣṇu ! I surrender unto you. Holding *Kaumodakī* mace, O Lotus-navelled lord of unlimited effulgence ! Protect me in the south. O Viṣṇu ! I surrender unto you. O puruṣa par-excellence ! Salutations to you. Holding lotus along with the mace, protect me in the west. O Viṣṇu ! I surrender unto you. O Lotus-eyed lord ! Holding the (enemy) destroying club, protect me in the north. O lord of the universe ! I take refuge in you. O Hari ! Salutations to you. With the bow *Śārṅga* and the missile Nārāyaṇa, protect me in the north-east. O killer of the *Rākṣasas* ! I take refuge in you. Holding the excellent conch Pāñcajanya and the blossomed lotus, protect me in the south-east, O Viṣṇu ! O sacrificial boar ! Wearing the armour *Sūryaśata* and holding the sword and the shield, protect me in the south-west, O god of divine form ! O one having the form of man-lion ! Wearing the garland *Vaijayantī* and the neck-ornament *Śrīvatsa*, protect me in the north-west. O horse-headed one! Salutation to you. Riding on Garuḍa, O Janārdana ! Protect me always in the sky, O unconquerable one ! O invincible one ! salutations to you. You riding on *Viśālākṣa*, protect me in the nether world. O great Tortoise! salutations to you. O great Fish ! Salutations to you ! Forming a cage with your eight arms, O god ! Protect my hands, head, feet and all. O Puruṣa-par-excellence ! Salutations to you." O best of the twice-born ! This great *Viṣṇu-pañjara* was imparted by Lord Śiva to Kātyāyinī for her protection when she destroyed the demon, Mahiṣāsura, Namara, Raktabīja and other enemies of gods.

Nārada said:

39-40. Who is this called Mahiṣa ? Who are Raktabīja and others ? Who is this one called Kātyāyini that killed Mahiṣāsura, Namara, Raktabīja and other enemies of gods ? Who is this one named Mahiṣa ? Where was he ? Of whom was he born ?

41. And who is this called Raktabīja ? And whose son was Namara? O father ! You please relate to me all this in detail.

Pulastya said:

42. Listen, I will relate the story that destroys sin. O sage ! this Kātyāyinī is (also called) Durgā, who is the grantor of every wish.

43. In the days of yore, there were two very strong and dreadful demons, Rambha and Karambha, who shook the world.

44. O divine sage ! They having no sons, performed penance to get sons. The two *Daityas* stood in the waters of *Pañcanada* for several years.

45. Of them one stood in water and the other had four fires (burning) around him. Both Rambha and Karambha (were) (concentrating) on *Yakṣa* Mālavaṭa.

46. Indra in the form of a crocodile caught the one who had entered waters by the legs, and killed him as he wished.

47. Then Rambha was enraged by the death of his brother and the mighty one desired to sever his own head and offer it to fire.

48. Then holding the hair of his head and the sword bright like the sun, he was about to cut off his own head when he was stopped by Fire-god.

49-50. Fire-god said: "O great *Daitya* ! Do not kill yourself. Sin of murdering a person is itself not easy to get rid of and sin of suicide is still more difficult.

O hero ! What you seek, I give you as you desire. Do not end yourself, for, the story of a person dead comes to an end here indeed."

51-52. Then Rambha said: "If you are certainly bestowing upon me a boon, then may I have a son who outshines you and conquers the three worlds. The *Daitya* shall be invincible for any god in battlefield. A mighty one like Wind-god, he shall be able to assume any form he wishes and be a master of weapons and missiles, O Fire-god !"

53. O Brāhmaṇa ! The omniscient (Fire-god) said to him: "It will certainly be so. (But) the female to whom (he) loses his heart, will kill the *Asura.*"

54. Then the *Dānava* so told by Fire-god, went to see *Yakṣa* Mālavaṭa surrounded by *Yakṣas.*

55. There resided with them Padmanidhi unmindful of anything else. They had lots of elephants, buffaloes, horses, cows, goats and sheep.

56. O great sage ! At the very sight of all of them, the king of *Dānavas* fixed his mind on a three year old handsome female-buffalo.

57. She too desiring (his company) speedily approached the *Daitya*-chief. He in his turn goaded by destiny, had sexual union (with her).

58. She conceived and then the *Dānava* taking her with him entered the nether world and went to his residence.

59. He was questioned by all the *Dānavas* and was forsaken by the relatives, because he had committed an evil. And he again went to Mālavaṭa.

60. That charming female buffalo too went to the holy and excellent colony of *Yakṣas.*

61. As that young female buffalo resided in that pious forest, O sage ! She gave birth to a bright son (male buffalo), able to assume any form.

62. When she was in her courses (after the birth of her son) another male-buffalo saw her and she approached the great *Daitya* (Rambha) protecting her chastity.

63. The *Dānava* seeing that male-buffalo coming with his snout raised, immediately drew his sword and ran after him.

64. The *Daitya*, on the other hand, was hit at chest by the buffalo with his pointed horns. With his chest being rent, he fell down on the ground and died.

65. When the husband died the young she-buffalo took refuge with the *Yakṣas*. She was then saved by the *Yakṣas* who drove away the buffalo.

66. The love-lorn male-buffalo restrained by the *Yakṣas*, fell into a beautiful lake and became a *Daitya* after death.

67. Under the name Namara; he became famous by his strength and powers. She under the care of *Yakṣas*, stayed in the forest counting her time.

68. That dead Demon-king was put on the funeral pyre by Mālavaṭa and other *Yakṣas* and that young lady mounted the pyre with her husband.

69. Then there sprang up in the midst of flames a man dreadful to look at. That frightening person with sword in hand, made the *Yakṣas* flee.

70. Then all the buffaloes sparing the protector Mahiṣa, the son of Rambha, were killed by that great man.

71. O great sage ! That *Daitya* was known by the name Raktabīja, who conquered the gods together with Indra, Rudra, Arka and Maruta, on all sides.

72. So powerful was this bull among *Dānavas*, but the *Buffalo-Rākṣasa* (Mahiṣāsura) shone with a surpassing Valor, and was anointed in the kingdom (of the *Daityas*) by the great *Asura*-chiefs Śambara, Tāraka and others who were vanquished.

73. Sun, Moon and Indra unable to (resist him) gave up their positions along with the gods, the Guardians of Quarters, Agni and Ādityas, and darkness engulfed (the world).

CHAPTER EIGHTEEN

Glorification of Devī

Pulastya said:

1. Then the gods conquered by Mahiṣa gave up their positions and keeping Brahmā in front went along with their weapons and vehicles to see the Mace-and-discus bearing God, the Lord of Śrī (*Lakṣmī*).

2. Having gone there, they found the esteemed gods Viṣṇu and Śiva, seated together. Seeing and saluting the bringers of success, they narrated to them the misdeeds of the foe, Mahiṣa.

3-4. "O Lord, taking possession of the positions of Aśvins, Sun, Moon, Wind, Fire, Brahmā, Varuṇa, Indra and other gods, we have been ousted out of heaven and have been forced to resort to earth by Mahiṣāsura.

You having heard this, instruct what is congenial to the gods who have taken refuge in you. Otherwise, we will now go to the nether world being driven away by the *Dānava* in battle."

5. Having heard these words of the mentally distressed (gods), Viṣṇu, Hari, the imperishable soul, considered the situation, along with Śiva, and immediately flew into rage like the world destroying fire.

6. Following that fit of rage of Viṣṇu, Śiva and Brahmā and Indra and other gods also became similarly enraged; (then) a splendid effulgence of high potency emerged from their faces.

7. O sage ! That effulgence got unified like the peak of a mountain, in the excellent hermitage of Kātyāyana. The great sage also sent forth a glow.

8. The glow (of the gods) blazing like a thousand bright suns, was encircled by the glow issued from the sage. From

that was born Kātyāyanī of wide and tremulous eyes and of body pure by *yoga.*

9. The face was formed by the effulgence of Śiva; the three eyes by that of Fire; the hair by that of Yama, eighteen arms were formed by that of Hari.

10. The close pair of breasts was formed by the effulgence of Soma, the waist by that of Indra, the broad thighs, shanks and hips by that of Varuṇa.

11. The lotus-bud like feet were formed by the effulgence of Brahmā, the great grand sire of the world; the toes by that of *Ādityas* and the fingers by that of *Vasus.*

12. The teeth manifested by the glow of Prajāpatis, the nose by that of Yakṣa, the ears by that of Maruts. By that of Sādhyas, manifested the two eyebrows charming like Kāma's bow.

13. That most splendid and great splendour came to be known by the name Kātyāyanī and she became famous in the entire world by that very name.

14. The benevolent Trident-bearing Lord gave her a trident; Viṣṇu gave a discus; Varuṇa a conch; Fire-god a spear; Wind-god a bow; Vivasvān a pair of quivers with inexhaustible arrows.

15. Indra gave Vajra with a bell; Yama a staff; Kubera a mace; Brahmā a rosary and a water-pot; Kāla gave a dreadful sword along with a shield.

16. Soma gave her a necklace as well as a chowrie; Ocean-god a garland; Himavān a lion. The divine sculptor gave her a crest jewel, ear-studs, a crescent moon and an axe.

17. The King of *Gandharvas* gave her the befitting silver-plated goblet full of the drink; the Lord of serpents gave a serpent garland; the Seasons gave a garland of never-fading flowers.

18. Then that three-eyed greatest goddess being highly pleased, burst into a roar of laughter. The prominent gods together with Indra and with Viṣṇu, Rudra, Indu (Moon), Wind, Fire and Sun praised her:

19-20. "Salutations to the goddess of pure body because of yoga and adored by the gods, who exists everywhere on earth in the form of sleep, who causes thirst, modesty, hunger and fear, who is complexion, faith, memory, nourishment, patience, reflection, power, fortune, intellect, memory, forgiveness, and illusion. Salutations to the goddess who is destiny."

21. Then the goddess adored by the chief of gods, went riding on the lion towards the forest on the peak of the high Vindhya mountain dwarfed by Agastya.

Nārada said:

22. O sage of pure and upright actions ! Why did the venerable great sage Agastya make that mountain into one of low peak? For whom was it done and for what purpose? You please tell me.

Pulastya said:

23. In days of yore, the course of the Sun moving in the sky was obstructed by the Vindhya mountain. Then the Sun approached the Pitcher-born Sage and said this to him at the close of his (daily) sacrifice.

24. "O twice-born ! I have come to you from a great distance. O best of sages, please come to the succor of the universe. Give me a gift which I have in mind so that I may move about freely in the sky."

25. Hearing the significant words of the Sun, the Pot-born Sage said this: "I give the gift desired by your mind; no suppliant goes from me with a face turned away."

26. Hearing these words full of nectar from the Pot-born Sage, the Lord (Sun) spoke placing his (folded) hands on the head: "Now this lofty mountain Vindhya obstructs my path; O venerable sir ! please see that it is bent low."

27. At these words of the Sun, the Pot-born Sage said: "Be assured that its peak is made of low by me. The mountain

will be subdued by your rays. What misery is there for you who have taken refuge in my feet ?

28. So saying, the Pot-born great Sage praising the Sun with utmost devotion, left Daṇḍaka (forest) for the Vindhya mountain assuming the form of an old man.

29. Having gone to the mountain, the sage said: "In the south there is an excellent place of pilgrimage of great merits. I am an old man and am unable to climb up your (peaks); therefore, may you lower yourself immediately."

30. So told by the noble sage, that mountain lowered its peaks. The chief of the great sages, going up and crossing the Vindhya, told the mountain—

31. "Till such time as I do not return again to my great hermitage from the sacred spot with my body cleansed, you should not rise up, otherwise I am going to curse for your disregard."

32. So saying the venerable sage, went to south and at once soaring into the sky, stayed in that direction (thinking): "I will go there at the appropriate time."

33. Having constructed there an exquisite hermitage with portals of pure gold arches and leaving there the daughter of the Vidarbha king (Lopāmudrā), he returned to his own calm hermitage (in Daṇḍaka).

34. At regular fixed period every month and on festive days, he would reside in the sky-borne hermitage. During the rest of the time, the sage of unlimited splendours practised penance staying in Daṇḍaka forest.

35. Vindhya too having seen the great strain (of the sage) in moving (up and down) (and) because of the fear of the great sage, did not at all rise. Thinking that he did not yet return he remained with the highest peak bent very low.

36. O great sage ! Thus that lofty mountain was made a low-peaked one. That Durgā adored by the sages stood on its high peak for the destruction of the *Dānavas.*

37. Gods, *Siddhas, Great Reptiles, Vidyādharas,* all groups of *Bhūtas,* along with all the *Apsarās,* all with their anguish gone remained there causing delight to Kātyāyanī.

CHAPTER NINETEEN

The Greatness of Devī

Pulastya said:

1. Then the two great *Dānavas,* Caṇḍa and Muṇḍa, saw that Kātyayānī dwelling as an ascetic there on the top of the lofty mountain.

2. As soon as the two *Dānavas,* Caṇḍa and Muṇḍa, the messengers of Mahiṣāsura, (saw her) they quickly descended from the mountain and went to their place.

They met the Lord of *Daityas* and told him—

Caṇḍa and Muṇḍa said:

3. You are well-off. But, O *Asura*-lord ! Now come on, let us (visit) Vindhya. There is a majestic divine lady, a maiden, most beautiful of the celestial belles.

4. The cloud is surpassed by her with curly hair; the moon is excelled by the damsel with her face; the three fires are set at naught by her three eyes; the conch is beaten by her neck.

5. The round breasts with nipples sunk, surpass as it were, the temples of an elephant. The two breasts are as if a strong (hill) fortress made by Kāma only, considering you as a conqueror of everyone.

6. Her stout eighteen arms carrying weapons appear like iron bars; they are as though machines made by Kāma knowing fully your valour.

7. O *Daitya*-lord ! Her wavy waist having three folds with the beautiful line of hair appear like stairs fashioned by Kāma eager to climb up due to fear from you.

8. O *Asura* ! That line of hair reaching her stout breasts, indeed appears like the gush of sweat of Kāma while climbing afflicted by fear from you.

9. Her navel deep and curving round and round to the right, appears very much like the seal put on the house of loveliness by king Kāma himself.

10. The lovely buttocks of the doe-eyed lady, rubbed all around by the girdle, are, I suppose, the city of Kāma concealed by rampart and (therefore) impenetrable.

11. The round, hairless, soft and matchless thighs of the young damsel appear like the space prepared by the Shark-bannered God for the people to dwell.

12. So also, O great Mahiṣāsura ! Those two raised knees appear beautiful. Indeed, the creator after having created, was too exhausted to survey it and he placed his two palms (over it).

13. O *Daitya*-lord ! Her round, hairless and pretty shanks which appear as if fashioned after subduing the worlds, are indeed created surpassing the arrow (of Kāma).

14. Her feet appearing like the interior part of lotus have been fashioned with care by the creator. The series of jewel-like nails were mistaken as the series of stars in the sky.

15. O *Dānava*-lord ! A maiden of such a form holding great formidable weapons, was watched by me to (my) heart's content but I do not at all know who that damsel is and whose daughter she is.

16. O great master of *Asuras* ! She is an exquisite jewel that has come down to earth leaving the heaven. So go to Vindhyas, find out for yourself and do whatever is aggreeable and appropriate to you.

Pulastya said:

17. O great sage ! Having listened to the captivating description of the Devī, Mahiṣāsura made up his mind saying, "There is nothing to be considered in this."

18. O Brāhmaṇa ! The good and evil of human beings have been appropriately ordained by the creator well beforehand. Accordingly, a person is drawn into or does by himself something which he is destined to follow.

19. Then the overlord of *Asuras* ordered Namuṇḍa, Namara, Caṇḍa, Biḍālanetra, Kapila, Bāṣkala, Ugrāyudha, Vikṣura, and Raktabīja.

20. Those mercilessly fighting sons of Danu beating the battle-drums left heaven and reached the (Vindhya) mountain. They set their camp at its foot and stood in battle-readiness.

21. Then the commander of the *Dānavas*, Dundubhi, son of Maya, the annihilator of the forces of the foes and having the voice of a drum was despatched by Mahiṣāsura.

22. O Brāhmaṇa ! Though Dundubhi approached Devī, he stood in the sky only and said: "O young lady, I am the messenger of Mahiṣāsura, the son of the great *Asura* Rambha that was matchless in warfare."

23. Kātyāyanī replied to Dundubhi: "Come (forward), come O *Daitya*-chief ! Casting away fear; verily speak out the message as conveyed by the son of Rambha, without embarrassment."

24. Then at the words of Kātyāyanī (Śivā), the Son of Diti left the sky and descended on to earth and sitting comfortably in a grand seat, conveyed the message of the son of Rambha.

Dundubhi said:

25-28. O Devī ; the *Daitya* Mahiṣāsura ! The foe of gods bids you thus: "The powerless gods are roaming on the earth; they have been vanquished by me in the battle.

"The heaven, the earth and the mid-air region–all these as well as the nether world, the kings and the others–are under my control. O young lady ! I am Indra, I am Rudra and I am the Sun; I am the overlord in all the worlds.

"Neither in the firmament, nor on earth, nor in heaven, nor even in the nether world, is there any one (who could think of facing me) in warfare. O lady of wide eyes ! I have now everything earned by my valour.

"You are an exquisite jewel among women and you are unmarried. And I have come to this mountain for your sake. Therefore, resort to me, the master of the universe. I, being a sovereign and emperor, am a proper husband for you."

Pulastya said:

29-30. So told by the Son of Diti, Kātyāyanī Durgā replied to the son of Maya: "It is true that the *Daitya*-king is a supreme emperor on the earth. It is also true that the gods are conquered (by him) in the battle.

But, O *Daitya*-lord ! In our family, the custom called *Śulka,* payment of money to the bride's parents, is well in vogue. If Mahiṣa should now offer that for me, surely I join Mahiṣa as husband."

31. Hearing these words, the son of Maya said: "Tell me what is the *śulka,* O lady of broad petal-like eyes ! (Mahiṣa) is prepared to give even his head for your sake. What *śulka* could there be which is beyond his reach?"

Pulastya said:

32. So told by the *Dānava*-chief, Kātyāyanī audibly bellowed and said this with a laugh for the good of all moveable and immoveable (creation).

Śri Devī said:

33. O Demon ! Listen, the *śulka* emphatically prescribed by the elders in our family is that he who overpowers a lady born in our family, in a battle, shall become the husband of that lady.

Pulastya said:

34. Having heard the words of Devī, the *Dānava*-lord Dundubhi returned to Mahiṣa and reported the matter accordingly.

35. That (*Dānava*) of enormous powers, on the other hand, surrounded the peak of Vindhya along with all *Daityas*, desirous of fighting with Sarasvatī (Kātyāyanī).

36. Then, O Nārada ! The *Daitya* commander Vikṣura made the *Dānava* by name Namara the leader of the army.

37. He (Namara) being appointed by him, took along with him a part of the force complete with all the four divisions and ran after Durgā with all might.

38. Then the gods led by Brahmā seeing him attack, said this to Mahādevī, " Please put on the armour."

39. Then Durgā replied to gods: "O gods ! I am not going to put on the armour. Which wretch of a demon can stand before me?"

40. When Devī did not don the armour, the protector from weapons, the *Viṣṇu-pañjara* was recited (by Śiva) to guard her.

41. O Brāhmaṇa ! Durgā being protected by it, crushed the supreme *Dānava* Mahiṣa who could not be killed by any god.

42. Thus in days of yore, the *Viṣṇu-pañjara* was recited for the lady-of-wide-eyes and she in her turn killed the great Mahiṣāsura by (merely) kicking him.

43. O Twice-born ! The *Viṣṇu-pañjara* of such powers is spoken of as most prominent of all the protective measures (*Mantras*). Who can indeed on this earth, humble the pride of the person in whose heart abides *Cakrapāṇi* (Disc-bearer Viṣṇu)?

CHAPTER TWENTY

Mahiṣāsura Killed

Nārada said:

1. How did Kātyāyanī kill Mahiṣāsura who had a vehicle and was followed by troops ? Please tell me in detail.

2. And a doubt lurks in my heart, O Brāhmaṇa ! Why did she crush him down under her feet even though there were weapons.

Pulastya said:

3. Listen with attention to this ancient story of great merits that eradicates fear. It occurred at the beginning of *Deva Yuga.*

4. That enraged Asura attacked (Kātyāyanī) with all (his) force. O Brāhmaṇa ! He along with elephants, horses and chariots, was surveyed by Devī at leisure.

5. Then bending her bow, Devī showered a volley of arrows (which were) the (very powers) of the groups of gods, on the *Daityas* like rains by clouds in the sky.

6. That bow (decorated) with golden flowers and forcibly bent by Durgā appeared in the *Dānava* army like lightning in the midst of clouds.

7. O sage of good vows ! She struck many enemies of gods with arrows. With mace and club she felled others from their positions.

8. That her lone lion too, shaking his manes, killed, like Yama, many *Daityas* and *Dānavas.*

9-10. The *Daityas* trembled, fell down and lost consciousness. They were smitten by the *Vajra*; their chests were rent asunder by the spear; their necks were severed by the plough; (their bodies) were cut into two by axes; their heads were broken by *Daṇḍa*; the tendons were torn by the discus; and (still) others fled from the battlefield.

11. Those *Daityas* and *Dānavas* of fierce face being slain by Durgā, thought of her as *Kālarātrī* (Night-of-Last-Destruction) and fled away afflicted with fear.

12. Looking round his army being routed and seeing Durgā positioned in front like that (like *Kālarātrī*), Namara proceeded riding on a youthful tusker.

13. Approaching quickly, the *Dānava* threw the spear on to Devī and the trident on to the lion during combat.

14. The two oncoming weapons were reduced to ashes by the very 'hum' sound of Devī. Then the strong elephant seized the lion by the waist.

15. Then springing immediately, the lion struck the *Dānava* with his paw and pulling the dead *Dānava* down from the elephant's back, the lion presented (him) to Devī.

16. O Brāhmaṇa ! Holding the *Dānava* (by the waist) in her left hand, Kātyāyanī with rage whirled and beat him like a rattle-drum, in (that) war.

17. As (the *Dānava*) was made into a drum, Devī burst into a loud laughter. By her laughter there came into being several kinds of spirits in a sequence.

18. Some were tiger-faced and ferocious; others were wolf-shaped; yet others were horse-faced; or buffalo-faced or boar-faced.

19. So also a few others had the face of rat, cock, cow, goat and sheep. There were (spirits) having varieties of faces, eyes and feet; also they wielded different kinds of weapons.

20. Some (of them) were singing; some were laughing; and some others were sporting together. Some were playing on musical instruments; yet others were praising Ambikā.

21. Along with the troops of spirits Devī moving about (here and there) devastated the *Dānava* forces like the thunderbolt devastating a heap of straw.

22. When the leader of the army was killed, the army commander Cikṣura along with the front-line soldiers gave fight to the goddess.

23. The best of the charioteers pulling (the string of) his strong bow as far as the ears, showered a volley of arrows like cloud raining on to the earth.

24. Durgā cut the multitude of arrows with her own arrows having good joints and then took sixteen other gold-feathered arrows.

25. With four of them, the charming goddess killed the four horses (of Cikṣura) and the charioteer with one. She tore away the banner with another.

26. Then Ambikā cut with an arrow his bow along with the arrow. As the bow was broken, the warrior took a sword and shield.

27. She cut with four arrows the *Daitya*'s sword as well as shield which were being forcibly swung. Then he took a trident.

28. Lifting the massive trident, he ran after Ambikā, like a joyful jackal running behind a lioness.

29. Being enraged, she hit the feet, the hands and the head by attacking (Cikṣura) with five arrows and the *Asura* fell dead.

30. When that commander was crushed, the great demon Ugrāsya attacked violently, as also the *Dānava* Karālāsya.

31-32. Bāṣkala, Uddhata, Ugrāsya, Ugrakārmuka, Durdhara, Durmukha and Biḍāla—Nayana-these and other strong *Dānavas,* best of the warriors with various weapons and missiles in their hands attacked Kātyāyanī.

33. Seeing them, Durgā sportively took a *Vinā* into her hands. With a smile she played on it as well as on the nice *Damaru* (drum).

34. As Devī went on playing these instruments, the troops of spirits danced and laughed.

35. Then the *Asura* wielding weapons approached Sarasvatī and hit her. And Devī Parameśvarī grasped them.

36. Seizing the great *Asuras* by their hair, she jumped up from the lion to the mountain top. The mother of the universe danced playing on the *Vīṇā* and drank the drink.

37-38. Then the pride of the great Asuras of superior might was shattered by being dropped from the arms by Devī and they lost their weapons and clothes as well as their life. Then seeing those mighty *Asuras,* Mahiṣāsura of great vigour chased away with the tip of his hoofs the troops of spirits of Devī and others with his snout, tail and as well as vigour. The other groups of spirits (were driven away) by his exhaled air.

39. Felling down yet others with the horn ends, (Mahiṣa) hastened towards the lion to kill him. Then Ambikā got furious and at once pushed away the *Daitya* easily.

40. Immediately then (Mahiṣa) with his sharp horns shattered in fury, the hillocks and the plain, and agitated the oceans and destroyed the clouds and then went after Durgā.

41. She, in her turn, tied down the wicked one with the noose; he, however, became a huge elephant. She chopped off the trunk of the elephant and he again became a buffalo.

42. Then Bhavānī threw the trident on him. But that fell on the earth with its hind part broken. She hurled the fire-faced spear. That also fell down with its tip blunted, O great sage !

43. The discus of Hari, the killer of the *Dānava* coterie, became twisted in shape in no time. The mace of Kubera, hurled after swinging, fell on earth broken.

44. The noose of Varuṇa was crushed by the great *Asura* with his horns, snout and front hoofs. The *Daṇḍa* of Yama thrown by her with fury was only shattered to pieces.

45. The *Vajra* of Indra hurled on his body was reduced to fine pieces. Immediately, Durgā left the lion and mounted on the back of Mahiṣāsura.

46. When Mṛḍanī was seated on his back, Mahiṣāsura due to arrogance of his valour was swinging time and again. She on her part, trampled him with her soft and tender feet, as if he were wet hide.

47. Crushed by Devī, the mountain-like strong one became quite emaciated. Then she severed his neck with the trident. Out of his body, then emerged a sword-wielding man.

48. Even as he emerged, she punched on his chest. And as soon as she seized him by his hair and angrily cut off his head, with her splendid sword, there was wailing among the army of *Daityas*.

49. The terror-stricken (*Daityas*) of tremulous eyes due to panic, rushed along with Caṇḍa, Muṇḍa, Tāra and

Asiloman into nether world being beaten by the *Pramathas* (a class of demons) of Bhavānī.

50. O great sage ! Having witnessed the success of Devī, the gods glorified with praises the fierce-looking yet charming Nārāyaṇī Kātyāyanī Devī, the support of the entire universe.

51. That Kātyāyanī Durgā having been adored by the assemblage of gods and *Siddhas,* merged into the feet of Śiva saying to those gods: "I shall appear again for the sake of the heavenly beings."

CHAPTER TWENTY-ONE

The Birth of Umā – The Marriage of Tapatī

Nārada said:

1. O Pulastya ! O best one among the Brahmaṇa-knowing sages ! Please tell me now in detail the reappearance of Devī; I am very anxious.

Pulastya said:

2. O sage ! Listen, I shall tell you (about) her reappearance for killing the *Asura* Śumbha with a desire of world's welfare.

3. O sage of many austerities ! She who was Himavān's daughter called Umā was married to Śiva. (Devī) born from her (Umā's) sheath (*Kośa*) (was, therefore, called) Kauśikī.

4. Born once more, she again went to the Vindhya mountain surrounded by the troops of spirits and killed Śumbha as well as Niśumbha with splendid weapons.

Nārada said:

5. O Brāhmaṇa ! You had told me that Dakṣa's daughter Satī was dead. You kindly tell me how (she was again) born as the daughter of Himavān.

6. How was Kauśikī born of the sheath of Pārvatī ? How did she kill the great *Asuras*, Śumbha and Niśumbha?

7. Whose sons were these famous heroes, Śumbha and Niśumbha? You please relate to me all this serially in detail.

8. O venerable sir ! By your grace, I have heard the magnificient story of Devī elaborately. (Now) describe the birth of Pārvatī, O sage !

Pulastya said:

9. O sage ! Gladly I will recount to you the birth of Pārvatī, and of Skanda. Listen with attention to (this) ever new story.

10. At the loss of Satī, Rudra being in Āśrama-lessstate got engaged in austerities observing the vow of celibacy.

11. He who was the vanquisher of the pride of *Daityas*, was the commander of the army of gods. He (now) assumed the peaceful form and gave up the army-commandership.

12. Then without Śambhu, th*e army commander, the gods were violently subdued by the Dānava*-chief Niśumbha.

13. Then they went to see the Lord of gods, the bearer of discus and mace. They resorted to Hari, the supreme soul, in the *Śvetadvīpa.*

14. Having seen those gods led by Indra, the puruṣa-par-excellence laughed and said (in a voice) as deep as (the rumbling of) cloud —

15. "Is it because you have been overpowered by the wicked *Asura*-lord Niśumbha that you have all together approached me ?

16. "If so, O excellent gods ! In view of your welfare, you carry out what I instruct you, and by following it, you will have success.

17. "You know the well-known *Pitṛ-devas*, Agniśvāttas. Their spiritual daughter is goddess Menā by name.

18. "O gods ! Having propitiated her with full faith on the great lunar day (8th *Tithī*) beseech that virtuous one for (becoming the wife of) Himavān.

19. "That helpless one who gave up her dear life like dirt, due to her ire against Dakṣa, will assume the body in her (i.e. will be born of her).

20. "The son whom she (Menā's daughter) begets from Śaṅkara's *Tejas* (semen), shall kill the *Daitya*-chief Śumbha and his accomplices.

21. "Therefore, you go to the holy Kurukṣetra which gives success. There you worship the imperishable *Pitṛs* in the *Pṛthūdaka-tīrtha.*

22. "If you all desire that the enemy be overcome by Śiva himself, you do this on the *Mahātithi* (sixth lunar day of the bright fortnight — MW)."

Pulastya said:

23. So instructed by Vāsudeva, the gods led by Indra asked the great Lord with folded hands —

The gods said:

24. Where is this place Kurukṣetra in which there is the holy Pṛthūdaka? O venerable lord ! Please tell us the origin of the *Tīrtha.*

25. Which is this important day which is the most momentous and propitious of the days and on which the divine *Pitṛs* are to be devotedly worshipped with water.

(Pulastya said:)

26. At the question of gods, the smasher of Mura and Kaiṭabha spoke about the *Tīrtha* in Kurukṣetra as well as about the *Tithi* (day).

The Lord said:

27. In the beginning of *Kṛtayuga,* there was a very strong king of the Soma lineage, Ṛkṣa by name. From Ṛkṣa was born Saṁvaraṇa.

28. Even as a young boy he (Saṁvaraṇa) was anointed as the king by his father. Even in his boyhood, he was engaged in righteous conduct and was always my devotee.

29. His *Purohita* was Vasiṣṭha, the son of Varuṇa. That liberal-minded one taught him the *Vedas* along with the auxiliaries.

30. The prince on a holiday (anadhyayana) went to the forest, keeping Vasiṣṭha, the treasure-house-of-austerities, in charge of all activity (of the king).

31. O sage ! Having been drawn away by a deer, he being then mentally absorbed, went on horse-back all alone into that Vaibhrāja forest.

32. Thereafter overcome by wonder and unsatisfied by the fragrance, he wandered all over the forest that had flowers all through the seasons.

33. There he saw a part of the forest full of full-blown red, pink, white and blue lotuses, white lilies and other aquatic flowers.

34. *Apsarās* and (other) divine damsels play there always. Then Saṁvaraṇa saw among them one maiden who surpassed others (in beauty).

35. At the very first sight, the king was afflicted by Kāma's arrow. Similarly, she too at the first sight, became a victim of Kāma's arrow.

36. Tormented by the arrows of Kāma, both of them were benumbed. The king fell down to the ground from the horse as he could not sit.

37. Noble-minded *Gandharvas* who could assume any form, approached him and sprinkled water. In a moment, he regained consciousness.

38. She too was picked up and taken to her father's house by the *Apsarās.* She was consoled by them with waters of sweet words.

39. The king also mounting the horse reached the excellent city of *Pratiṣṭhāna* like a divine being moving at will reaches the peak of Meru.

40. Since the day that Tapatī was seen with his own eyes on the hill, he neither ate during day nor slept during night.

41. Then the omniscient and unperturbed Vasiṣṭha, the son of Varuṇa, the treasure-house-of-austerities, came to know that the heroic king had been tormented for Tapatī.

42. The great *yogī* soared up and entered the orb of the Sun and saw the Hot-rayed God sitting in the chariot.

43. The best of the twice-born seeing god Sun, bowed down to him. The sage too was saluted in turn by god Sun.

44. With glowing matted hairs, the sage, the son of Varuṇa, gone near the Sun, shone like a second resplendent sun.

45. Then the sage rich-in-penance was honoured with respectful offerings by the Sun. Asked about the purpose of his coming he replied to the Sun —

46. "O great god of great effulgence ! I have come to solicit your daughter for Saṁvaraṇa. Kindly offer her to him."

47. Then the Sun offered his daughter Tapatī to Vasiṣṭha, the bull among the twice-born, who had come to his house on behalf of king Saṁvaraṇa only.

48. Having obtained the approval of the Sun, Vasiṣṭha started towards his hermitage. That lady too remembering that prince, told the son of Varuṇa with folded hands —

Tapatī said:

49. O Brāhmaṇa ! The prince who was seen in the forest by me along with *Apsarās* and attendants and (later) was distressed, was like a divine offspring and I know his features too.

50. The handsome feet were marked with discus, mace and sword. The shanks and thighs were similar to the trunk of an elephant. The waist was slim like that of a lion. The abdomen was encircled by the three folds.

51. His neck was similar to a conch. The arms were stout, stiff and quite long. His hands had the marks of Lotus petals and his head looked like an umbrella.

52. The hair was black and curly; his ears were fleshy; the nose symmetrical. The fingers and toes were long enough and had good joints; his teeth were bright.

53. He was prominent in three; he was deep in three aspects; he was long in three; in seven places, he was red; the prince was black in four places; and was bent in three.

54. He was white in two; fragrant in four; and had ten lotus-like features. O venerable Sir ! After good deliberation I have already chosen that prince as my husband.

55. O Master ! O foremost one among ascetics ! Please give me in marriage to the person whom I love and who is endowed with good qualities. The good declare that one can voluntarily (offer oneself in marriage) on account of love and so you cannot give me in marriage to another person, O master !

The Lord of Lords said:

56. So told by the daughter of the Sun, the sage got into meditation. Coming to know that it was the same love-born son of Ṛkṣa, he said this with delight—

57. "O daughter ! he is the same prince whom you saw earlier and whom you desire today. He is the son of Ṛkṣa, Saṁvaraṇa by name, and comes to my hermitage."

58. Then indeed the prince came to the hermitage of that sage, the foremost of Brāhmaṇas. Seeing Vasiṣṭha, the king prostrated to him and also saw Tapatī staying there.

59. Looking at that lady of lotus-like wide eyes, he thought that he must have seen her before. He asked: "Who is this belle? O best of the twice-born !" The son of Varuṇa replied to the king—

60-61a. "O King ! She is the daughter of the Sun, well-known on the earth as Tapatī. The sun solicited by me for your sake, gave her whom I brought to this hermitage. Therefore, get up, O King ! and formally hold the hand of Devī Tapatī."

61b. The King so told married Tapatī with joy according to the custom.

62. That daughter of the Sun obtaining the loved one as her husband having Indra-like prowess, rejoiced in the palace like the daughter of Pulomā in the heaven with Indra.

CHAPTER TWENTY-TWO

King Kuru's Achievement — Kurukṣetra

The Lord of Lords said:

1. A son bearing regal marks was born of that Tapatī to that best of men. As his sacraments like the rite of birth (Jātakarma) and others were performed, he grew along like fire with the offering of ghee.

2. O gods ! The tonsure sacrament (Cūḍākaraṇa) and initiation into vows when the boy was nine years old, were performed by the Brāhmaṇa (Vasiṣṭha), the son of Mitrāvaruṇa. The boy became proficient in Veda and Śāstra in accordance with the injunction.

3. Then he (the boy) learnt everything in ten years. That excellent person, the son of Saṁvaraṇa, Kuru by name, became well-known on the earth.

4. Finding his son aged sixteen years, the King made efforts for his marriage in an auspicious family.

5. For Kuru, the King sought the most beautiful girl Saudāminī, the daughter of Sudāman. He, in turn, gave her (in marriage) to Kuru.

6. Having married the princess, he enjoyed the company of the beautiful lady like Indra that of Paulomī (Śacī), without transgressing his *Dharma*.

7. Then the powerful king knowing his son to have become fit to bear the burden of administration, formally anointed him as the prince.

8. Then coronated in the kingdom by the father in his place, he protected the kingdom and the subjects as his own children.

9. The mighty one himself was the guardian of land, guardian of animals, and himself was the guardian of the kingdom and of goats.

10. Then the thought occurred to him. Indeed one should live in this world as long as the fame that one has earned lasts.

11. The foremost of the kings then agreed that it was true and he went round the earth for fame.

12. Then the self-controlled one touring the world, came to the holy (place) named *Dvaitavana.* Feeling very happy he entered it.

13-14. Then he visited the holy goddess, Plakṣajā Sarasvatī, the remover of all sins, the daughter of Brahmā, Harijihvā, the mother of Sudarśana. He got a wide tank built and brought the water of the river into the tank. Bathing therein, the king felt happy.

15-16. Then he came to the Northern Altar of Brahmā, the excellent place of righteousness called *Samantapañcaka,* which extends to 5x5 yojanas on all sides.

The gods said:

16b-17. O Lord ! O Puruṣa par excellence ! Which are the other Altars of Brahmā? For, you spoke of the Altar in *Sarvapañcaka* as Northern.

Hari said:

17. All around there are five Altars of *Dharma,* the master of the universe.

18. On all these Śambhu, the Lord of gods and guardian of the universe, has performed sacrifices. Prayāga is the Central altar; Gayāśiraḥ is the Eastern altar.

19. Virāja is the Southern altar which bestows infinite rewards. The Western altar is Puṣkara adorned with the three pools.

20-21. The altar in *Syamantapañcaka* is itself spoken of as the Northern. That royal sage pondered: "I will make this holy place (able to) confer great rewards. I will attain all my wishes as I like." Thinking thus, he got down from his excellent chariot.

22-23. That great king for attaining glory, made it a peerless region. The king made a golden plough and taking the bull of Rudra and the male-buffalo of Yama as the drawers, he himself began to plough. Indra approached that great man who was ploughing.

24-27. (Indra) said: "O King ! What are you trying to do here?" The King replied: "Here I am cultivating austerity, truth, forbearance, compassion, purity, charity, contemplation and celibacy." Lord Indra asked him: "O King ! Where did you get the seeds from?" So sneering,he immediately left the place. After Indra went away, the king with plough in hand (continued) ploughing day after day other areas upto seven krośas all around. Then I went there and asked him, "O Kuru ! What is this ?"

28. Then the eight-limbed great *Dharma* was explained by the King. Then I asked him, "O King ! Where does the seed exist ?"

29. He replied, "The seed is in my body." I told him, "Give it to me; I will get it sow; and you may draw the plough."

30-31. Then the King stretched his right arm. Seeing the arm extended it was immediately cut into thousand pieces by the great discus. Therefore he came to have only one arm. Then the King gave his left arm. That was also cut by me.

32. So also he presented both his thighs; and both of them were cut off. Then he came forward with his head. Then I was pleased with him.

33. When I told him, "I am ready to confer a boon," Kuru begged for a boon. Kuru said: "May the whole of the area ploughed by me be your pious land.

34-37. "May there be great meritorious reward for those who take ablution here and for those who die here. O Mahādeva ! O Supreme being ! O Hṛṣīkeśa ! O bearer of conch, discus and mace ! Please the high rewards of fasting, charity, ablution, japa, oblation, sacrifice and such other auspicious or inauspicious acts performed on this most distinguished holy land become imperishable. So also, O lotus-eyed eternal god ! You along with gods and with the Trident-bearing god, dwell here (in this land) indicative of my name."

So asked by the King, I replied, "Be it so."

38. "O King, you too attain again the celestial body. Also, O one of good vows ! You shall finally merge in me.

39. "Your fame shall become everlasting; there is no doubt about it. Then you, as a sacrificer are going to offer thousands of sacrifices."

Pulastya said:

40-41. For the protection of that area, the puruṣa-par-excellence gave the *Yakṣa* Candra by name, the serpent Vāsuki by name, the *Vidyādhara* Śaṅkukarṇa and Sukeśa, the lord of Rākṣasas, King Ajavana and the fire-god Mahādeva.

42. These and other strong servants following them guard the Kurujāṅgala land covering it on all sides.

43. Eight thousand most fierce archers keep away the utter sinners of the beings (moving and non-moving) and do not allow them to bathe, O brave one !

44. In the middle of that only, there is the highly meritorious and auspicious lake, Pṛthūdaka which destroys sins. Born of that lake flooded with water, a holy river full of water flows eastwards.

45. This river was created by the Great Grand Sire along with the whole host of Bhūtas, viz. earth, water, fire, wind and Ākāśa. Thus Pṛthūdaka appeared in the early age.

46. So too the vast oceans, the sacred ponds, the rivers, the streams and the lakes-all are well created by the mighty lord. The waters in them are indeed the divine path.

47. The best of the twice-born asked the primeval chief sage dwelling in Kurujāṅgala (the region) between Sarasvatī and Dṛṣadvatī.

The sages said:

48. Please tell us the extent of the lakes, especially of the *Tīrthas* as well as the glory of the gods and the birth of Vāmana.

49. Hearing their words, Lomaharṣaṇa bowed down to the primeval sage (Brahmā) and told this to those Brāhmaṇas.

Lomaharṣaṇa said:

50. I will speak about Brahmasaras, the best *Tīrtha* after bowing down my head to Lord Brahmā sitting on the lotus, Viṣṇu with Lakṣmī and Lord Rudra.

51. And O excellent Brāhmaṇas ! Listen to what is said about the dimensions of the lake, by the venerable Vyāsa in the age between Kali and Dvāpara.

52. The lake from Rantuka to Aujasa, from Pāvana to Caturmukha, was called Sannihita in the early age alone by Brahmā.

53. The lake Sannihita is spoken as extending from Viśveśvara to Hastipura and Kanyā Jaradgavā to Oghavatī.

54. But I have heard of the expanse (of the lake) as set forth in the *Vāmana Purāṇa.* O best of the Brahmaṇas, listen to that; it is holy and greatly promotes prosperity.

55. The lake Sannihita is known to extend half a Yojana all around on all sides, from Viśveśvara and Devavara to Pāvani and Sarasvatī.

56. Taking refuge in it, gods and sages have come here with a desire for emancipation and others stay here desiring to attain heaven.

57. The Yogin Brahmā used this with a view to create (the universe). It was attended upon by Viṣṇu as Hari, desirous of maintaining (the universe).

58. The great resplendent Rudra-Hara who entered into the middle of the pond, attained Sthāutva (state of *Liṅga*) by attending on this *Tīrtha.*

59. First it was (known as) the altar of Brahmā. Then it came to be known as Rāmahrada. Because it was ploughed by Kuru, it came to be called Kurukṣetra.

60. This region that lies between Arantuka and Avantuka, between Rāmahrada and Pañcaka, is Kurukṣetra: it is called Samantapañcaka, and the high altar of Brahmā.

CHAPTER TWENTY-THREE

Glory of King Bali

The sages said:

1. Please state the greatness of Vāmana, especially his birth, how Bali was restrained and how the realm of Indra was given (back to him).

Lomaharṣaṇa said:

2. O sages ! Be happy to listen to the birth, and greatness of the eminent Vāmana and his dwelling in Kurujāṅgala.

3. So also listen, O holiest Brāhmaṇas ! To the family of *Daityas,* the family in which was born Virocana's son Bali in days of yore.

4. Of the *Daityas,* Hiraṇyakaśipu was the first (great) personage. His son was the eminent *Dānava,* Prahlāda by name.

5-12. Virocana was born of him and Bali was born of Virocana. When Hiraṇyakaśipu was killed after he routed the gods from everywhere, he ruled over the three worlds that included all moveables and immoveables and performed sacrifices.

As the *Daityas* performed sacrifices, and the three worlds assumed the nature of *Daityas* (i.e. became dominated by *Daityas*), as the strong Maya and Śaṁbara became victorious, as all the quarters were clear (of the clouds of war) and rites and rituals began to be performed, as the *Daitya* path was established, as the sun was in his half-yearly movements, as all the quarters were guarded with affection by Prahlāda, Śambara and Maya and the sky by the *Daityas*, as the *Vedas* showed the glory of sacrifice as existing in the heaven, as the situation had become normal and the people were set on the righteous path, as there was absence of all sins, as the attitude of righteousness became always dominant, as *Dharma* stood on all its four legs and evil (*Adharma*) was rendered bereft of legs (supportless), as the kings entrusted with the protection of the subjects were resplendent, as everyone adhered to one's duties and stayed in one's own stage of life, Bali was crowned King of *Daityas* by all the *Asuras*. The assembly of *Asuras* felt happy and shouted in merriment.

13. Then the benevolent Goddess Lakṣmī of easy entrance, having a complexion of the interior of a lotus and holding a lotus in her raised hand, approached Bali.

Śrī said:

14. O Bali ! O best of the mighty ones ! O Eminent *Daitya* Lord ! I am pleased with you on your defeating the king of gods (Indra). May you fare well.

15. Considering your extraordinary might as you courageously defeated Indra in the battle, I have come to you on my own.

16. O best of *Dānavas* ! Such an act of yours who are born of the family of Hiraṇyakaśipu is no surprise.

17. O King ! You by whom the entire imperishable three worlds have been united, have excelled the *Daitya*-chief, your grandfather.

Lomaharṣaṇa said:

18. Thus saying, the benevolent and venerable goddess Lakṣmī who enthrals all gods, entered Bali, the *Daitya* King.

19-21. Pleased were the pre-eminent goddesses: Bashfulness (*Hrī*), Glory (*Kīrti*), Splendour (*Dyuti*), Effulgence (*Prabhā*), Fortitude (*Dhṛti*), Patience (*Kṣamā*), Prowess (*Śakti*), Prosperity (*Ṛddhi*), Supreme Intelligence (*Divya-mahāmati*), Divine Wisdom (*Śruti*), Learning (*Vidyā*), Remembrance (*Smṛti*), Fame (*Kīrti*), Peace (*Śānti*), Nourishment (*Puṣṭi*), as well as Action (*Kriyā*). All the divine *Apsarās,* experts in music and dance, resorted to the *Daitya*-chief. The three worlds with all their moveables and immoveables things (as well as) matchless prosperity were acquired by Bali who professed the knowledge of Brahmaṇa.

CHAPTER TWENTY-FOUR

The Gods Go to Brahmā

The sages said:

1. Please tell us about the activity of the gods by doing which they were defeated. How did the supreme god Viṣṇu assume the form of a dwarf ?

Lomaharṣaṇa said:

2. Seeing the three worlds subjugated by Bali, god Indra went to the auspicious residence of his Mother on the Meru.

3. Having approached his Mother he told her the fact that all the sons of Aditi had been defeated in battle by the sons of Danu.

Aditi said:

4. O my son ! If it is so, Bali, the son of Virocana can not be killed in a battle by you even along with the entire group of *Maruts.*

5. It is only the thousand-headed (Viṣṇu) that is able to kill him. O Thousand-eyed one ! He can be killed by him (Viṣṇu) alone and by nobody else.

6. Therefore, you ask your father Kaśyapa, the knower of Brahmaṇa, about the means of defeating the great *Daitya* Bali.

Lomaharṣaṇa said:

7-12. Then gods along with the heavenly beings approached Kaśyapa. There they saw the effulgent sage Mārīca (descendant of Mārīci – MW), rich in penance. (Kaśyapa) the divine primordial father of gods, who was effulgent with *Brahmatejas* (the splendour of a Brāhmaṇa – MW) who was resplendent like the sun, and who appeared like the flame of fire, who was resting on a staff, was engaged in austerity, had tied the skin of black buck, had wrapped round bark and skin, and appeared to glow with splendour, who was dazzling and endowed with fragrance of ghee like fire, was engaged in the study of the *Veda*, and appeared as though fire in human form, the knower of Brahmaṇa, the formidable master and overlord of the moveable and the immoveable, peerless with Vedic lore and prosperity, radiant with splendour, who was the creator of all the worlds, was the excellent protector of beings, and was the third Prajāpati because of the distinguishing features of self.

13. Then all those pious gods, the bulls among the celestial beings together with *Ādityas* having well-disposed mind, said with folded hands —

14. "Bali, the *Daitya* excelling in strength, is invincible by Indra in battle. Therefore, please ordain us what is favourable to us and what enhances our prosperity."

Hearing the words of those sons, the father Kaśyapa (replied) —

Kaśyapa said:

15-16. You set your mind to proceed to the realm of Brahmā. The creator will tell you the means of vanquishing the *Daitya*-lord.

O Indra ! Let us all go to the transcendental abode of Brahmā.

So all of them got ready to inform Brahmā about the defeat.

17. Then the gods along with *Ādityas* (who) had gone to the hermitage of Kaśyapa, proceeded towards Brahmā's abode resorted to by hosts of *Brahmarṣis.*

18. Those lustrous ones reached the realm of Brahmā, in an instant in strong divine vehicles appropriate to each of them and capable of going anywhere.

19. Desirous of asking Brahmā, the imperishable store of austerities, (the gods) entered the extensive, exquisite assembly hall.

20. Then they were delighted to see (the hall) which was pleasing with the humming of bees, in which *Sāma*-singers were singing, which was conducive to prosperity and able to vanquish the enemy.

21. The tigers among the celestial beings heard the *Ṛks* recited in *Pada* and *Krama* modes by the foremost of those versed in *Ṛgveda,* during the rites being performed.

22. The hall reverberated with the voices of the great sages as well as of those versed in the *Veda* and performance of sacrifice and of those who were skilled in *Pada* and *Krama* (modes of recitations).

23-26. They also heard the voices of twice-borns who knew the prayers in sacrifices and who were scholars of phonetics, of experts in metrics, of those learned in several fields of knowledge and of the chief *Lokāyatikas.* The sons of Kaśyapa saw here and there self-controlled venerable Brāhmaṇas who had undertaken vows and the chiefs of them engaged in *Japa* and *Homa.* In such an assembly hall was sitting Brahmā, the primordial Father of the universe, the master of the moveable and the immoveable and one radiant with learning and transcendental powers (*Māyā*) of the *Veda,* and the omnipresent one on whom the Prajāpatis were contemplating there only.

27-30. Dakṣa, Pracetas, Pulaha, Marīci, Bhṛgu, Atri, Vasiṣṭha, Gautama, Nārada and such other principal Brāhmaṇas, the different branches of learning, Ākāśa, Wind, Fire, Water and Earth, Sound, Touch, Form, Taste and Smell, Prakṛti and its transformations and the other cause, Mahat, the four Vedas along with the auxiliaries and additional ones, the Lord of the world, Austerities, Sacrifices, Thoughts and Vitality—all these and many others were waiting on Brahmā (*Svayambhū*).

31-33. Dharma, Artha and Kāma, Anger and Merriment, Śukra and Bṛhaspati, Saṁvarta as also Mercury, Saturn, Rāhu and other Planets were in constant attendance. O eminent! Brāhmaṇas, Maruts, Viśvakarma and Vasus, Sun and Moon, Day and Night, Fortnights, Months and six Seasons were attending (on him).

34-35. Kaśyapa, the best among the righteous ones, and his son, the lord of heavenly beings, entered Brahmā's celestial assembly, giver of all wishes, endowed with all radiance, divine, attended upon by the hosts of *Brahmarṣis,* served by the grace of Brahmā's power, beyond imagination and reliever of languor.

36. Seeing Brahmā seated on an exquisite seat, all those gods along with *Brahmarṣis* bowed down to the Lord with their heads.

37. Then at the touch of the feet of the great god, they with controlled mind were rid of all sins and were cleansed of all stains.

38. Having seen all those heavenly beings come with Kaśyapa, the most radiant Brahmā, the master and overlord of gods, said —

CHAPTER TWENTY-FIVE

Brahmā's Advice to Gods

Brahmā said:

1. O mighty ones ! I am thinking calmly about the very purpose for which you all have come over here.

2. O eminent gods ! All that you have wished for is going to happen. He who will be the conqueror of the *Dānava*-chief Bali, shall be born.

3. He, the creator of the universe, is the refuge not only to the foes of gods but also to me. He is the guide of the three worlds and is the master of even the gods.

4. He is the lord of all the worlds and eternal and is the universe himself. This primordial deity is spoken of as my forefather.

5. The gods, however, do not know about this supreme soul as to who he is. But that puruṣa par excellence knows us, the gods and the universe.

6-9. It is only by his grace that I explain to you the best course of action. Practising steadiness of mind, if (you) perform severe penance on the northern bank of Milk-ocean in the north (where) the creator of the universe (is), then you shall hear the speech of *Brahmavādins* (discourses of sacred texts – MW), the (eminent) speakers—speech sounding loud and deep like that of the clouds, very much cultured, pleasing, well-worded, charming, not frightening (i.e. pacifying) and auspicious always celestial, sincere, truthful and ridding of all evils. Soon the overlord of all gods shall present himself.

10. At the closure of the vow and the completion of the contemplative vow, the extraordinary, never failing, fiery, power of the supreme soul (will show itself and say) —

11. "O supreme divine beings ! Welcome to you who have approached me. O gods ! Being (pleased) to give a boon, I offer a boon to Kaśyapa."

12. Then Aditi and Kaśyapa will bow down their heads to the feet of that wise god, and seek the boon: "Please favour us that the lord himself be born as our son."

13. So prayed, he shall say with his excellent voice, "It will be so." All the gods and Kaśyapa and Aditi shall tell (the purpose of the request).

14-16. The graceful creator of all the worlds shall say, "It will be so." Thus obtaining the boon from that Lord, O supreme heavenly beings ! You having achieved the purpose, go to your respective abodes.

All the divine personages bowed their heads down to the Lord (and accepted) "so it shall be" and proceeded towards north to reach Śveta-Dvīpa. Before long they arrived at the Milk-ocean, the lord of rivers.

17-18. As instructed by the truthful Lord Brahmā, the eminent gods crossed over all oceans, mountains as well as forests, and various holy rivers on the earth and saw the frightening *Tamas,* bereft of all *Sattva.*

19. They reached along with noble Kaśyapa, the limitless region called *Amṛta* having no sun and covered by *Tamas.*

20-21. Kaśyapa consecrated (himself) for the divine vow of a thousand years with celibacy, silence, standing (in particular postures) and sitting in warrior posture, to propitiate the wise and prosperous god Nārāyaṇa of a thousand eyes, the lord of gods, and *Yoga* personified.

22. Following him all the gods engaged themselves in austerity and contemplation. To propitiate the adorable Lord, venerable Kaśyapa gave expression to an excellent hymn which is spoken of as set forth in the *Veda.*

CHAPTER TWENTY-SIX

Kaśyapa's Prayer to Viṣṇu

Om. Obeisance to Lord Vāsudeva.

Kaśyapa said:

O (god) having a single horn ! O Vṛṣasindhu ! O Vṛṣākapi! O best one of the celestial beings ! O one existing without beginning ! O Rudra ! O Kapila ! O Viṣvaksena ! O Lord of all beings ! O everlasting one ! O Virtue ! O Vaikuṇṭha ! O Vṛṣāvardha (one having no beginning, middle or end) ! O Dhanañjaya ! O one having pure fame ! O one having variegated splendour ! O one having innate victory ! O god lying in ambrosia ! O eternal one ! O one having triple abode! O Tuṣita ! O great principle ! O protector of the universe ! O lotus-navelled one ! O creator ! O god of multi-forms ! O imperishable one ! O changeless one ! O partaker of havis ! O axe-wielder lord ! O mighty one ! O one having Muñja (grass) like hair ! O swan ! O Great compassionate one ! O overlord of sense-organs ! O subtle one ! O observer of excellent law ! O passionless one ! O support of the universe! O formless one ! O first-born one ! O one born of *Dharma* ! O fulcrum of *Dharma* ! O partaker of divine food ! O master of rays ! O protector of Indra ! O one having golden chariot! O one radiant like the sun ! O one having ocean as cloth ! O unborn one ! O god of thousand heads ! O god of thousand feet ! O one of short temper ! O superman ! O puruṣa par excellence ! O god of thousand arms ! O god of thousand forms ! O god of thousand mouths ! O one having thousand births ! you are spoken of as the universe; you having flower-like smile, O ultimate one ! You are Vauṣaṭ and Vaṣaṭkāra; you are said to be the foremost partaker (of Havis) in sacrifices ! O hundred-pointed one ! O thousand-pointed one ! O god bowed down to by Earth ! O Lord of the Earth! O son of Bhṛgu ! O Lord known (only) by the Veda ! O one lying in Brahman ! O god dear to the Brāhmaṇas (or one having Brāhmaṇas as dear ones)! you are the highest heaven; you are *Mātariśvan*; you are *Dharma*; you are the invoker; the Potṛ, the killer, the counsellor, the *Netṛ*, and the cause of sacrifice; you are the chief one because of your radiance; O fine receptacle with (the ornaments of) Ṛks ! you are worthy of worship; you are the most wise one and the sacrificial fuel-sticks; you are the master, the resort and you are the benevolent; you are emancipation; you are *yoga*; you create and you are the creator; you the supreme sacrifice; you are Soma; you are the consecrated; you are the *Dakṣiṇā*; you are the universe; O primordial one ! O golden-egged ! O Nārāyaṇa ! O three-eyed lord ! O first letter (of the alphabet) ! O one having Sun's resplendence ! O great Puruṣa ! O Puruṣa par excellence ! O first divinity ! O one who measured the earth ! O god of triple stride ! O giver of light ! O Śambhu ! you are the one that exists by oneself; you are the *Ahaṅkāra Tattva* as well as the great elements; O all-pervading one ! you are indeed the universe; you are the guardian of the universe; you are the cleanser; O origin of the universe ! O one moving upwards ! O ambrosia ! O lord of the heaven ! O Lord of speech ! O blazing fire ! O one of inexhaustible actions ! O dynasty ! O god of the first dynasty! O mind ! You are the *Aśvamedha* sacrifice; you are the bestower of boons to those who seek boons.

Salutations to you, the soul of sacrifice, who are offered oblations with (five formulae having) four, two, five and two (syllables respectively).

CHAPTER TWENTY-SEVEN

Aditi's Penance

Lomaharṣaṇa said:

1-2. Satiated after having heard thus the excellent prayer uttered by Kaśyapa, the son of Brahmā, and the best of the twice-born, the lustrous, and revered Nārāyaṇa of pleased mind said the words that a powerful lord would speak (at such a time), and that were full of syllables pregnant (with meaning)—

3-4. "O ye excellent gods ! May ye have auspiciousness. Choose a boon (if any). I am going to give you the boon."

Kaśyapa said:

"O pre-eminent god ! You are pleased. As resolved by (us) all, may the lustrous lord be the son of Aditi and younger brother of Indra, promoting the joy of all the relatives."

5. Aditi, the mother of gods, too, expressed these very ideas, desirous of boon of a son, to the lord, the benefactor.

The gods said:

6. For the well-being of all the gods, you the supreme lord, be the protector, nourisher, benefactor and shelter to us always.

Lomaharṣaṇa said:

7-9. Then Viṣṇu himself answered to those gods : "All those who are the enemies of you all, can not stand before me even for a while. O foremost of the divinities ! having killed with the most superior divine action the hosts of Asuras who are (now) the first partakers of portions of sacrifices, I will make the gods to enjoy the divine offering and the *Pitṛs* to enjoy the *Kavya*-offering. O prominent gods ! You return the way you came."

10. Then having been told thus by the most powerful Viṣṇu, the cheerful (gods) worshipped the Lord.

11-13. The great Viśvedevas, Kaśyapa as well as Aditi prostrated to the Lord, the chief divine being, and all of them immediately proceeded eastwards to the extensive hermitage of Kaśyapa. Having reached the great Kurukṣetra forest, the hermitage of Kaśyapa, they appeased Aditi and set her for austerity. Then she performed severe penance for ten thousand years.

14. That wonderful auspicious forest yielding every wish (came to be known) by her name. For the propitiation of Kṛṣṇa (*Hari*) she restrained her speech and subsisted on air.

15-16. Seeing the most pious sages terror-stricken and expelled by the *Daityas,* she bowed down to Hari with disheartenment that she bore sons in vain. Engaged in deep austerity, she with praises in pleasing language propitiated Viṣṇu and bowed to him who is the protector, the succor, who is affectionate to the devotee, who comprises both Devas and *Daityas* and is of the form of beginning, middle and end.

Aditi said:

17. Salutation to him who destroys the affliction caused by black magic. Salutation to the lotus-garlanded god. Salutation to the most auspicious of the auspicious, to the first creator.

18. Salutation to the lotus-eyed. Salutation to the lotus-navelled. Salutation to the origin of the one born of the lotus, to the one who is the source of himself.

19. (Salutation) to the beloved of Lakṣmī, to the restrained one, to him who is seen by the self-restrained ones, to the discus-bearer. Salutation to the holder of lotus etc. Salutation to the wearer of golden dress.

20. (Salutation) to him for whom sacrifice is self-knowledge, to the *Yogin* who is meditated upon by the *Yogins*, to Hari the attributeless (but) the distinguished, to the very embodiment of Brahman.

21. (Salutation to him) in whom the universe exists, (to him) who is not seen from the universe. Salutation to the biggest and the most minute. (Salutation) to the lord, the bearer of *Śārṅga* (bow).

22-24. He whom the people do not see though they can see all this world, but he who abides in the heart and is seen by those who do not see the world; he who is not indicated by any external light and is perceived beyond any light; in whom, from whom, and under whose bidding is this entire universe— to him the grand master of all this universe, salutation, salutation. He who is the primordial Lord of creatures and he who is the protector over and above the *Pitṛs*, he who is the guardian of the divine beings— to such a creator, to Kṛṣṇa, salutation.

25. Salutation to that mace-wielder god who has no attachment to the actions that continue (the worldly life) and to those that stop (the worldly life), to that god who awards the fruit of heaven or emancipation (to the devotees).

26. Salutation to the pure and supreme (embodiment of) horse-sacrifice, who once thought of, destroys all sins instantly.

27. I bow down to the birthless, imperishable Lord by regarding whom as the support of everything, (people) do not again undergo birth and death.

28. I bow down to the powerful supreme Lord Viṣṇu, the embodiment of sacrifice, who abiding in sacrifice is worshipped through sacrifices.

29. Salutation to that victorious Viṣṇu who is known through the *Veda*, who is praised in all the *Vedas* by those that know the *Veda* and who is the resort of the wise.

30. Salutation to that pre-eminent lord from whom this universe has sprung and in whom it merges and who is thus the origin and support of the universe.

31. I bow down to Upendra by whom all these mobile and immobile objects from Brahmā to a bunch of grass have been encompassed and who is not bound by the fetters of *Māyā.*

32. I bow down to the supreme Lord of beings, Viṣṇu, the Lord of the universe and the universe itself who supports all this, assuming the form of the third (element, i.e. water).

33. I bow down to Upendra who without a concrete form dispels the mass of gloom in the form of *Asuras,* and (dispels) in the form of the sun, the darkness of the night.

34. I bow down to Upendra whose two eyes, the sun and the moon, see the good and bad actions in all this world.

35. I bow down to the powerful, imperishable and birthless Viṣṇu, the overlord, for whom whatever I have said is true for all times and never false.

36. If what I have said again and again is true, then O Janārdana ! By that very truth please all my desires be fulfilled.

CHAPTER TWENTY-EIGHT

Lord's Boon to Aditi

Lomaharṣaṇa said:

1. Having been thus prayed (by Aditi), adorable Vāsudeva invisible to any being appeared before her and spoke to her—

The Adorable One said:

2. O Aditi ! Whatever cherished objectives of your mind you desire, O knower of righteousness ! You shall obtain all that by my grace; there is no doubt about this.

3. Listen, O auspicious one ! The cherished wish in your heart (shall certainly come about). My appearance will never go in vain.

4. Whoever that stays here in my grove and observes (vows) for three nights, of such a one all the heart-felt wishes become fruitful.

5. O Aditi ! Even a person who lives away (from this grove) and yet recalls it, shall attain the highest abode; then what to say of the person who dwells here (only)?

6. He who offers here food in good faith to five, three or two Brāhmaṇas or even to only one, shall get the final attainment.

Aditi said:

7. O one affectionate to the devotees ! If you, the Lord, are pleased with my devotion, then may my son be the overlord of the three worlds.

8. His realm has been taken over and he has been deprived of the portion of the sacrifices by the *Asuras.* O giver of the boon ! If you are pleased, may my son have them (back).

9. O Keśava ! The loss of the realm of my son is not the cause of my grief, but the deprivation of the offerings of the devotees aches my heart.

The Adorable One said:

10. O lady ! Favour has been done by me to you as you desire. With my own part I shall be entering the foetus in your womb by Kaśyapa.

11. O giver of joy ! After I am born of your womb, I shall kill all those who are enemies of gods; so you rest assured.

Aditi said:

12. O god of gods ! You be pleased. O creator ! Salutations to you. O master ! O Keśava ! I shall not be capable enough to carry you in my womb. You are the very source of the universe. O Lord ! Everything is established in you.

The Adorable One said:

13. O giver of joy ! I shall carry you as well as myself. I will not inflict any pain on you. May you fare well. I am taking leave (of you).

Lomaharṣaṇa said:

14. As the lord disappeared after having said so, Aditi conceived.
15. Even as Kṛṣṇa (Viṣṇu) was in the womb (of Aditi), the whole of earth shook; mountains shuddered and the oceans got agitated.
16. Wherever (pregnant) Aditi went and placed her excellent foot, there the earth sank with fatigue, O bulls among the twice borns !
17. When the slayer of Madhu (Viṣṇu) was in the womb (of Aditi), the splendour of *Daityas* got diminished as assured by the supreme soul.

CHAPTER TWENTY-NINE

Prahlāda Curses Bali

Lomaharṣaṇa said:

1. Then having seen the *Asuras* losing their valour, the *Asura*-lord Bali enquired of his grandfather Prahlāda—

Bali said:

2. O venerable one ! Why is it that the *Daityas* have lost their power all of a sudden as though burnt down by fire or struck by *Brahma-daṇḍa* ?
3. Is this the misfortune of the *Daityas* or is it the witchcraft produced by the gods to destroy the *Asuras*, that has caused the loss of their power ?

Lomaharṣaṇa said:

4. O Brāhmaṇas ! Questioned thus by his grandson, the best of *Daityas* pondered for a long time and then spoke thus to the *Asura.*

Prahlāda said:

5. The hills are shaking, the earth is giving up its natural poise. The rivers and seas are agitated. And the *Daityas* are rendered powerless.

6. The planets are not moving at sunrise as before. On the basis of (these) omens, great prosperity of the gods can be surmised.

7. O valorous one ! O Lord of *Dānavas* ! This portent is rather grave; you should not consider it trivial. Anyway, some action has to be taken (against it).

Lomaharṣaṇa said:

8. After saying thus to the *Dānava*-lord Prahlāda, the best of *Asuras,* who was a great devotee (of Lord Viṣṇu) resorted mentally to Hari, the Lord of gods.

9. Then *Asura* Prahlāda first meditated and then came to know about Janārdana as he was (i.e. as being in the womb of Aditi).

10. Prahlāda saw in her (Aditi's) womb Viṣṇu in the form of Dwarf (Vāmana). Within Vāmana he saw *Vasus, Rudras, Aśvins* as well as *Maruts.*

11. (He saw) *Sādhyas, Viśvedevas, Gandharvas, Uragas, Rākṣasas,* his son Virocana as well as Bali, the Asura leader.

12. (He saw there) Jambha, Kujambha, Naraka, Bāṇa, and other *Asuras,* (as well as) himself, Ākāśa, Wind, Mind, Waters and Fire.

13. (He saw) seas, hills, trees, islands, lakes, animals, the earth, birds, all human beings as well as reptiles.

14. (He saw) Brahmā, the creator of the whole universe, Bhava (Śiva), the planets, the constellations and stars, the sages and Prajāpati.

15. Having seen all these Prahlāda was astounded and in a moment he became normal again. He then spoke to *Daitya*-Chief Bali, the son of Virocana—

Prahlāda said:

16. My boy, I have understood why this loss of power of you all has come about. Listen to me about it in detail.

17-18. The god of gods, the source of the Universe, the originator of the Universe, the birthless master, the beginningless one, the beginner of the Universe, the adorable and the benevolent Hari, the ultimate goal of all those who are engaged in *para* and *apara* types of meditation and who is himself far above this world, the overlord, the measure of the measures, he who is superior to the lord of the seven worlds, the master of the Universe, has entered into the womb of Aditi to maintain the balance of the Universe.

19. The master of masters, the one beyond the remotest, the venerable one, the beginningless, middleless and endless one and the blessed one has incarnated with a part of his as the son of Aditi to make the Universe endowed with a protector.

20. O Lord of *Daityas* ! That Vāsudeva whose real nature is not known to Rudra or the Lotus-born God, or Indra or Sun or Moon or venerable Marīci or other sages, has incarnated with a part of himself.

21. I bow down to Vāsudeva who is the first one and called *Akṣara* by the *Vedic* scholars, in whom they merge shedding off their sins and in whom those who are established are not born again.

22. I bow down to Vāsudeva who is beyond thought, from whom all these beings spring and into whom alone they get merged at the time of dissolution like the series of waves of an ocean.

23. The eye is assigned the function of apprehending form, the skin, that of touch, the tongue, taste; the nose,

smell. But none of these—skin, nose, eyes or tongue—is able to comprehend him whom, I salute.

24. To that Hari, who is the only overlord and who is to be known through reason, to him who is beginningless, middleless, the sinless god and is the controller, the supreme lord of the Universe and who destroys the fear of re-birth, I bow down.

25. I always bow down to Viṣṇu, the adorable lord, by whom (as the *Boar*) this immovable earth was lifted up with a single tusk and who rears the Universe and annhilates all this Universe.

26. I bow down to the infinite God, the Ruler who is an axe to the trees of entire cycle of birth and death; who having entered the womb of Aditi with a part of his, has taken away the prowess of the great *Asuras*.

27. The blessed god, the source of the Universe has entered the womb of the Mother of Indra with his sixteenth part. O Great *Asura* ! By him the strength of your bodies has been taken away.

Bali said:

28. O grandfather ! Who is the one called Hari, from whom there is this fear? With me are hundreds of *Daityas* stronger than Vāsudeva.

29-30. Vipracitti, Śibi, Śambhu, Jambha, Kumbha, Hayaśiras, Aśvaśiras, Bhaṅgakāra, Mahāhanu, Vātāpi, Pravaśa, Śumbha, Kukurakṣa, Durjaya and many more sons of Diti and Danu are there with me.

31. They are all of superior strength and of enormous valour and are able to bear the weight of earth. Kṛṣṇa is not a match for any one of them in valour or strength.

Lomaharṣaṇa said:

32. Having heard the words of his grandson, Prahlāda, the bull among *Daityas*, was enraged and told him, who spoke ill of *Vaikuṇṭha* (i.e., Viṣṇu)—

Prahlāda said:

33. Those your *Daityas* and *Dānavas* who have a king like you who is wicked and indiscriminate, shall surely get destroyed.

34. Which other evil-minded person other than you shall speak thus about the pre-eminent Lord of Lords, the birthless and omnipresent Vāsudeva ?

35-38. All these *Daityas* and *Dānavas* mentioned by you, gods along with Brahmā as well as other beings including the immovables, you and I and this universe together with hills, trees, rivers and forests, seas, islands and those which move and those which do not move—all these forms are one, but several aspects of a part of the omnipresent supreme soul who is adorable to the venerable ones. Of such a one, who shall indeed speak like this, except you who are indiscriminate, wicked, having no control over senses, who transgresses the regulations laid down by the elders and is heading towards destruction ?

39. Indeed, I am to be pitied, I in whose house was born your wretched father, of whom you are such a son, a despiser of the god of gods !

40. Apart from devotion to Kṛṣṇa, which puts an end to the flood of sins of any number of births, should you not pay regards to me at least ?

41. All this world and you vile *Daitya,* know that to me there is nothing dearer, not even my body, than that great Lord Kṛṣṇa.

42. Knowing fully well that Hari is dearer to me than even my life, you abuse him showing disrespect to me.

43. O Bali ! Virocana is respectable to you and I am venerable to him. Hari Nārāyaṇa is adorable to me and to the world as well.

44. Because you are reviling Kṛṣṇa who is the great Lord of Lords, you shall before long, fall from your exalted position here.

45. O Bali ! That god of the universe, Janārdana, is my protector. Should you not have any regard to me, who am an elderly one and respectable to your father ?

46. Because you did not take into account even this much while censuring the Lord of the universe, I am going to curse you.

47. Because of your utterance of words of censure of *Acyuta,* which are much more violent (to me) than (even) severing my head, you fall down losing your kingdom.

48. Just as I see no rescuer other than Kṛṣṇa in the ocean of re-birth, so shall I see you deprived of the kingdom before long.

CHAPTER THIRTY

Birth of Vāmana

Lomaharṣana said:

1. Having heard the unpalatable words of his grandfather the Lord of *Daityas* appeased his grand sire by bowing down to him again and again.

Bali said:

2. O grandfather ! Be pleased. Please do not be angry with me who was deluded by ignorance; under the influence of pride of strength I spoke in such a way.

3. O best of those born of Diti ! I am a sinner whose understanding is impaired by ignorance. I, an evil-doer, has been cursed by you and you have done the right thing.

4. By that (curse) I shall undergo loss of kingdom and loss of fame. I have acted so indecently that you feel much depressed, O father !

5. In all the three worlds, prosperity or any other thing is not difficult to obtain. But elderly people like you are hard to be met with in this world, O father !

6. Therefore, be pleased. It is not proper for you to be angry with me. O king of *Daityas* ! burnt down by your anger, I am afflicted day and night.

Prahlāda said:

7. My boy, because of anger I lost my presence of mind and by that you were cursed by me. My wisdom was obliterated by ignorance.

8. If my understanding had not been obscured by ignorance O Mahāsura ! how would I have cursed any person, knowing Hari to be omnipresent.

9. This curse which I pronounced on you, O bull among *Daityas* ! is going to take place surely. Therefore, don't grieve at this.

10. From today onwards you, be a devotee of Lord Hari, the imperishable blessed Lord of Gods. He shall be your protector.

11. O brave one ! (At least) after being cursed by me, you called to mind the Lord of Gods; so, I shall tell you how you would obtain prosperity.

Lomaharṣaṇa said:

12. After Aditi received the boon that ensured fulfilment of all desires, God Hari of great glory gradually grew (in the womb of Aditi).

13. Then as the time of delivery approached in the tenth month, the blessed Lord Govinda was born having the form of a dwarf.

14. As the protector of the universe, the Lord of all heavenly beings incarnated, the gods as well as the mother of gods, Aditi, gave up their grief.

15. Then blew soothing breeze; the sky became free from dust; and the minds of all beings were directed towards *Dharma.*

16. O best of the twice-born ! There was no pain in the body of the human beings. Then, the minds of all the beings were engaged in *Dharma.*

17. Right after his birth, blessed Lord Brahmā, the grandsire of the universe, performed the birth-rites and other rites and propitiated him.

Brahmā said:

18. O Overlord ! Victory to you; O unconquerable one ! may you be victorious. O Master of everyone ! O Hari ! Victory to you. O one beyond birth, death and old age, victory to you ! O infinite one ! O indestructible one ! Victory to you.

19. O Unconquered one ! Victory to you. O endless one ! O one of Unmanifest form ! Victory to you. O core of the ultimate ! O Omniscient one ! O essence of all knowledge and known !

20. O direct observer of the whole universe ! O creator of the universe ! O preceptor of the universe ! O lord of both the mobile and the immobile ! you protect during the preservation stage; victory to you.

21. O inexhaustible one ! victory to you. O endless one ! victory to you. O one existing in every heart ! victory to you. O one who is the beginning ! Middle and end (of the universe)! O one who is the form of all knowledge ! O excellent one ! Victory to you.

22. O ever blissful one ! O master ! victory to you, who are not defined by even those who are striving for emancipation, nor by the *Yogins* seeking realization, O one adorned by restraint and other qualities.

23. Victory to you, who are too minute beyond (normal) comprehension. O source of the world ! O one who appears as universe ! victory to you who are smaller than the smallest. Victory to you, O *Yogin* beyond the reach of the senses !

24. Victory to you absorbed in meditation through your own transcendental power (*Māyā*)! O imperishable one resting on the coiled Śesa ! Victory to you who hoisted up the earth with the tip of your single tusk.

25. O man-lion who tore open the chest of the enemy of gods ! O soul of the universe ! O Keśava ! O, you who are appearing now as a dwarf ! Victory to you.

26. O Janārdana ! O creator of the universe ! One covered by the veil of your own transcendental power (*Māyā*), victory to you. O unimaginable one ! O master ! Who are the only source of multifarious forms, victory to you.

27. O Hari ! may you prosper, you who develop the *Prakṛti* into multifarious transformations. By you only should this universe standing on Śeṣa, conform to *dharmic* mode of living.

28. O Hari ! Neither I nor Lord Śiva, nor Indra nor the other heavenly beings are able to comprehend you; neither the sages Sanaka and others nor the *Yogins* are able to know you.

29. In this world, O lord of the universe ! You are covered by the veil of Māyā. O lord of all ! Which human being can comprehend you without your grace ?

30. O Lord ! Favourable with grace, he only by whom you have been worshipped, will be able to comprehend you and no other person.

31. O Lord of Śiva, the master of Nandīśvara ! O Vāmana, O universal soul ! O lord of large eyes ! Please prosper for the strength of this universe.

Lomaharṣaṇa said:

32. Hṛṣīkeśa in the form of dwarf so praised (by Brahmā) smiled and spoke words deep with thought and indicative of welfare.

The Lord said:

33. I have been adored before by you, Indra and others and Kaśyapa. And I have promised Indra (the sovereignty of) the three worlds.

34. Again I was adored by Aditi, whom also I promised that I was going to hand over to Indra the three worlds with the thorns destroyed.

35. I, having promised thus, shall act in such a way that the thousand-eyed Indra becomes the overlord of the universe. What I have told you is the truth.

36-37. Then Brahmā gave deer skin to Hṛṣīkeśa, and venerable Bṛhaspati gave *Yajñopavīta.* Marīci, the son of Brahmā gave *Daṇḍa* to the *Brahmacārin;* Vasiṣṭha gave him water-pot (*Kamaṇḍalu*) and Aṅgiras gave *Darbha* grass and bark garments. Pulaha gave him a seat and Pulastya, a pair of yellow garments.

38. The *Vedas* decorated by the utterance of *Praṇava* and all the *Śāstras* as well as *Sāmkhya* and *Yoga* precepts attended on him.

39. That Lord Vāmana, the embodiment of all the *Vedas,* having matted hair and carrying a staff, an umbrella, and a *Kamaṇḍalu,* proceeded to the sacrifice of Bali.

40. O Brāhmaṇas ! In whichever part of the earth Vāmana set his foot in all those spots the afflicted earth gave way.

41. Vāmana though moving slowly and softly made the whole earth together with mountains, hills, islands and forests shake.

42. Bṛhaspati was (moving ahead) slowly and led the auspicious way. Thus his slow movement came to be ironically spoken of as (Vāmana's movement).

43. Then Śeṣa, the great serpent, crawled out of *rasātala* and helped the Discus-bearing Lord of lords.

44. Even this great and excellent help of Śeṣa became famous. By the very sight of this, one will not have fear from serpents.

CHAPTER THIRTY-ONE

Vāmana Conquers Bali

Lomaharṣaṇa said:

1. Having seen the earth together with forests and hills shaken, Bali bowed down to Śukra Uśanas and asked him with folded hands—

Bali said:

2. O Ācārya ! Why is the earth along with oceans, forests and hills agitated and why the fires are not accepting the shares of *Asuras* ?

Lomaharṣaṇa said:

3. So questioned by Bali, the son of Kavi, the best of the knowers of the *Veda* and of great intellect, replied to the overlord of the *Daityas* after deliberating for a long time—

4. "Hari, the source of the universe, the eternal one and the supreme soul, has incarnated in the house of Kaśyapa here in the form of Vāmana.

5. "O bull among *Dānavas* ! Surely, he is coming to your sacrifice. This earth is shaking by his footsteps.

6. "The hills are trembling, the oceans are agitated; the earth is not capable of bearing the Lord, the master of the beings.

7. "The earth along with *Devas, Asuras, Gandharvas, Yakṣas, Rākṣasas* and *Pannagas,* as well as the Waters, the Fires, the Wind and the Sky— all these are sustained by him only. He sustains all the gods, human beings as well as the mighty *Asuras.*

8. "No one can escape from this *Māyā* of Kṛṣṇa, the creator of the universe. The universe is joined together by the relation of sustainer and sustained.

9. "Because of his presence now, the chief divinities are having their shares. Therefore your trifle fires are not enjoying the shares of the *Asuras.*"

10-12. Having listened to the words of Śukra, Bali said with horripilation: "I am blessed and I am meritorious for the lord of sacrifice is coming to the (my) sacrifice personally. O Brāhmaṇa ! Which other person is superior to me? The imperishable supreme soul to visualise whom the *Yogins* are ever engaged, that Lord himself is attending my sacrifice. O *Ācārya* ! you please guide me as to what I have to do."

Śukra said:

13. O *Asura* ! On the authority of the *Vedas*, the gods are partakers of the shares in the sacrifice. But, O *Daitya* ! By you the *Dānavas* were made the enjoyers of sacrificial shares.

14. This Lord established in *Sattva,* preserves (the creation). In the same way, the powerful master will himself devour at the end all the created beings.

15. Indeed, the gods have been denied (their legitimate share) by you and certainly Viṣṇu has stood up to maintain balance. O King ! Having known this, do whatever comes to your mind.

16. (However), O Lord of *Daityas* ! Even for a trivial matter, do not make any promise, only speak pleasing words without fruit.

17. To Kṛṣṇa who has begun his efforts for the welfare of the gods and who begs of you, O great *Asura* ! You say thus, "To you, O lord ! Who have accomplished everything and acting for the gods, I am not capable of giving anything."

Bali said:

18. O Brāhmaṇa ! How do I say ("I do not have") even to any other person that may beg of me? This being so, how indeed can I say to the Lord of gods and the destroyer of the upsurging sin of *Saṁsāra* ?

19. Lord Hari, is comprehended through various vows and fasts; if that Govinda should say "Give me", what more (should one desire) than that ?

20. He, the Lord, to propitiate whom sacrifices are performed by people with purity (of heart and soul), is himself going to ask me, "Give me."

21. Our actions (performed) have indeed been done well and (our) austerities have been performed well, for, what is offered by me is going to be received in person by Hari, the Īśa.

22. O master ! How can I say "No" to the Lord who comes to me? I would (rather) give up my life (than say) "I do not have anything."

23. Therefore, what (fruit) that is desired in this sacrifice is indeed attained and there is no doubt about this, if Janārdana, the lord of the sacrifice (himself) is going to beg of me.

24. If Govinda should say to me "Give me", I shall give even my head to him without second thought. What more can there be ?

25. How will I say "No" to *Acyuta* who comes to me of his own accord when I have not said "No" to any other seeker?

26. For noble ones, to face danger through charity is praiseworthy only. That munificence which does not form an obstacle is indeed spoken of as very great.

27. In my kingdom there is no one who is not happy, no one is poor, no one who is diseased, none who is not decorated, none who is mentally afflicted, nor is there one who is without mental poise.

28. O auspicious one ! All my subjects are happy, pleased, make use of scents, are satisfied and endowed with all virtues. And what else? I too am always happy.

29. This extraordinary fruit of the seed of charity is attained by me. O tiger among sages ! Such is my understanding of what I heard from your mouth.

30. If this best seed of charity falls on Lord Janārdana who is most worthy recipient then what is there that has not been earned, O preceptor !

31. That gift will be very special to me and the gods will be satisfied. It is said that gifting of an object is hundred times pleasurable than enjoyment (of the same).

32. Surely Hari, who is worshipped through sacrifices is inclined to favour me and therefore he arrives here. There is no doubt, he is the one who favours merely by granting his appearance.

33. Or say, if he comes in anger to kill me who have obstructed the divine shares, even then to be killed by *Acyuta* is most commendable.

34. Indeed, how can Hṛṣikeśa come here to kill me ?

35. O best of the sages ! Bearing this in mind, you should not take the stand of obstructing charity when Govinda, the Lord of the universe, comes over here.

Lomaharṣaṇa said:

36. Even as he (Bali) was speaking thus, he (Vāmana) approached the venue of the sacrifice along with the group of heavenly beings led by Bṛhaspati.

37-38. Again Bali said to Śukra, his *Purohita*: "He is coming to beg of me, for Hari the witness of every soul, the compriser of all gods and the inconceivable one comes to my house voluntarily assuming the form of dwarf."

39. Having seen the supreme lord entering the sacrificial hall, the *Asuras* got agitated by his brightness and were made powerless by his effulgence.

40. Vasiṣṭha, Gādhi's son (Viśvāmitra), Garga and other great sages who had assembled at that big sacrifice trembled.

41. And Bali felt his entire life fruitful. At that time, no one who was perturbed uttered anything.

42-43. Everyone worshipped the Lord of Lords with one's own spiritual power. Then having seen the king of *Asuras* and those sages prostrating, the supreme god of gods, Viṣṇu, himself assuming the form of the dwarf, praised the sacrifice, the fires, the sacrificer, the officiating priests, those that were engaged in other duties in the sacrificial performance, the members of the assembly, and the profuseness of the material.

44. Immediately, the Brāhmaṇas, the members in the sacrificial hall spontaneously exclaimed, "Bravo, bravo!" in honour of Vāmana.

45. Horripilated Bali duly welcomed Govinda offering water. And the mighty *Asura* said—

Bali said:

46-47. Honourable Sir ! Please listen, I am going to bestow on you whatever of my belongings are liked by you, heaps of gold and gems, elephants, buffaloes, women, clothes, ornaments, cows, lots of gold and silver, all this entire kingdom, or whatever you wish for.

Lomaharṣaṇa said:

48. Having been prayed thus by the King of *Daityas*, the adorable one of the form of dwarf said with a smile in deep voice these words pregnant with affection—

(Vāmana said:)

49. O king ! To house my sacred fire, give me land measuring three feet. Give those gold, villages and gems to those who ask for them.

Bali said:

50. O best of those having feet ! Of what use is (land measuring) three feet? You ask for a hundred or a hundred thousand feet.

Śrī Vāmana said:

51. O *Daitya*-Lord ! With these three steps, I will have gained what I want in my search. You indeed bestow wealth to other seekers in accordance with their desires.

(Lomaharṣaṇa said:)

52. Having heard these words spoken by the adorable Vāmana, the valiant one gave away three steps to Vāmana.

53. No sooner the water fell on to the hand of Vāmana, than the Dwarf became a non-dwarf (i.e. a giant); anon, he exhibited a form encompassing all gods.

54. The Sun and the Moon were his eyes, the sky (*Dyaus*) was the head and the Earth his feet, his toes were the *Piśācas* and fingers the *Guhyakas* (*Gandharvas*).

55. The Viśvedevas formed the knees and the *Sādhyas* his shanks. The sacrifices, the deities and the *Apsarās* were in his (various) limbs.

56. The entire (constellation of) stars formed his eye-sight and the hairs of the lord were the Sun's rays. The stars were pore of his skin and the great sages were in his hairs.

57. The intermediate directions were his arms and the (main) directions were the ears of the adorable one. The Aśvins formed his sense of hearing and the strong god *Vāyu* was his nose.

58. Moon-god found himself in his favourable attitude and *Dharma* resorted to his mind. *Satya* (truth) became his speech and Goddess Sarasvatī was his tongue.

59. Aditi, the mother of gods, was his neck and the *Vidyās* were the lines (round the neck); *Svargadvāra* was his anus and Tvaṣṭā and Pūṣan were the eyebrows.

60. Vaiśvānara (Agni) was located in the mouth and Prajāpati in his scrotum. Parabrahma was the heart and sage Kaśyapa his masculinity.

61. His back was formed by Vasus and Marut gods were found in every joint. Rudra was in his chest and the great oceans were his courage.

62. In his abdomen were *Gandharvas* and the strong *Maruts*; *Lakṣmī, Medhā, Dhṛti, Kānti* and all *Vidyās* were his hips.

63. The Lord was all effulgence as well as great austerities and there emerged the excellent brilliance of the Supreme Lord.

64. The *Vedas* were in the interiors of his body and his knees were the major sacrifices, *Iṣṭis, Paśubandhas* and the activities of the Brāhmaṇas.

65. Having seen Viṣṇu's body comprising all gods, the mighty *Daityas* did not go near him being afraid like moths of fire.

66. However Cikṣura, a valiant *Daitya,* took hold of a big toe. With the very toe Hari hit (broke) his neck together with his teeth.

67. The omnipresent Lord felled all the *Asuras* (who attacked him) with his foot and palm and immediately after having assumed a giant form, he occupied the whole of the earth.

68-69. When he was measuring the earth for protecting the gods, the sun and the moon were found at his chest and they appeared at the thighs, when he was measuring the skies; and they appeared below the knees, when he measured the heaven.

70. Having conquered all the three worlds, and having killed the bulls among *Asuras,* Viṣṇu of wide strides gave the three worlds to Indra.

71. The most superior and venerable Viṣṇu gave the netherworld called Sutala below the earth to Bali.

72-74. Then Viṣṇu, the overlord of all the Lords, told the king of *Daityas* — "Because I accepted the water given by you on my hand, you will have a noble life for a *Kalpa.* When at the end of the period of *Vaivasvata-Manvantara* comes *Sāvarṇika-Manvantara,* you will become Indra. Now all your kingdom has been given to Śakra (Indra).

75. "The Four-*Yuga* System lasts till the end of seventy-one cycles; and all those that go against it, are to be restrained by me.

76. "O Bali ! I had earlier been worshipped with deep devotion by him (Indra). Accepting my words, O *Asura* ! duly carrying out my instructions, you reside in the netherworld called *Sutala*, which is inhabited both by *Devas* and *Asuras*, crowded with hundreds of storeyed buildings, which is beautified by ponds having full-blown lotuses, by trees and clear-watered rivers. O *Dānava*-Chief ! You endowed with good physique, well-perfumed, adorned with golden ornaments, with wreaths and sandalpaste, with the mind entertained by music and dance, enjoy varieties of luxurious pleasures.

77-81. "O Bali ! On my orders, you will be there surrounded by hundreds of women. So long as you do not come into conflict with gods and Brāhmaṇas, you will enjoy pleasures fulfilling all desires. When you go against gods and Brāhmaṇas, the awesome and agonising noose will bind you."

Bali said:

82. O adorable one ! By your order, my residence will be in *Pātāla*. O Lord ! What will be the source that provides me with enjoyments, satisfied by which I shall always remember you ?

The Lord said:

83. The gifts not given according to law, those Śrāddhas without involving those learned in the *Vedas*, the fire-offerings without faith—these will bear fruit to you.

84. The sacrifices lacking in *Dakṣiṇā*, the rites not performed according to regulations, the learning without proper vows—all these will bear fruit to you.

85. Worship without water, rites performed without *Darbha*, sacrifice without ghee—all these will bear fruit to you, O Bali !

86. If anyone resorting to this place performs any rite, there will never be a share of it for the *Asura*.

87-89. (This) *Jyeṣṭhāśrama* is highly meritorious, so is the *Viṣṇupada* pond. If anyone performs *Śrāddhas*, or observes vows and restraints or some rite is performed according to prescriptions by an eminent person—all these (rites) (bestow) inexhaustible (merit) to him. There is no doubt.

90. He who keeps fasting on the eleventh day of the bright half of *Jyeṣṭha* and who, on the twelfth day, having visited Vāmana and having bathed in the *Viṣṇupada*, gives gifts within one's means, shall attain the highest abode.

Lomaharṣaṇa said:

91. Having conferred this boon on Bali and the Heaven on Śakra (*Indra*), Hari became invisible with his all-pervading form.

92. Indra, respected by the three worlds, ruled over (the heaven) as before and Bali resorted to *Pātāla* and resided in his appointed place.

93. Thus is recounted the excellent glory of Viṣṇu-Vāmana; he who listens to this will be relieved of all sins.

94-95. Those persons who recall the dialogue of Bali and Prahlāda, the discussions of Bali and Śukra, and the dialogue of Bali and Viṣṇu, will not have any mental agony nor any physical illness. Their mind never gets confused, and they never commit any sin, O best of Brāhmaṇas !

96. By listening to this story, one who has lost the kingdom will regain it and a person separated (from his desire) will obtain his desire, O venerable one !

97. By listening to the glory of Vāmana, one is absolved of all sins: a Brāhmaṇa learns the *Veda*, a Kṣatriya conquers the earth, a Vaiśya will have multitude of wealth and a Śūdra attains happiness.

CHAPTER THIRTY-TWO

Hymn to River Sarasvatī

The sages said:

1. How did this venerable river Sarasvatī, the best of rivers, flowing through Kurukṣetra, originate ?

2. And after reaching the pond and creating holy spots on its banks, how did the auspicious river flow westward in visible and invisible course ? O foremost of the knowers of Brahmaṇa ! Please tell us in detail about the *Tīrtha.*

Lomaharṣaṇa said:

3. The foremost of rivers and the eternal one (Sarasvatī) originated from the *Plakṣa* (fig) tree. (The river) absolves one of all sins always, merely when remembered.

4. We learn this great river of holy waters breaking through a thousand hills entered the forest called *Dvaita.*

5. The noble sage Mārkaṇḍeya having observed Sarasvatī who was established in the *Plakṣa* tree, prostrated with his head and propitiated Sarasvatī.

Mārkaṇḍeya said:

6-8. O goddess ! You are the mother of all the worlds, you are the auspicious source (*araṇī*) of the *Vedas*; whatever that is existing (sat) and non-existing (*asat*), i.e. the imperishable supreme Brahman and perishable universe and the word that reveals *Mokṣa*—all these are contained in you as water in the sea. Just as fire is hidden in wood and smell pervades the earth, so the immutable supreme Brahman and this entire universe of perishable nature are indeed in you.

9. The changing and unchanging world, O goddess ! Has the form of the letters of 'om'; all the visible and invisible universe is three-fold as the three phonemes of 'om'.

10-12. Three worlds, three *Vedas*, three-fold activity connected with (each of) the three *Vedas*, three fires, three lights, the group of three human values, *dharma* and others; three *Guṇas*, three *Varṇas*, three deities, three *Dhātus*, three states (*Avasthā*), *Pitṛs*, and *Aṇimā* and others (*Siddhis*); O goddess Sarasvatī ! These three syllables (of 'om') is your form; (you) appearing multifariously are the first (creation) of Brahmaṇa and yet ever new.

13. O Goddess ! The age-old practices of the group of *Soma* sacrifices, the group of *Havis* sacrifices and the group of *Pāka* sacrifices are conducted through uttering you by the knowers of Brahman.

14. That which is represented by the half syllable (of 'om') is indeterminable, unchangeable, imperishable, divine and mutationless.

15. Also this minute form which I am unable to speak of, cannot be expressed by any one else, not even with one's tongue, palate, lips, etc.

16. That (form) is Viṣṇu, Śiva, Brahmā, Candra, Arka (Sun), Luminaries (stars), Maheśvara who is the basis of the universe and the embodiment of the universe.

17. It is established by the diverse branches (of learning) and set forth by the *Sāṅkhya* system and the *Veda*, that it is ever *sat-asat* (existent and non-existent) which has neither a beginning nor a middle nor an end.

18. It is one and though one, it is diverse, depending on the different *Bhāvas* (mental dispositions); the nameless, yet nameable because of the six qualities, multi-named, the basis for the three *Guṇas*.

19. It is able to comprehend the manifestations of various energies and is able to manifest the various faculties. It is of the form of joy of joys, the beatitude; it consists of *Guṇas*.

20. Thus, O goddess ! This universe is pervaded by you wholly and in parts; you are Brahman existing as the unique and established in the diverse (universe).

21. Those objects which are eternal and those which are transient, those which are gross and those that are minute,

those which may be on the earth, in the atmosphere or elsewhere—their comprehension is you only (that is, due to you only).

22. All this having a form or being formless, all activity that is found in the created beings, all activity that is found in the gods or in any other form—all these are associated with vowels and consonants.

(Lomaharṣaṇa said:)

23. Propitiated thus Goddess Sarasvatī, the tongue of Viṣṇu, replied to the eminent noble sage Mārkaṇḍeya: "Wherever you take me, O Brāhmaṇa ! I go there without sloth."

Mārkaṇḍeya said:

24. The pond which was known as Brahmasaras earlier came to be known later as Nāgahrada. (The area around it) was ploughed by Kuru-ṛṣi, (hence) came to be known as Kurukṣetra. You are holy and of holy waters; you please flow through the middle of it (Kurukṣetra).

CHAPTER THIRTY-THREE

Greatness of Kurukṣetra

Lomaharṣaṇa said:

1. Having listened to the words of the wise sage Mārkaṇḍeya, the river (Sarasvatī) in floods entered Kurukṣetra.

2. That Sarasvatī of holy waters reaching Rantuka and after flooding Kurukṣetra, proceeded in western direction.

3. There are a thousand holy spots and they are resorted to by sages. With the grace of Parameṣṭhī, I shall describe them to you.

4. Remembering holy places is meritorious. Visit to these places destroys sins; bathing causes merit, even for one who has committed wicked deeds.

5. Those who remember the *Tīrthas,* those who propitiate the deities and those who bathe with faith, they all attain the final beatitude.

6. If one who, whether, pure or impure, gets involved in any situation, remembers the Lotus-eyed god, he becomes cleansed internally and externally.

7. Even by uttering the words, "I will go to Kurukṣetra, I live in Kurukṣetra," one gets liberated from all sins.

8. Indeed emancipation of human beings is spoken of as of four types: viz. knowledge of Brahman, obsequies at Gayā, death (while fighting against) capture of cows and residing in Kurukṣetra.

9. The land that lies between the rivers Sarasvatī and Dṛṣadvatī, is spoken of as Brahmāvarta, a land created by gods.

10. Even he who may be at a distance (from Kurukṣetra) (yet) always says "I will go to Kurukṣetra and reside there", shall be freed from all sins.

11. The consciousness of a self-possessed one who resides there only on the banks of the river Sarasvatī, will assume Brahman-form; there is no doubt about this.

12. Gods, sages, *Siddhas*—all resort to Kurujāṅgala. By resorting to it, one will certainly (be able to) see Brahman in one's own self.

13-14. Fickleness is the nature of human being. Those of controlled self or sinners who reach (Kurukṣetra) and live there desirous of emancipation, shall be completely free from sins committed in many earlier birth. They see the ever-new stainless divinity being in their hearts.

15. Kurukṣetra is the altar of Brahman; Sannihita pool is holy. Those persons who resort to these will always attain the supreme abode.

16. The planets, the asterisms, and the stars (have) fear of falling down in course of time. (But) for those who die in Kurukṣetra, there is no question of falling down at all.

17-18. Having gone to the great Sthāṇu lake where Brahmā and other gods, sages, *Siddhas, Cāraṇas, Gandharvas, Apsarās* and the *Yakṣas* desirous of (higher) states dwell, he who bathes there with faith shall obtain the wishes cherished by his mind. There is no doubt about this.

19-20. Having kept a vow and circumambulating the pond, a person should reach Rantuka and begging to be excused again and again, bathing in (the river) Sarasvatī and seeing the *Yakṣa* and bowing to him, one should offer flowers, incense and food and then should pronounce these words—

21. "O Lord of Yakṣas ! By your grace, I shall go round to forests, rivers and sacred spots. Make the course completely free from obstacles."

CHAPTER THIRTY-FOUR

Tīrthas in Kurukṣetra

The sages said:

1. Please tell us which are the seven forests and which are considered the seven rivers. (Please tell us also) about all the *Tīrthas* as well as the merit of bathing in *Tīrthas.*

2. What are the merits (gained by ablution in) different *Tīrthas* and what are the regulations (thereof)? O best of reciters of *Purāṇa* ! Please tell us all this in detail.

Lomaharṣaṇa said:

3. Listen now to the names of seven forests in Kurukṣetra which are (by themselves) holy and destroy all sins.

4-8. The sacred Kāmyaka forest, the great Aditi forest, the holy forest of Vyāsa, the Phalakī forest, the Sūrya forest, the great Madhu forest and the holy Śīta forest which destroys all blemishes. These are indeed the seven forests. Listen from me the names of rivers, O twice-born ones !

Sarasvatī, the sacred river, Vaitaraṇī, Gaṅgā of great merits, Mandākinī, Madhusravā, Amlu, Kauśikī that destroys sins; Dṛṣadvatī, which is very much sacred, and Hiraṇvatī. These rivers except Sarasvatī flow during rainy season.

9. The waters of these rivers are spoken of as being holy during rainy season. They have no impurity at any time. These excellent rivers are holy because of the efficacy of the *Tīrtha.*

10. O sages ! Listen with pleasure to the great merit of bathing in the *Tīrthas.* Going (to a *Tīrtha,* i.e. pilgrimage) and even their remembrance destroys all blemishes.

11. A person should start the pilgrimage to the *Tīrthas* after visiting Rantuka, and saluting the mighty doorkeeper, Yakṣa.

12. O eminent vipras ! Then one should go to the great Aditi forest, where a severe and great penance for the sake of a son was performed by Aditi.

13. Having bathed there and worshipped Aditi, the mother of gods, a person begets a brave son free from all defects and rides an aerial-car having a splendour of a hundred suns.

14. O eminent vipras ! Then one should proceed to the great abode of Viṣṇu well-known as *Satata* where Hari dwells.

15. Having bathed in the pond Vimalā and having visited Vimaleśvara, a person without any blemish obtains heaven and reaches Rudraloka.

16. Having visited Hari and Baladeva that are together, on the *Ekādaśī* day, one gets absolved of the blemishes caused by *Kali* (*age*).

17-18. Thereafter one should go to the *Pāriplava-tīrtha* well-known in all the three worlds. Having bathed (there) and having seen Brahmā with the *Vedas,* obtaining the merits of the (performance of) *Brahmayajña,* one attains heaven. There is the charming confluence of Kauśikī.

19. A person taking ablution at the confluence attains the supreme state. All the offences committed by a person

in the forest, are forgiven the moment (such) a person bathes there.

20. Then having gone to Dakṣāśrama and having visited *Dakṣeśvara Śiva*, the person obtains the fruits of (the performance of) *Aśvamedha-sacrifice.*

21. One should visit next *Śālūkini*, O best of the twice-born ! Having taken a dip in the *Tīrtha* and having devotedly worshipped Hari together with Hara, the person reaches the desired world (heaven), absolved of all sins.

22. Then having reached *Sarpirdadhi*, a prominent *Tīrtha* of *Nāgas*, and having bathed there, one becomes free from the fear of serpents.

23. O foremost of the twice-born ! One should thereafter go to Rantuka, the rescuer from hell. (Staying) there for a night, one should bathe in the auspicious and great *Tīrtha.*

24. Having worshipped diligently the second doorkeeper and having fed Brāhmaṇas and having prostrated, one should beg to be excused—

25. "O Yakṣa chief ! By your grace, I am freed from all sins. May I obtain the desired super-human power ?"

26. After propitiating the Yakṣa-chief thus, one should proceed to *Pañcanada.*

27. Five rivers terrifying *Dānavas* were fashioned by Rudra and hence the *Tīrtha* came to be known as *Pañcanada* in all the worlds.

28. Because ten million *Tīrthas* were brought together here by Rudra, (this) is called *Koṭi-tīrtha* famous in all the three worlds.

29. A person endowed with faith, having bathed in that *Tīrtha* and having seen *Koṭīśvara Hara*, obtains without fail, the (fruits of the performance of the) five *Yajñas.*

30. There only is Lord Vāmana established by all the gods. By bathing there, one attains the merit of performing *Agniṣṭoma.*

31. Proceeding with faith and self-control (next) to the *Tīrtha* of *Aśvins*, (and by bathing therein), one comes to be endowed with beauty, fortune and fame. There is no doubt.

32. (The next one is) named *Varāha-tīrtha* established by Viṣṇu. A faithful person by bathing therein, reaches the supreme state.

33. O prominent Brāhmaṇas ! Thereafter one should go to the great *Soma-tīrtha* where Soma performed a penance and got rid of the disease in days of yore.

34. By visiting Someśvara and by bathing in the auspicious and exalted *Tīrtha*, a person acquires the merit of performing *Rājasūya* sacrifice.

35. And the person freed from diseases and liberated from all sins, reaches the abode of Soma and enjoys with Candra for a long time.

36. Bhūteśvara as well as Jvālāmāleśvara are there only. By worshipping that *Liṅga*, one will not have rebirth.

37-38. By bathing in the (next *Tīrtha*) *Ekahaṁsa*, a person acquires the merit of (making a gift of) a thousand cows. By going to *Kṛtaśauca* (*Tīrtha*) and performing worship in the *Tīrtha*, a person becomes purified and obtains the merit of performing *Pauṇḍarīka* sacrifice. Thereafter is the (*Tīrtha*) of the self-controlled Mahādeva, *Muñjavaṭa* by name.

39. By fasting (there) for a night, one attains the (abode) of *Gaṇa*pati. The venerable *Yakṣiṇī* known all over the world is there only.

40. Going and bathing there (results in) liberation from great sins. This place is well-known as the gateway of Kurukṣetra and is the enhancer of merit.

41-42. After going round it in circumambulation, one should feed Brāhmaṇas. Then by going to and worshipping the *Pitṛ-deities* there at Puṣkara founded by the great (Paraśurāma, son of Jamadagni), a king becomes successful and obtains the merit of performing *Aśvamedha*.

43. The divinities get pleased and bestow the desired fruit on him who gives his daughter (in marriage) in (the month of) *Kārttika*, there.

44. The great *Yakṣa*, Kapila, who himself stands as the doorkeeper causes obstacle and a miserable state to sinners.

45. His wife is the great *Yakṣī*, Ulūkhalamekhalā by name. She always moves about beating a drum.

46. She (once) saw a woman born in a sinful region, along with her son. Then, the *Yakṣī* beating the drum told her during night—

47-50. "(You have) eaten curd in *Yugandhara* and stayed in *Acyuta*-region; in the same way, (you have) bathed in *Bhūtālaya* and you want to live along with your son. I am telling you this in the day time. (But) I shall certainly devour you at night." Having heard these words, she bowed down to the *Yakṣiṇī* and said in a piteous voice: "Please do favour me, O lady !" Thereupon the Yakṣiṇī full of compassion told her: " By taking bath in (the river) Sarasvatī, when the solar eclipse is going to occur in course of time, you, being purified, will go to heaven."

CHAPTER THIRTY-FIVE

Tīrthas in Kurukṣetra (continued)

Lomaharṣaṇa said:

1-3. O best of the twice-born ! A person on pilgrimage to *Tīrthas* should then go to Rāmahrada. There, we have heard that five pools were created with special effort by the Brāhmaṇa (Paraśu-) Rāma of brilliant lustre after uprooting the *Kṣatra* (i.e., Kṣatriyas) and by filling them with the blood of the tigers among men. He propitiated not only his parents but also grandparents. Those Fathers being pleased, spoke to Rāma. O best of twice-born—

4-5a. "O Rāma ! O Rāma ! O exalted one ! O great son of Bhṛgu ! We are pleased with this devotion of yours to the Pitṛs and you valour. O one of great glory ! Please you take fare well. You ask for a boon which you wish."

5b-8. So told by the Fathers, Rāma, the best of the mighty, folded his hands in reverence and said these words to his *Pitṛs* who appeared in the sky: "If you are pleased with me, then may this be conferred that with the grace of the Fathers, I would like getting back again this (my) penance. For overcome by fury, the *Kṣatra* (i.e. all the Kṣatriyas) was annihilated by me. May I be absolved of the sin thereof by your power. May these pools become *Tīrthas* and become well-known on the earth."

9. Having heard these virtuous words of Rāma, the Fathers being very much pleased and endowed with joy, replied—

10-14a. "O son ! Your austerities prosper, especially because of your devotion to your parents. You are absolved of the sin of annihilating royalty in rage; they were defeated by their own *Karmas.* These pools will now attain the character of *Tīrtha.* There is no doubt. One who bathes in these pools and satiates his own Fathers, the Fathers grant the cherished fruit; and the desired mental wishes as well as eternal stay in heaven."

14b. After bestowing such boons, the pleased parents of Rāma then (took leave of) Rāma Bhārgava and disappeared there only, O twice-borns ! Thus the Rāma-pools of the exalted Bhārgava became holy.

15. A celibate person of pure vows by taking ablutions in the pools of Rāma as well as by worshipping Rāma, will acquire much gold.

16. O twice-borns ! A self-possessed visitor of *Tīrthas,* by reaching the *Vaṁsamūla* (*Tīrtha*) and bathing (there) with the family, will elevate his family.

17. Having approached *Kāyaśodhana-tīrtha* famous in the worlds, and having bathed therein, one gets purification of the body. There is no doubt in this.

18. With a pure body, he goes to that abode from which one does not return again. The *Siddhas* who are devoted to the *Tīrthas* move among *Tīrthas,* till they reach *Kāyaśodhana-tīrtha* here.

19. By dipping one's body in this *Tīrthu*, the self-controlled attains the supreme abode from which there is no return again.

20. O great Brāhmaṇas ! Then should one go to the *Tīrtha* renowned in the three worlds, where all the worlds were delivered by the all-powerful Viṣṇu.

21. Having reached *Lokoddhāra-tīrtha* and having bathed in that excellent *Tīrtha*, devotedly remembering (its efficacy), one sees the eternal world.

22. By propitiating with prostration the two gods Viṣṇu and the eternal Lord Śiva who ever dwell there, one attains emancipation.

23. Then one should proceed to *Śrītīrtha Śālagrāma.* The Lord grants constant presence with him who bathes therein.

24-27. By proceeding to the *Tīrtha Kapilahrada* well-known in the three worlds, by worshipping, after ablution there, the deities (of the *Tīrtha*) as well as the *Pitṛs*, a person acquires the merit of (the gift of) a thousand black kine. Having visited Mahādeva Śiva who dwells there assuming the form of Kapila and is worshipped by sages, one attains emancipation.

By going to *Sūrya-tīrtha* and bathing there with self-control and by worshipping *Pitṛs* and *Devas* observing fast, one acquires the merit of (the performance of) *Agniṣṭoma* (sacrifice) and reaches the abode of Sūrya.

28. Having visited the thousand-rayed Lord Bhānu (*Sūrya*) renowned in the three worlds, a person endowed with (perfect) knowledge attains emancipation.

29. Having arrived (next) at *Bhavānīvana* in due order and having taken ablutions there, a visitor of *Tīrthas* gains the merit of (gifting) a thousand cows.

30. In days of yore, when Brahmā belched while drinking ambrosia, Surabhi was born and she resorted to the nether world.

31. From her were born Surabhi mothers who are the mothers of the worlds. The whole of nether world was completely pervaded by them.

32. When Brahmā was performing a sacrifice, they were brought for *Dakṣiṇā*; Brāhmaṇas were invited. And they (cows) were rushed through an opening.

33. At the entrance of this opening stands *Gaṇa*pati himself, by visiting whom a person of self-control obtains all desires.

34-35. Having reached *Saṅginī-tīrtha,* the resort of emancipation and having bathed in *Devī-tīrtha,* a person comes to possess an exquisite form, and acquires infinite wealth along with sons and grandsons and after gaining plenty of enjoyments, reaches the supreme abode.

36. Having bathed in *Brahmāvarta,* a person comes to be endowed with knowledge of Brahma and gives up his life at will. There is no doubt about this.

37. O Brāhmaṇa-chiefs ! Then one should go to Rantuka, the doorkeeper. There one should take bath in the Tīrtha of exalted Yakṣa-chief in Sarasvatī (river).

38. By devotedly fasting there one acquires (supreme) knowledge and gains the desired fruits by the grace of Yakṣa.

39. O Brāhmaṇa-chiefs ! Thence one should go to *Brahmāvarta* praised by sages. Having bathed in *Brahmāvarta* a person shall certainly attain Brahma.

40. Then one should proceed to the superior Sutīrthaka, O Brāhmaṇa-chiefs ! The *Pitṛs* are always present there along with the gods.

41. One should take ablution there being intent on the worship of the *Pitṛs* and gods. One pleases (thus) the *Pitṛs* for ever and acquires the merit of (the performance of) *Aśvamedha* (sacrifice).

42-44. O knowers of *Dharma* ! Then by arriving at Avanti in due course and by bathing in the *Kāmeśvara-tīrtha,* one endowed with devotion, gets free from diseases and certainly attains Brahma. And there only is *Mātṛ-tīrtha.* The progeny of a devoted person who bathes therein prospers always. That person acquires limitless wealth as well. Then a person of self-control should go to *Sītāvana* observing moderation in food.

45. O chief of Brāhmaṇas ! There is an exalted *Tīrtha* hard to find elsewhere. By a mere visit, it sanctifies twenty-one (generations) of people.

46. By sprinkling one's hair (with water) therein, one becomes cleansed of sin. There is another superior and exalted *Tīrtha, Śunāṁlomāpaha.*

47-48. O Brāhmaṇas ! There in the *Śvavilomāpaha-tīrtha,* well-known in the three worlds, Brāhmaṇas who are very wise scholars and intent on the *Tīrthas,* remove the hair of their (body), through *Prāṇāyama.* O best of Brāhmaṇas ! those Brāhmaṇas of sanctified souls reach the highest abode.

49. And the well-known *Daśāśvamedhika-tīrtha* is also there. By bathing there with devotion, one gains the same merit (i.e., of the performance of ten Aśvamedha sacrifices).

50. Then a person full of faith, should proceed to *Mānuṣa,* known all the world over. By the sight of the *Tīrtha* one gets rid of sins.

51. In the bygone days, black bucks tormented by the arrows of hunters, dived into this pool and were transformed into human beings.

52-55. Then all those hunters asked these venerable Brāhmaṇas, "O sages ! Where did the black bucks hurt by the arrows, go? Fallen in the pool, were they drowned? Please tell us, O Venerable Brāhmaṇas !" And those respectable Brāhmaṇas questioned there, said, "We are they. By the virtue of this *Tīrtha,* (we were) transformed into human forms. Therefore, you too perform ablutions in the pool keeping faith and giving up envy. You shall get rid of all sins, without doubt." Then all of them bathed and went to heaven with sanctified bodies.

56. O best of the twice-born ! This is the greatness of the *Mānuṣa-tīrtha.* Those who listen (to this) with faith, also reach the supreme abode.

CHAPTER THIRTY-SIX

Tīrthas in Kurukṣetra (continued)

Lomaharṣaṇa said:

1. O best of the twice-born ! At a distance of only a *kośa* to the east of *Mānuṣa(-tīrtha)*, there is a river by name Āpagā resorted to by the twice-born.

2. No sin remains of those who gift *Śyāmāka* grain cooked in milk and having a liberal dash of ghee, to the Brāhmaṇas (here).

3. Those who having reached that Āpagā river, perform *śrāddha*, will get all (their) desires fulfilled without doubt.

4-5. The parents and the grandparents yearn: In our family may be born a son or a grandson who goes to river Āpagā and satisfies us with sesamum (*libation*); by that we will be satiated for as long as a hundred generations."

6. When *Nabhasya* (i.e. *Bhādrapada*) month arrives, he who offers rice-balls (to *Pitṛs*) during the mid-day of the fourteenth day, especially of the dark fortnight, attains emancipation.

7. O great Brāhmaṇas ! From there one should proceed to the excellent region of Brahmā, renowned by the name Brahmodumbara in all the world !

8. O most pious of the twice-born ! A person who bathes there in the *Brahmarṣi* pool, gains the merit (of the performance) of the seven *Soma* (sacrifices), by the grace of the Seven Sages.

9. The (Seven) Divine Sages (are): Bharadvāja, Gautama, Jamadagni, Kaśyapa, Viśvāmitra, Vasiṣṭha, and Atri.

10. By these (sages) together was fashioned that pond hard to find on the earth. Brahmā also resorted to it. Therefore, it is called Brahmodumbara.

11. Having bathed in the excellent *Tīrtha* of Brahmā of imperceptible origin, one attains the abode of Brahmā; there is no need to entertain any doubt.

12. To him who worships a Brāhmaṇa having in view gods and *Pitṛs*, the happy *Pitṛs* give what is difficult to get on the earth.

13. He who takes ablutions separately having in view the Seven Sages, becomes master of the seven worlds by the grace of the Sages.

14. (The *Tīrtha*) renowned as Kapilastha in which the Lord himself known as *Vṛddha-Kedāra* dwells, is destroyer of all sins.

15. Having bathed there and having worshipped Rudra along with *Daṇḍin*, one acquires invisibility and enjoys in Śiva's abode.

16. He who, after offering libations, drinks three palmfuls (of water) and bows down to the Lord of Lords, obtains the merit of (visiting) Kedāra.

17. He who performs *śrāddha* having Śiva in view, on the fourteenth day of the bright half of Caitra month, attains the supreme abode.

18. Then one should go to Kalasī where dwells goddess Durgā, (known also as) Kātyāyanī, Bhadrā, Nidrā, Māyā and Sanātanī.

19. Having bathed in Kalasī, and having visited Durgā dwelling on her bank, a person crosses over the impassable forest of *Saṁsāra*.

20-21. Then one should proceed to *Saraka* which is hard to find in the three worlds. Having visited Lord Maheśvara on the fourteenth day of dark fortnight, one gets all desires fulfilled and reaches the abode of Śiva. O most pious of the twice-born ! Three crore (thirty million) *Tīrthas* are found in Saraka.

22-23. *Rudrakoṭi(-tīrtha)* is established in a well in the middle of the pond. A person who bathes in that pond and remembers Rudrakoṭi and adores Rudrakoṭi becomes, without doubt, free from all blemishes by the grace of Rudras.

24-27. He reaches the supreme abode having the vehicle of Indra.

There only is the *Tīrtha Iḍāspada* which drives away the fear of sin, and by the very sight of which a person attains salvation. Having bathed there and having worshipped the group of *Pitṛs* as well as the group of gods, one never falls into trouble but gains whatever conceived by the mind.

Kedāra is an exalted *Tīrtha* that destroys all blemishes. By bathing there a person gains the merit of gifting everything.

Kiṁrūpa is a great *Tīrtha* hard to find on the earth. A person that bathes there, gains the merit of (performance of all) sacrifices.

28. To the east of *Saraka* is a *Tīrtha* famous in the three worlds. Its origin is well-known on the earth and it eradicates all sins.

29. Viṣṇu who having assumed the form of Man-Lion, killed the powerful *Dānava,* and being in the animal bod, he had copulation with lionesses.

30. Then the gods along with *Gandharvas* adored Śiva, the granter of boons, and prostrating with all their limbs, asked him to retrieve the body of Viṣṇu.

31. Then the exalted Lord assumed the form of *Śarabha* and had a very tense combat (with Viṣṇu in the form of Lion) for a thousand divine years.

32. Both the Lords fell into the pond while fighting.

33. The divine sage Nārada, who was seated in meditation under the Pīpal tree on the bank of the pond, saw them, O Vipras !

34. Viṣṇu emerged (from the pond) with four arms and Śiva assumed the Liṅga-form. Having seen the two *Puruṣas,* (Nārada) prayed with devotion.

(Nārada said:)

35. Salutations to Śiva, to the most powerful Viṣṇu. Salutations to Hari and to the consort of Umā, (the lord who) sustains the universe.

36. Salutations to Hara of multi-forms and to Viṣṇu of cosmic form, to the Three-eyed Lord, the well-accomplished and to Kṛṣṇa, the source of knowledge.

37-38. I am blessed, I am meritorious for ever for the puruṣa-par-excellence were seen (by me). This my holy hermitage is purified by you (lord), from today onwards, (will become) renowned in the three worlds as *Dhanya-janma* (of blessed birth).

39. A devout person who having come here, bathes and propitiates the *Pitṛs*, will have *Indriya*-knowledge.

40. I always dwell at the root of the *Pīpal* tree. One (who) after bowing down to (that) *Pipal* tree, prostrates to Śiva and Viṣṇu (shall have *Indriya*-knowledge).

41. O great Brāhmaṇas ! From there one should proceed to the excellent Nāga pond. Having bathed in the lotus water, one attains the merit of (the performance of *Pauṇḍarīka*) sacrifice.

42. Especially bathing, doing *Japa* and offering *śrāddha* on the tenth day of the bright half of *Caita*, leads to the path of salvation.

43. Then one should go to *Triviṣṭapa-tīrtha* resorted to by gods. There is the holy river Vaitariṇī which cleans off sin.

44. By bathing there and worshipping the Trident-bearing and Bull-bannered (Lord Śiva) one gets purified from all sins and reaches the supreme abode.

45. O great Brāhmaṇa-chiefs ! From there one should go to the excellent *Rasāvartana*. Having bathed there with devotion, one attains the greatest accomplishment.

46. After bathing in the *Alepaka-tīrtha* on the fourteenth day of bright half of *Caitra*, and worshipping Śiva, not a trace of sin remains.

47. O great Brāhmaṇas ! Then one should go to the excellent *Phalakīvana* where *Devas*, with *Gandharvas*, *Sādhyas* as well as sages have been performing a long penance for a thousand divine years.

48. A person bathing in Dṛṣadvatī and propitiating the deities, acquires the merits of (the performance of) *Agniṣṭoma* and *Atirātra* (sacrifices).

49. Listen to the results of the virtuous (acts) of a person who performs *śrāddha* on Moon's day (Monday) during waning of the Moon (dark fortnight).

50. Just as the *śrāddha* offered in Gayā always pleases the Pitṛs, so *śrāddha* (performed there and hence it) should be performed by those who have resorted to *Phalakīvana.*

51. The *Pitṛs* of a person who (even) recalls to mind the excellent *Phalakīvana,* will become satiated; there is no doubt.

52. There is also a very great *Tīrtha* adorned by all deities. A person who takes bath there will gain the merit of (gifting) a thousand cows.

53. By bathing in *Pāṇikhāta-tīrtha* and satiating the *Pitṛs,* a person obtains the merit of (the performance of) *Rājasūya* (sacrifice) and attains (the knowledge of) *Sāṅkhya-yoga* (doctrines) too.

54-55. Thence should one go to the very great and excellent *Miśraka-tīrtha.* There the *Tīrthas* (from various sources) were mixed by the exalted sage Vyāsa for the sake of Dadhīca. A person who takes ablution in *Miśraka* will have taken ablutions in all *Tīrthas,* O great sages !

56-58. From there a disciplined one of moderate diet should reach *Vyāsavana.* By bathing in *Manojava* and visiting God Manīṣī, all the wishes of the mind will be realized; there is no doubt about it. After reaching Madhuvana as well as *Devī-tīrtha,* a person who is pure should take bath there. Then the person so sanctified (should worship) gods and *Pitṛs.* Such a person acquires supernatural powers granted by the Devī.

59. A noble person of restricted diet, who takes bath in Dṛṣadvatī at the confluence with Kauśikī, becomes rid of all sins.

60-61. Then one should proceed to *Vyāsasthalī* where the learned Vyāsa overcome by the grief about his son, made the decision to give up his life but was dissuaded from that by the gods, O great Brāhmaṇas ! A person who reaches his (Vyāsa's) region (Vyāsasthalī) does not suffer grief due to (loss of) son.

62. Arriving at *Kiṁdattarūpa* and gifting a *prastha* (measure) of sesamum, a person obtains supreme powers and finally attains salvation.

63. *Anna* and *Sudina* are two *Tīrthas* hard to find on the earth. By bathing in them one with purified soul attains *Sūryaloka*.

64. Then one should arrive at *Kṛtapuṇya*, well-known in the three worlds. Staying there with purity, one should take ablutions in (the river) Gaṅgā.

65-66. By worshipping Mahādeva, one gains the merit of *Aśvamedha* (sacrifice).

Koṭi-tīrtha is there only. Bathing there and visiting Lord *Koṭīśvara*, a devout person shall gain the merit of ten million sacrifices.

Then one should go to *Vāmanaka* renowned in the three worlds.

67. (In this *Tīrtha*) the powerful Viṣṇu assuming the form of Vāmana (dwarf) took away the kingdom of Bali and handed it over to Indra.

68. By bathing in *Viṣṇupada* and worshipping Vāmana, a person with his soul cleansed of all sins, attains *Viṣṇuloka*.

69. *Jyeṣṭhāśrama*, that eradicates all sins, is there only. Having seen that, a person attains salvation; there is no doubt.

70. A person bathing on the twelfth day after fasting on the eleventh day of the bright half of Māgha month, gains superiority among men.

71. Brāhmaṇas endowed with initiation and position and engaged in propitiating Viṣṇu, have been established there by the powerful Viṣṇu.

72. The *śrāddhas* (offered by them) and the various gifts given to them shall be imperishable till the Manvantara lasts.

73. There only is *Koṭi-tīrtha* famous in the three worlds. By bathing in that *Tīrtha* one gains the merit of ten million sacrifices.

74. Having visited the supreme Lord Koṭīśvara in that *Tīrtha*, a person acquires the rank of *Gaṇa*pati by the grace of Mahādeva.

75. There only is the very great *Tīrtha* of the great Sūrya. Having bathed with devotion in that *Tīrtha*, one becomes honoured in *Sūryaloka*.

76-78. O chief of Brāhmaṇas ! From there one should go to the most clear *Tīrtha*, *Kulottāraṇaka* by name, that destroys blemishes and was formerly established by Viṣṇu, for liberating the *Varṇas* and *Āśramas*. They, also having come to the *Tīrtha*, will see the supreme abode: A student, a householder, a recluse or a mendicant, taking ablution, liberates twenty-one generations.

79. Brāhmaṇas, Kṣatriyas, Vaiśyas and devout women and Śūdras bathing with devotion in the *Tīrtha*, will see the supreme abode.

80. Even he who lives far away and remembers Kurukṣetra together with Vāmana, attains salvation: What (to speak of) one who is dwelling (there only)?

CHAPTER THIRTY-SEVEN

Tīrthas in Kurukṣetra (continued)

Lomaharṣaṇa said:

1. By bathing in the pond of Pavana and paying visit to Maheśvara, a person is liberated from all blemishes, and attains the abode of Śiva.

2. (It is the place) where Pavana due to grief of his son's death had concealed himself and then the gods along with Brahmā eulogised him with devotion (and brought him back).

3. Then one should go to that place of the Trident-bearing Lord, *Hanumat-sthāna*, where the gods together with *Gandharvas* made Hanumān manifest.

4-5. By bathing in the *Tīrtha* there, one attains immortality. The best of the twice-born who tours round the *Tīrthas*, will cause deliverance to all his grandparents on both maternal and paternal sides by reaching *Kulottāraṇa.*

The tīrtha of the saintly king Śālihotra is well-known in the three worlds.

6. By bathing there one will get rid of the blemishes caused by the body.

Śrīkuñja-tīrtha in (the river) Sarasvatī is renowned in the three worlds.

7. A person taking ablutions there with devotion will get the merit of *Agniṣṭoma* sacrifice.

The next *Tīrtha* to be reached by a virtuous person is *Naimiṣakuñja.*

8-9. (By bathing there) one gets the merit that is obtained by an ablution in Naimiṣa.

There is the widely known *Tīrtha* associated with Vedavatī, who, pulled down by grief, gave her life up (here) to kill Rāvaṇa who had dragged her by hair, O best Brāhmaṇas !

10. Later she was born (as the daughter) of the high-souled King Janaka. She, well-known by the name Sītā, was the devoted wife of Rāma.

11-12. She was carried away by Rāvaṇa only for his own destruction. After killing Rāvaṇa and coronating Vibhīṣaṇa, Sītā was brought back home by Rāma as a person of self-respect (would bring) fame. The person who bathes in this *Tīrtha* will gain the merit of *Kanyā yajña.*

13. (Also) he, free from all blemishes, reaches the supreme abode.

Then one should proceed to the very great and excellent place of Brahmā.

14. By taking ablution there, a person of lower *Varṇa* attains *Brahmaṇahood* and a Brāhmaṇa with his soul purified reaches the highest heaven.

15. From there one should go to *Soma-tīrtha* which is hard to find even in the three worlds. Soma obtained the kingdom of Moon, after performing penance there.

16. By bathing and worshipping one's *Pitṛs* and deities, a person becoming pure, reaches heaven as by (worshipping) Vāmana in *Kārttika* month.

17-18. *Sapta-sārasvata-tīrtha* is hard to find in the three worlds. Seven streams of Sarasvatī flow here united. (They are) Suprabhā, Kāñcanākṣī, Vimalā, Mānasa-hradā, Sarasvattoyā, Suvarṇā, Vimalodakā.

19-20a. When Grandsire Brahmā who was staying in Puṣkara, was performing a sacrifice, all the sages said: "This sacrifice does not have any great merit. Indeed, Sarasvatī, the best of the rivers, is not seen in front."

20b. Having heard it, the blessed one then recalled Sarasvatī with pleasure.

21. That Devī Sarasvatī who was invited to Puṣkāra by the grandsire engaged in sacrifice, is famous as Suprabhā.

22. Having seen that fast-flowing Sarasvatī giving respect to Brahmā, the pleased sages too regarded her highly.

23. Thus this Sarasvatī, the best of the rivers flowing in Puṣkara, was brought to Kurukṣetra by the exalted Mārkaṇḍa.

24. The sages Śaunaka and others rich in penance dwelling in Naimiṣa asked the great lord Lomaharṣaṇa—

25-26a. "O sage ! How can the merit of the sacrifice comes to us who are devoted to virtuous conduct?" The blessed one bowed down his head to the sages and said: "The merit of the sacrifice gets enhanced where river Sarasvatī flows."

26b-30. Having heard this, the sages who knew the different *Vedas*, came together and all of them called Sarasvatī to their mind. Then she being meditated upon by the sages engaged in *Sattra* (long lasting) sacrifice, arrived at the sacrifice for the ablution of the exalted ones.

Sarasvatī of holy waters, Kāñcanākṣī at Naimiṣa, arrived at Kurukṣetra, when (mentally called) by Maṅkaṇa of great vigour.

The best of the rivers, Sarasvatī, was invited for the Gaya sacrifice, the great sacrifice with Gaya as *Yajamāna* (performed) at Gayā. The sages of accomplished vows, call her by the name Viśālā.

31. That river was invited by the exalted Maṅkaṇa. The great river came and entered Kurukṣetra.

32. In the regions of holy *Uttarakośalā* resorted to by gods and sages, river Sarasvatī was meditated upon by Sage Uddālaka.

33. The most sacred river came to that place because of the sage. She was honoured by the assembly of sages clad in bark and skin (garments).

34. The river Sarasvatī well-known as Manoharā in Kedāra, resorted to by sages and *siddhas,* is considered as eradicating all sins.

35. For the benefit of the sages, she too was made to enter Kurukṣetra by the same sage through propitiating the supreme Lord.

36. The same Sarasvatī made manifest at *Gaṅgādvāra* by Dakṣa who was performing a sacrifice, (was known as) the noble *Vimalodā.*

37. Sarasvatī invited by the exalted Maṅkaṇa, as well as by *Kuru* engaged in sacrifice, went to Kurukṣetra.

38. She was brought to the pond by the wise Mārkaṇḍeya. The noble Maṅkaṇaka of accomplished powers, who stayed in *Saptasārasvata* (and danced) praising Sarasvatī of holy waters (was dissuaded by Lord Śaṅkara).

CHAPTER THIRTY-EIGHT

Sage Maṅkaṇaka's Boon

The sages said:

1. How did Maṅkaṇaka become a *Siddha* (accomplished one)? Of whom was the great sage born? Why was he, while dancing, dissuaded by the Lord (Śiva)?

Lomaharṣaṇa said:

2. Sage Maṅkaṇa was born of Kaśyapa. He was his mind-born son. O twice-born ones ! He, with his bark garment in hand, went for bathing.

3. Rambha and others, the good-looking and blemishless *Apsarās* of charming form, who had come there, were bathing with their clothes off.

4. Then due to excitement, the semen of the sage fell into water. A hunter took that semen and kept it in a pot.

5-6. (The semen) kept in the pot got itself divided into seven parts. There seven Ṛṣis who are known as the group of *Maruts,* were born (their names being—)

Vāyuvega, Vāyubala, Vāyuhā, Vāyumaṇḍala, Vāyukāla, Vāyuretas and the heroic Vāyucakra.

7-8. These are the sons of the sage, who sustain the movable and the immoveable (universe).

I have heard: Once the hand of Maṅkaṇaka of superior powers was hurt by the sharp tip of *Kuśa* grass and vegetable sap exuded from the wound. He having seen the vegetable sap, was overcome by joy and danced.

9-11a. Then all the moveable and immoveable ones began to dance. Having observed the universe dancing as deluded by his spiritual power, Mahādeva was requested by Brahmā and other gods together with sages rice in austerity, for the sake of the hermit, O best of the twice-born ones—

11b-12. "O Lord ! You should do that by which he stops dancing."

Then the Lord saw the sage whose mind was over-powered by joy. Mahādeva spoke to him with a desire for the welfare of the heavenly beings: "O best of hermits ! What is the occasion for joy to you, an ascetic who are on the path of Dharma ?"

The hermit said:

13. O Brāhmaṇa ! Do you not see the vegetable sap oozing from my palm ? Seeing which I am dancing with great joy.

Lomaharṣa said:

14. Laughing at the sage deluded by passion, the Lord said: "I am not at all surprised, now look at me."

15. Having said so to the foremost of the sages, the great effulgent Lord of Lords struck his own thumb with the tip of his finger, O eminent Brāhmaṇas !

16. Then from the wound, there came out snow-like ash. Having seen that the Brāhmaṇa was ashamed and fell at his feet and said—

17-19. "I do not know any god other than the exalted Trident-bearing Lord. You, the Trident-bearer, are the master of the mobile and the immobile universe. O sinless one ! Brahmā and other heavenly beings are found to be under your aegis. You are the supreme maker of the gods and their inspirer. All the heavenly bodies rejoice without fear from any quarter because of your grace. O overlord of gods and Asuras ! Please my great austerity do not go wasted."

Lomaharṣaṇa said:

20. Having thus glorified Mahādeva, the sage prostrated. Thereupon the pleased Lord told the sage these words—

Īśvara said:

21. May your austerity increase thousandfold by my grace, O Brāhmaṇa ! And I shall dwell here in this hermitage along with you for ever.

22. For a person who having bathed in the *Sapta sārasvata*, worships me, there is nothing that is inaccessible in this or the other world.

23. They will also go to the *Sārasvataloka*, without doubt and by the grace of Lord Śiva, attain the highest abode.

CHAPTER THIRTY-NINE

Tīrthas in Kurukṣetra (continued)

Lomaharṣaṇa said:

1. From there (*Saptasārasvata*) one full of faith should proceed to *Auśanasa-tīrtha,* where Uśanas (*Śukra*) became fully accomplished and attained the status of a Planet.

2. (By bathing) in the holy Kurukṣetra, a person becoming free from sins committed since birth (in this world), reaches the supreme Brahman whence one does not return again.

3. There a sage by name Rahodara caught by a huge head, got released, by realising the greatness of the *Tīrtha.*

The sages said:

4. How did Rahodara came to be seized (by the head)? How did he get released ? We desire to hear the greatness of the *Tīrtha.*

Lomaharṣaṇa said:

5. In the past, O tigers among the twice-born ! *Rākṣasas* were killed by the great Rāghava (Rāma) staying in *Daṇḍakāraṇya.*

6. There the head of a wicked *Rākṣasa* severed with a sharp-edged dagger, fell in that great forest.

7. That (head) got accidentally stuck to the neck of Rahodara who was moving about in the forest and it got fixed (*lit.* entered) by breaking a bone.

8. With it (head) clung to him, the learned sage was not able to move about and visit *Tīrthas* and temples.

9. The great sage though afflicted with pain (due to the head) from which was oozing (pus) went round all those *Tīrthas* that were on the earth.

10. Then he spoke to sages of purified soul. Those sages told him, "O Brāhmaṇa ! Proceed to *Auśanasa*(*-tīrtha*)."

11-14. Having heard their words, Rahodara, then went to *Auśanasa-tīrtha.* By touching its waters, the head detached from its place, fell into the waters, O twice-born ! Then he with a pure heart, getting rid of passion and cleansed of blemish, came to the hermitage and gladly told everything. The sages listening to the great efficacy of the *tīrtha* came there and named it 'Skull-remover' (*Kapālamocana*).

There only is the well-known great *Tīrtha* of Viśvāmitra.

15. By bathing in that *Tīrtha* where the great sage Viśvāmitra attained the status of Brāhmaṇa, one surely attains Brāhmaṇahood.

16. A Brāhmaṇa, however, with his soul purified, attains the supreme abode.

A disciplined person of moderate diet will go from there to *Pṛthūdaka.*

17. A sage Ṛṣaṅgu by name became accomplished there. Ṛṣaṅgu who could recall his previous births stayed always at *Gaṅgādvāra.*

18. Having come to know that he was now by his last days, he told these words to his sons. Having remembered all the merits of the *Tīrtha,* he spoke to the most pious of the sages this—

19. "One who muttering (prayers) gives up his body in the *Pṛthūdaka-tīrtha,* on the north of Sarasvatī, will not have mortality.

20. There only is *Brahmayoni* where Brahmā resorting to *Pṛthūdaka* dwelt on the bank of Sarasvatī.

21-22. (Brahmā) got engaged in meditation for creating the four *Varṇas.* From the face of meditating Brahmā of unmanifest birth, Brāhmaṇas were born, Kṣatriyas from the arms, Vaiśyas from the thighs, and from the feet were born Śūdras.

23. Having seen the four *Varṇas,* the *āśramas* were established. The *Tīrtha* thus established was called *Brahmayoni.*

24. By bathing there, a person desirous of emancipation does not undergo birth again. There only is the widely known *Tīrtha* called *Avakīrṇa.*

25. The *Tīrtha* in which Baka Dālbhya oppressed by Dhṛtarāṣṭra, offered a sacrifice along with Brāhmaṇas; then the king got awakened.

The sages said:

26. How did the *Tīrtha* come to be established by the name *Avakīrṇa*? Why was he (Baka) not appeased by King Dhṛtarāṣṭra?

Lomaharṣaṇa said:

27. The sages of Naimiṣa once went for (receiving) *Dakṣiṇā*. Of them Baka Dālbhya requested Dhṛtarāṣṭra.

28-29. What was spoken and held (to be given) by him (Dhṛtarāṣṭra) was to revile (them). Then with intense anger, (his own) flesh was torn and he sacrificed the kingdom of the king Dhṛtarāṣṭra in the great *Pṛthūdaka-tīrtha, Avakīrṇa* by name.

30. As the procedure of the *Yajña* was on and the kingdom was being offered, the kingdom got emaciated by the wicked action of the king.

31-32. Then he thought of the doings of the Brāhmaṇa. He went with the *Purohita* taking gems and all to *Avakīrṇa* to appease the Brāhmaṇa. Propitiated by the king, he said to the king—

33. "Brāhmaṇas are not to be looked down upon by a wise person. If a Brāhmaṇa is disregarded, he destroys three generations of the family."

34. Having told the king thus, he, bent on the well-being of the King, brought the dead back to life with ghee and milk.

35. A faithful one of restrained senses who bathes in that *Tīrtha*, gets the divine fruit wished by one's mind.

36. There is the *Tīrtha Yāyāta* by name (i.e., of Yayāti) quite well-known to the sacrificer for whom the river (Sarasvatī) brought honey with her flow.

37. A person who bathes with devotion therein, will get free from all blemishes and acquires the merit of *Aśvamedha* sacrifice.

38. There only is the holiest *tīrtha Madhusrava,* O twice-born ones ! After bathing therein, a person should devotedly offer libations of water to the *Pitṛs.*

39. There also is the very great *Tīrtha* called *Vasiṣṭhodvāha.* A person taking bath there with devotion reaches *Vasiṣṭhaloka.*

CHAPTER FORTY

Curse on Sarasvatī

The sages said:

1. Indeed the fast-flowing current (came to be called) *Vasiṣṭhasya Apavāha* (carrier of Vasiṣṭha). Why did that great river carry away the sage?

Lomaharṣaṇa said:

2. Between the seer-king Viśvāmitra and the noble-minded Vasiṣṭha, there ensued a very intense enmity due to rivalry in austerities.

3. The hermitage of Vasiṣṭha was on (the eastern side of) *Sthāṇu-tīrtha*; and that of the learned *Viśvāmitra,* to the west of it.

4. (Sthāṇu-tīrtha is the place) where Sthāṇu, the blessed Lord of gods, worshipped and offered sacrifice to Sarasvatī and established Sarasvatī in the form of a *Liṅga.*

5. Vasiṣṭha resided there for practising a severe penance. Viśvāmitra was, however, inferior to him in austerity.

6-7. Having summoned Sarasvatī, he (Viśvāmitra) told her this: "You bring Vasiṣṭha, a tiger among hermits, along with your current. I will kill that foremost sage when he comes here; there is no doubt." Having heard this, the river was indeed sorrowful.

8. Having seen that great river afflicted and trembling, Viśvāmitra angrily said thus: "Bring Vasiṣṭha quickly."

9. Then having gone to the eminent hermit Vasiṣṭha, the sorrowful great rivers conveyed those words of Viśvāmitra.

10. (Vasiṣṭha) asked the grief-stricken chief of the rivers, pale and much emaciated because of penance, "Carry me to Viśvāmitra."

11. Having heard the words of the compassionate one, that river (Sarasvatī) carried him to that place through the current of water.

12. Being carried by the river overflowing the banks, the Son of Mitrāvaruṇa praised goddess Sarasvatī.

13-16a. "O Sarasvatī ! You have sprung from the pond of the Grandsire (Brahmā); the whole world is encompassed with your excellent waters only. You are the only goddess who can move at will and you produce water in the clouds. All waters are you only. We are being carried by you. Nourishment, steadfastness, fame, super-human powers, beauty, patience, *Svadhā*, *Svāhā* and speech and the whole world depend upon you. You exist in all beings in the form of speech."

16b-17. The blessed Sarasvatī praised thus by him carried the Brāhmaṇa smoothly towards the *Āśrama* of Viśvāmitra. Then with respect, she presented that sage to Viśvāmitra.

18. Having seen Vasiṣṭha brought by Sarasvatī, (Viśvāmitra) then full of anger, searched for a weapon fit to kill him.

19. Having observed him enraged, the River being afraid of *Brāhmaṇicide*, carried away Vasiṣṭha in the middle of the stream, deceiving the son of Gādhi. She had surely carried out the words of both.

20. Then having seen the eminent sage Vasiṣṭha being carried away, Viśvāmitra of great austerities uttered, with his eyes red due to anger—

21. "O chief of rivers ! Because you have gone away deceiving me, O auspicious one ! You carry blood and be in league with groups of *Rākṣasas.*"

22. Then Sarasvatī having been cursed by the learned Viśvāmitra carried water mixed with blood for a year.

23. Afterwards the sages, gods, *Gandharvas* and *Apsarās* were deeply grieved seeing such a Sarasvatī.

24. Blood flowed in that holy and charming *Tīrtha.*

25. At that time came goblins, ghosts and *Rākṣasas.* They all drank the blood and enjoyed it.

26. They were deeply intoxicated by it and they became happy and free from afflictions; they were dancing and laughing as if they were conquerers of heaven.

27. After some time, ascetics rich in penance came on a pilgrimage to Sarasvatī from a place hundred Yojanas away.

28. Having seen that mighty river Sarasvatī being drunk by the fierce *Rākṣasas,* made a gigantic effort to rescue Sarasvatī.

29. All those noble and virtuous persons together resorted to the foremost of the rivers and said this—

30. "Alas, O foremost of the rivers ! Why are you flowing with blood? We are asking you, having heard that you have been distressed thus."

31-32. At that she (Sarasvatī) related all that was done by Viśvāmitra. Then the ascetics gladly combined with Sarasvatī, the river Aruṇā having floods of holy waters and able to absolve one of all wicked acts. Having seen the (fresh) waters of Sarasvatī the *Rākṣasas* were deeply sorrowful.

33-38a. They along with *Daityas* spoke again and again to all those ascetics: "We are all hungry; and we lack in *Dharma,* for ever. It is not our cherished act that we commit sins. Because of your apathy and by our own evil deeds, our tribe is increasing; we are *Brahmarākṣasas.* So also Vaiśyas, Śudras and Kṣatriyas who disparage Brāhmaṇas with wicked acts, become *Rākṣasas* here. Those who malign the *ācārya,* the mother or the father and those who vilify the elderly ones, become *Rākṣasas* here. (Our tribe) is increasing by the sexual crimes of wicked women. You are capable of delivering even the entire world."

38b-40. The ascetics having listened to them and being compassionate became agitated and the Brāhmaṇas spoke to each other: "The food over which one has sneezed, or over which worms have fallen, or that which is partly eaten by an untidy person, or on which hair has fallen or which has been shaken, or which is contaminated by wind or exhaled air, or that has come in contact with these—such food will be the share of *Rākṣasas.*"

41. Therefore, a learned man should always remain careful and avoid them. A person who himself partakes of such food will only feed the *Rākṣasas.*

42. The sages rich in penance, having cleansed that *Tīrtha,* created the confluence also for the emancipation of those *Rākṣasas.*

43. A person who having fasted for three days, bathes in the world-famous confluence of Aruṇā and Sarasvatī will be absolved of all sins.

44. When the awesome age of *Kali* arrives and *Adharma* reigns, one attains salvation after bathing at the confluence of Aruṇā and Sarasvatī.

45. Then all those *Rākṣasas* bathed there and being absolved of sins, wore divine flowers and clothes and were attended upon by divine damsels.

CHAPTER FORTY-ONE

Tīrthas in Kurukṣetra (continued)

Lomaharṣaṇa said:

1. The four seas were created there by the sage in the days of yore. A person bathing in any one of them, attains the merit of (gifting) a thousand cows.

2. O chief of Brāhmaṇas ! Whatever little austerity is performed at this *Tīrtha*, even by a wicked person, becomes complete in every respect.

3. O Brāhmaṇas ! There only is situated the *Śatasāhasraka-tīrtha* as well as the *Śatika-tīrtha*. By taking ablutions in both of them, one obtains the merit of (gifting) a thousand cows.

4. *Soma-tīrtha* is situated there on the bank of Sarasvatī, by bathing in which a person gains the fruit of *Rājasūya* sacrifice.

5. Having arrived in *Reṇukāṣṭaka*, a staunch person of self-control earns the very merit that (accrues by) devotion to one's mother.

6-7. Having resorted to *Ṛṇamocana-tīrtha* (regularly) visited by Brāhmaṇas, and to *Kumārābhiṣeka* well-known as *Ojasa*, and having bathed therein, a person becomes endowed with glory and reaches the abode of Kumāra.

8. A person who performs *Śrāddha* on the sixth day of the bright fortnight of *Caitra* (month), earns the very merit of *Gayāśrāddha*.

9. (One attains the merit of offering) *Śrāddha* in Sannihiti as proclaimed by Vāyu in days bygone. Therefore, one should perform *Śrāddha* with all efforts.

10. The libation of waters to the *Pitṛs* of a person who with faith takes bath and performs *Śrāddha* on the sixth day of *Caitra*, stands inexhaustible.

11. There is the *Tīrtha* by name *Pañcavaṭa* well-known in all the three worlds, where Mahādeva himself dwells having assumed *Yogic* form.

12. By performing ablution there and by worshipping Maheśvara, the god of gods, one attains the status of *Gaṇa*pati and enjoys along with gods.

13. O best of Brāhmaṇas ! Kurukṣetra is famous, where a very severe penance was performed by Kuru for tilling the land.

14-15. Indra pleased with his severe austerity, spoke these words: "O King-seer ! O virtuous one ! I am satisfied by this your penance. Those who offer sacrifice to Indra, go to sin-free heaven of the meritorious."

16-17. Then sneering (at Kuru), Lord Indra went back to heaven. Again and again he came and every time he came he sneered (at him) and untiringly asked him repeatedly. When his own body was scorched by the fierce austerity, then pleased Indra said, "Tell me what do you want to do?"

Kuru said:

18. Those devout persons who reside at this *Tīrtha*, reach the abode of Brahman, the supreme soul.

19. May those persons who have committed crimes elsewhere and those who are stained by the five great sins, be emancipated and go to the eternal abode, after taking bath in this *Tīrtha*.

20. O chief of Brāhmaṇas ! Kurukṣetra (*Kuru-tīrtha*) is the most meritorious in Kurukṣetra. One having visited it becomes absolved of sins and reaches the highest abode.

21. A person having taken bath in Kurukṣetra (*-tīrtha*) becomes freed from blemishes and with the approval of Kuru, attains the highest abode.

22. Then one should go to *Anaraka-tīrtha* well-known in all the three worlds. In the east dwells Brahmā and in the south Maheśvara.

23. In the west is the spouse of Rudra and in the north, Padmanābha dwells; in the middle is *Anaraka-tīrtha*. It is diffcult to find (its equal) in the three worlds.

24-28a. Persons take bath in *Anaraka-tīrtha* and get freed from sins. By taking ablution on a Tuesday which falls on the eighth day (*Aṣṭamī*) of *Vaiśākha*, one becomes free from sins. He too who offers gold as fourth part of the gift, and similarly one who gifts a pitcher full of cakes. First the gods are to be propitiated with pots full of gems. Then the two pitchers destroying all sins are to be gifted. He who performs ablution in this manner, becomes free from all sins and reaches the highest abode.

28b-30. This (ablution) may also be taken on a Tuesday which falls on the sixth day (*ṣaṣṭhī*) of any other month. Even then the rite is going to yield emancipation. O adorable Brāhmaṇas ! He who bathes in the most sacred of all the sacred places, attains the supreme state with the approval of the *gods*.

Kāmyaka grove is a holy place that destroys all sins.

31. By merely entering (*Kāmyaka*), one becomes free from blemishes. Having resorted to this holy grove, *Savitṛ* (Sun-god) is staying there in visible (form).

32. His name is Pūṣan, O foremost of Brāhmaṇas ! By visiting him, one attains salvation. A person taking bath on a Sunday becomes mentally pure and gets the one's cherished fruit.

CHAPTER FORTY-TWO

Tīrthas in Kurukṣetra (continued)

The sages said:

1. To the east of *Kāmyaka* is a bower frequented by gods. Please tell us in detail the origin of this *Tīrtha*.

Lomaharṣaṇa said:

2. O sages ! (You) all listen to the excellent glory of the *Tīrtha*. By listening to the activities of the sages one becomes free from sins.

3. The sages of Naimiṣa came to Kurukṣetra to have an ablution in Sarasvatī but could not gain entry into it.

4. Then they established the *Tīrtha Yajñopavīti*. But the other sages did not have access into it.

5-6. Sarasvatī who is always for the welfare of beings, having seen that the area from Rantuka's *Āśrama* to *Cakra-tīrtha* was full of Brāhmaṇas, took a westerly course creating ponds for the good of all Brāhmaṇas.

7. He who bathes in the eastern stream earns the merit of a bath in Gaṅgā. In the southern stream of Sarasvatī, Narmadā, the best of the rivers (dwells).

8. In the western direction, dwells river Yamunā, when the river flows northwards, she becomes Sindhu.

9. Because of the streams thus (flowing) in different directions, Sarasvatī is the most sacred river. A person taking bath therein becomes one who has taken bath in all the *Tīrthas.*

10. O eminent Brāhmaṇas ! From there one should go to the *Tīrtha* of the glorious Madana. It is known all over the three worlds and is called by the name Vihāra.

11. There the gods came together desirous of seeing Lord Śiva. (But) the gods assembled there could not see the Lord who was with his consort.

12-13. The praised Mahādeva Nandīśa, the *Gaṇa* leader. Then the pleased Nandīśa told them about the doings-the intense sport of *Bhava* (Śiva) with Umā in *Vihāra.* Having heard it, the gods called out their wives and went (there).

14-16. Śaṅkara, who was pleased with their sport and pastime, said: "A person who bathes with faith in this *Vihāra-tīrtha,* is going to be endowed with wealth, grains and dear ones. There is no doubt."

Then one should go to *Durgā-tīrtha* resorted to by Durgā, where by taking a bath and worshipping the *Pitṛs* one does not undergo distress.

There only is the bank of Sarasvatī famous in the three worlds.

17-19. By visiting (the *Tīrtha*), one purged of all sins, attains salvation. A person who satiates gods and *Pitṛs* with faith earns (merit) that cannot be exhausted. *Pitṛ-tīrtha* excels all others.

A matricide, a patricide or a *Brāhmaṇicide* or one who has violated the bed of a teacher becomes purified by bathing in the Eastern Sarasvatī who took recourse to the sky and has flown through the sky.

20-23. Eastern Sarasvatī is sanctifying even for sinners. In case of those who having approached Eastern Sarasvatī, reside there for three nights, not a touch of evil remains in their body. The divine Nara and Nārāyaṇa, Brahmā, Sthāṇu

(Śiva) as well as Ṛṣis and gods along with Indra ever attend on Eastern (Prācī) side (of Sarasvatī). For those who having come to Prācī, perform *Śrāddha* (there), there is nothing that is difficult to obtain in this or in the other world. Therefore one should go over to Prācī at any time, especially on the fifth day (*Pañcamī*).

24-25. A person who resorts (to Prācī) on the fifth day (*Pañcamī*) becomes wealthy. There only is found *Auśanasa-tīrtha* (similar to) which is hard to find in the three worlds and where Uśanas (Śukra) propitiated Parameśvara and became an accomplished one. He, being devoted to that *Tīrtha*, came to be included among planets.

26. Thus those who frequent with faith the excellent *Tīrtha* resorted to by ascetic Śukra, acquire the highest state.

27. By a person who performs *Śrāddha* with devotion at this *Tīrtha*, the *Pitṛs* will be liberated; there is no doubt.

28-29. Those who reach *Caturmukha-Brahma-tīrtha* standing as the boundary, and reside there fasting on the fourteenth day and on the eighth day of the dark-fortnight of *Caitra*, will see the Supreme Subtle One, from which (state) there is no return, O excellent twice-borns !

30. From that *Tīrtha*, one should go to *Sthāṇu-tīrtha* which looks splendid with a thousand *Liṅgas*. By visiting *Sthāṇu-vaṭa* there, one becomes free from sins.

CHAPTER FORTY-THREE

Glory of Sthāṇu-tīrtha

The sages said:

1-2. O great sage ! Please relate in detail all about the glory of *Sthāṇu-tīrtha* as well as of *Vaṭa* (banyan tree), the glory of the pond; the origin of *Sannihatya* pond and filling it later with dust. What is the merit of visiting the *Liṅgas* and what is the fruit of touching them ?

Lomaharṣaṇa said:

3. Let all the deities listen to the great *Vāmana-Purāṇa*, listening to which one attains emancipation with the grace of Vāmana.

4-5. Sanatkumāra was sitting near *Sthāṇu-vaṭa* along with Vālakhilyas and other venerable sages, and sons of Brahmā. Ascetic Mārkaṇḍeya courteously approached (him) and questioned about the glory of the pond, its extent and position as well.

Mārkaṇḍeya said:

6. O son of Brahmā ! O venerable one ! O master of all Śāstras ! You please tell me the glory of the pond that drives away all sins and fears.

7-8. Which *Tīrthas* are visible; which are hidden? O eminent Brāhmaṇa ! How many of the Liṅgas are holy in the vicinity of Sthāṇu, by the mere sight of which a man attains emancipation? Please also tell me the merit acquired from a mere sight of *Vaṭa* (banyan), and also its origin.

9. What merit does accrue from circumambulating? What is the fruit of bathing in the *Tīrtha*? What is the merit of (visiting) the hidden (*Tīrthas*)? O Lord !

10. How did the Lord of Lords, Sthāṇu, establish himself in the middle of the pond? But why did Indra fill the *Tīrtha* with dust ?

11. Please tell me the glory of *Sthāṇu-tīrtha*, the fruit of (visiting) *Cakra-tīrtha*, the glory of *Sūrya-tīrtha* and *Soma-tīrtha*.

12. O venerable one ! Please speak to me in detail, which are the mysterious *Tīrthas* of Śaṅkara, which are of Viṣṇu and which of Sarasvatī ?

13. You are the (first) embodied (creation) of the Lord and know the excellence fully. And by the grace of Brahmā all these are known to you.

Lomaharṣaṇa said:

14-15. Having listened to the words of Mārkaṇḍeya, that ascetic son of Brahmā condescended due to excessive devotion to the *Tīrtha.* He having relaxed his posture of *Paryaṅka* and prostrating to Maheśvara began to relate all that he had heard earlier from Brahmā.

Sanatkumāra said:

16. Bowing down to the auspicious, benevolent master, Mahādeva, I will explain in detail the origin of the *Tīrthas* as told by Brahmā.

17. In the days of yore, when the moveable and the immoveable ones had vanished and the whole universe had become one awesome mass of water, there appeared one large egg, the source of all beings.

18. Brahmā who was within the egg went to sleep. Having slept for a thousand *Yugas,* he woke up.

19. Then he being saturated with *Sattva* saw the universe desolate. As he thought of creation, he was engrossed by *Rajas.*

20. *Rajas* is the *Guṇa* that creates and *Sattva* is the *Guṇa* that maintains; *Tamoguṇa* comes to play at the time of dissolution.

21. That divinity who is beyond the *Guṇas,* is spoken of as the all-pervading *Puruṣa.* All are pervaded by him whatever that is designated *Jīva.*

22. He is Brahmā; he is Govinda; he is Īśvara, he is the eternal one. He who knows that supreme soul, certainly knows everything.

23. That *Puruṣa,* the innermost soul and the eternal one is beyond the *Guṇas.* He who knows that supreme soul, knows everything and attains emancipation.

24. What is the use of all (these) *Tīrthas* or *Āśramas* to those whose minds are established firmly in the *Ātman* only?

25. The self is the river (bed); self-control is the holy *Tīrtha;* Truth is the water endowed with proper conduct,

tranquility etc. A virtuous one bathing in such a river gets purified; the inner self is not cleansed with water.

26. The primary task of a human being is only to know that (self) absorbed in the consciousness of self—say the righteous ones; having reached this (state), the embodied one discards desires.

27. There is no wealth for a Brāhmaṇa equal to oneness, equality, truthfulness, proper conduct, firmness, imposing penalty (on oneself), straightforwardness and gradual disinterestedness in activities.

28. O eminent Brāhmaṇa ! I have told you in brief about Brahman by knowing which you attain the supreme Brahman; there is no doubt.

29. Now you listen to the birth of Brahmā from the supreme soul. This couplet is quoted in regard to Nārāyaṇa.

30. "Waters are spoken of as Nara-s; indeed waters are the offspring of Nara. Because he reclines over them, he is known as Nārāyaṇa."

31. Having known that the universe is immanent in that sacred water, the Lord, broke open the egg; from that emerged *om.*

32. From that came into being (the sound) *Bhūḥ*, the other one was *Bhuvaḥ* and the third sound was *Svaḥ*; the three (sounds) are designated, *Bhūr Bhūvaḥ Svaḥ.*

33. From that was born effulgence, which was the distinguished effulgence of that *Savitṛ*. That effulgence emerging from *Aṇu*, dried the water.

34. When dried by the effulgence, what remained became jelly. The jelly developed into 'bubble'. Then it hardened.

35. Because of the hardness it is called *Dhāriṇī* (earth); indeed she is the supporter of the beings. The Sannihita pond is in the place where the egg stood.

36. Because the effulgence that emerged was the first (to emerge), therefore it is called Āditya. Within the egg, Brahmā, the grandsire of the universe, came into being.

37. Meru mountain was his Vulva and the mountains are considered his womb. The oceans and the thousands of rivers were the mucous of the womb.

38. The clean and profuse water (came out) of the navel of Brahmā. The large pond was filled by that clear and fine water.

39-41. In the middle of it stood the mighty banyan tree, the embodiment of Sthāṇu. From it evolved the *Varṇas*—Brāhmaṇas, Kṣatriyas and Vaiśyas, and Śūdras— were born from him to serve the twice-born.

Then from Brahmā of inexplicit origin, who thought of creation, the mental sons, *Vālakhilyas,* embodiments of purity, were born; they were eighty-eight thousand in number and were celibates.

42. From the mind of Brahmā of inexplicit birth, who thought of creation, were born the mental sons, Sanaka and other great sages.

43. Again from the wise (Brahmā) meditating, desirous of offspring, were born the Seven Sages who became Prajāpatis.

44. Again from him (Brahmā) who was meditating and influenced by *Rajas,* were born *Vālakhilyas* who were engaged in austerity and study of the *Vedas.*

45. They are always particular about ablutions and ever intent on worship of gods; they waste their physical body with fasts and severe vows.

46. For a thousand divine years they worshipped the Lord of gods with their body emaciated with strained veins. But Śaṅkara was not pleased.

47. After a very long time, Śaṅkara (came there) along with Umā. Then the goddess having seen (them) from the aerial path, was very much distressed.

48-50a. Having appeased Śaṅkara the Lord of lords, the virtuous one (the goddess) said: "These groups of ascetics inhabiting Dāruvana are very much afflicted. O Lord ! Please do what will stop their suffering. Have mercy on me. O Lord!

what is the inexhaustible sin of these devoted to gods and *Dharma*, because of which their (wish) is not fulfilled, and they are reduced to sinews and bones ?"

50b. Having heard the words of the goddess the wielder of *Pināka*, the destroyer of the fallen, appearing splendid with the beams of charming moon on the head, said with a laugh—

Śrī Mahādeva said:

51. Devi, really you do not understand the mysterious ways of *Dharma*. Neither these (sages) know the *Dharma*, nor are they free from passion.

52a. Nor are they free from anger. They have only erroneous knowledge.

52b-53a. Having heard this the goddess said: "No, this is not true about these virtuous ones. O Lord ! Please reveal yourself (to them). I am very curious."

53b. The Lord of Lords so told by her said with a smiling face—

54. "You be here; I will go to the place where the bulls among ascetics are practising severe austerities; I will show you their reaction."

55-56. Then the goddess, Bhuvaneśvarī, so told by magnanimous Śaṅkara gladly said to him, her Lord: "Please go there where all those venerable ascetics (with their bodies) like wood and stone are reciting (the *Veda*) and attending to the fire with oblations."

57-58. Later having seen these ascetics, the Lord with an attractive physique, bare and youthful, bedecked with a long wreath of *sylvan* flowers, holding a begging bowl, wandering a-begging through hermitages, went to the hermitage of those sages. Then he moved into the hermitage saying, "Please give me alms."

59. The wives of the expounders of the *Veda* having seen him who had come to the hermitage, with their natural curiosity, were attracted by his beauty.

60-62. The ladies talked among themselves:—"Come on, let us meet the mendicant." Having told each other thus, and having taken many fruits and roots, the ascetic women told the Lord: "Take the food." He, on the other hand, extended his begging bowl very courteously (and said), "Please give, O ladies rich in penance ! May you fare well." The Lord of lords who was smiling there, was observed by the goddess.

63-64. Having offered the alms, those ladies afflicted by *Kāma,* asked him—

The ladies said:

O hermit ! What is the name of the vow you are practising, because of which you are bare-bodied and adorned with the long wreath of wood-flowers ? You are indeed a charming hermit; please tell us if you like.

65-66. The hermit so asked by the ladies said with a smile on his face: "This my vow is of some sort; secret and not made public. Where there is a large audience, there cannot be an exposition of this vow. Having known this, O honourable ladies ! You go back."

67. So told by him, they again spoke to the hermit ! "O hermit ! Then come on, we will go; our curiosity is too great."

68-69. So saying they held him with their sprout-like hands. Someone (held him) at neck with love. Another subdued by love (held him) at his knees; yet another lady sportively (held) his hair; some other lady (touched) his hips and yet another feet.

70-71. Having seen the excitement of their wives, in the hermitage, the ascetics, with clubs and stone in hands, mutually conversing "Let him be beaten", threw upwards the lord's dreadful *Liṅga.* As the *Liṅga* was thrown, Īśvara disappeared.

72-73. The venerable god reaching Kailāsa mountain with the goddess, laughed (heartily). As the *Liṅga* of the Lord of lords was thrown in this world, there was a great confusion among the devout sages. Having known this, they remained afflicted.

74-75a. One eminent sage, the most intelligent of them, said: "We do not know the true nature of the high-souled ascetic. Let us take refuge in Brahmā, he knows his movements."

75b-76. So told by him, all the sages of self-control went to the abode of Brahmā served by all gods. Having prostrated to the Lord of gods, they stood with their heads lowered in shame.

77. Then Brahmā seeing them distressed, said the words: "Alas ! you were indiscreet when you were sullied by anger.

78. "Those who are indiscreet cannot discern what is virtuous action. O hermits of cruel action ! Listen to the essentials of *Dharma.*

79-81. "Having known it, a learned man attains quickly the fruit of *Dharma.* That all-pervasive and eternal being, established in this self, in this body, is beginningless; he is the great Sthāṇu characterised as unattached. Even as a gem though colourless and bright, assumes (the colour) and becomes one with the object nearby, so is the soul made by the mind. (The soul) assuming the changes of the mind, gets entangled with *Karmas.*

82. "Then being in the grip of *Karmas* the soul experiences objects of enjoyment, heaven and hell. Therefore, a wise man should purify the mind through expedients like *Jñānayoga* (contemplation).

83-84. "Once it (mind) becomes pure, the inner self will be free from distraction of its own accord. A person whose mind is not cleansed, does not attain purity by bodily mortification even of the nature of scorching. The rites are recommended only to check (the mind) from (committing) sins.

85. "Because a body very much sullied cannot be easily cleansed, therefore this course is the indicator of good path.

86. "This division of *Varṇa* and *Āśrama* (created) by some master of the universe is the cause of the influence of ignorance, and is an excuse for the rising ones.

87. "You remain in an *Āśrama* overcome by anger and lust. For the enlightened the house is the hermitage and the hermitage is the house for the unenlightened.

88. "Where are you who have kept away all desires, and where is this sexual delusion ? Whence this fierce anger by which you could not discern yourself ?

89. "Whatever a man of anger does, worshipping, gifting or practising of austerity or offering sacrifices (it is futile); he does not get any fruit. In this world, the actions of an angry person are void of results !"

CHAPTER FORTY-FOUR

Origin of Sthāṇu-tīrtha

Sanatkumāra said:

1. Having listened to these words of Brahmā, all those sages asked him again the cause of prosperity of the universe.

Brahmā said:

2. We will take refuge in Trident-bearing Lord of three eyes. With the blessings of the Lord of lords, you will become as before.

Sanatkumāra said:

3. So told by Brahmā, they went along with Brahmā to the excellent mountain Kailāsa and saw Hara seated along with Umā.

4. Brahmā, the Grandsire of the universe began to eulogize the overlord of the gods, the master of the three worlds, the wishgranter Śiva.

Brahmā said:

5. Salutation to you the infinite, the propitious, the wielder of Pināka (bow), to the great god, to the lustrous, to Sthāṇu to the supreme soul.

6. Salutations ever to you, the Lord of the universe, the saviour. You are the only god who bestows all knowledge, the puruṣa-par-excellence.

7. Salutation to you, Padmagarbha (Viṣṇu); salutation to the one lying in the lotus of heart; salutation to you who vehemently destroy the evil, O god of fierce anger !

8. Salutation to you, O god ! O master of the universe ! obeisance to you, O leader of the brave ones ! Salutation to you, O wielder of trident ! Salutation to you, O creator of the universe !

Sanatkumāra said:

9. Thus eulogized by Brahmā and the sages, the Great God said to them: "You go back. The phallus will be yours again.

10. "You carry out my words immediately. By the consecrations of the *Liṅga*, there will be immense pleasure to me. There is no doubt.

11. "For those who worship my *Liṅga* with devotion, there is nothing difficult to attain at any time.

12. "Even all those who have consciously committed evils, get purified by the worship of *Liṅga*. Doubt should not be entertained in this.

13. "Having transported the well-known *Liṅga* thrown by you in the large lake, (see it) established immediately in that Sannihiti.

14-15. "Then, O Brāhmaṇas ! You will get what you wish for. Because Sthāṇu by name, honourable to heavenly beings in the three worlds, is established in *Sthāṇvīśvara*, (the *Liṅga*) is spoken of as *Sthāṇvīśvara*. Those who constantly remember Sthāṇu, get freed from all sins.

16-17. They with a pure body will be able to attain salvation, by visiting (*Sthāṇu*)." So told by the Lord, the sages along with Brahmā attempted to carry the *Liṅga* from that *Dāruvana.* The gods alongwith the sages were incapable of moving it.

18. Excessively exhausted, they took refuge in Brahmā. Brahmā spoke these words to those exhausted (sages).

Brahmā said:

19. What is the use of making great effort ? You are not capable of carrying the *Liṅga* dropped by the Great God, the Wielder of Trident, at his own sweet will.

20. Therefore, O gods ! We will all together take refuge in him only. The pleased Mahādeva will himself transport it.

Sanatkumāra said:

21. So told by Brahmā, the sages and the gods along with Brahmā reached mountain Kailāsa desirous of meeting Rudra.

22. And they did not see the Lord there. Then they were engrossed in sorrowful thought. The sages asked Brahmā: "Where is Lord Maheśvara?"

23. At that Brahmā pondered for a long time (and came to know) the great Lord Maheśvara having assumed the form of an elephant who was mentally propitiated by the sages.

24. Then along with Brahmā, the gods as well as the sages went to the great holy pond where the Lord himself was.

25. And they searching for him could not see him. Along with Brahmā the gods were pensive.

26. They saw the goddess in gay mood holding the water-pot (*Kamaṇḍalu*) and addressed thus to please her.

27. "O Goddess Mother, where is the Lord? He is not seen by us. We have been strenuously searching for Maheśvara."

28-29a. At that time, the compassionate goddess said: "O virtuous ones ! You will see Maheśvara here and now only. O gods ! You drink (this) nectar, then you will comprehend Śaṅkara."

29b-30. Having listened to the words uttered by Bhavānī, those gods sat relaxed and drank that pure nectar. Afterwards (the gods) who were resting asked Parameśvar—

31. "Where is the Lord who came here assuming the form of an elephant?" And he, standing in the middle of the pond, was shown by the Goddess.

32. Having seen the Lord of all, the gods along with Indra went delighted, and said this with Brahmā at their front—

33. "O Mahādeva ! The *Liṅga* honoured by the three worlds was dropped by you. O Maheśvara ! No one else is capable of bringing it."

34. The venerable Lord Hara so told by Brahmā and others went to the hermitage of Devadāruvana together with the sages.

35. Having gone there the great Lord Hara who had assumed the form of an elephant sportively held Parameśvara (i.e., *Liṅga*) by his trunk.

36. Mahādeva brought it and while being eulogized by the great sages set it on the western side of the pond.

37. Then the gods and all the sages rich in penance, finding themselves successful, began a eulogy of Maheśvara.

38. "Salutation to you, O supreme self ! O inexhaustible source ! O observer of the universe ! O supreme one ! O venerable one ! O omniscient one ! O knowing self ! O object of knowledge ! O almighty ! O supreme creator ! O one of superhuman power ! O exalted supreme self ! O great spirit! O one immanent in every being ! O one abiding in the mind, O primeval lord ! O ever auspicious one ! O master ! O one beyond comprehension ! O one hard to be appeased ! O lord of the great elements ! O Parameśvara (the supreme ruler) ! O great master of Yoga ! O three-eyed one ! O pre-eminent *yogin* ! O supreme Brahma ! O most exalted effulgence ! O foremost one among the knowers of *Veda,* O embodiment of '*Om*', of '*Vaṣaṭ*', of '*Svāhā*' and of '*Svadā*', O fundamental cause ! O omnipresent one ! O all-perceiver!

O almighty ! O all-god ! O unborn one ! O thousand-rayed one ! O most brilliant one ! O one having the lustre of Hara! O one living on the *vaṁśa* ! O *Saṁvarta* (cloud)! O one who withdraws (the world unto himself) ! O submarine fire ! O embodiment of *Agni soma* ! O purifier ! O eminent purifier! O chief cloud ! O great destroyer of Kāma ! O pure one ! O ascetic ! O paramount sovereign, O exalted overlord ! O great loving one ! O excellently pure one ! O destroyer of the world ! O one worshipped by *Suras* and *Siddhas* ! O wearer of gold ! O one of golden seed ! O gold-navelled one! O gold-tufted one ! O Muñja-haired one ! O benefactor of everyone! O one favouring all ! O one lying on the lotus ! O one lying in the heart ! O ocean of knowledge ! O Śaṁbhu! O all-pervader ! O embodiment of great sacrifice! O eminent sacrificer ! O one immanent in all sacrifices ! O one eulogized in all sacrifices ! O shelterless one ! O lord of oceans ! O one born of Atri ! O one sympathetic to the devotees ! O one undistracted in contemplation ! O supporter of *yoga* ! O one whose body is shining with *Vāsuki* and other large serpents ! O green-eyed one ! O three-eyed one ! O one of matted hair ! O blue-necked one ! O crescent-moon-bearer! O one sharing half of Umā's body ! O wielder of trident ! O wielder of *Pināka* (bow) ! O wielder of sword and shield ! O wearer of elephant skin ! O great destroyer of impassable cycle of birth and death ! O one affectionate to devotees ! Be pleased."

39. Eulogised thus with deep devotion by the gods along with eminent Brāhmaṇas as well as by Brahmā, the most revered one, abandoned his elephant form and made the *Liṅga* his abode.

CHAPTER FORTY-FIVE

Origin of Sthāṇu-tīrtha (continued)

Sanatkumāra said:

1. Then Mahādeva related the excellent merits of the *Tīrtha* to the gods led by Brahmā in the presence of the sages—

2. "This pond *Sannihata* is spoken of as the foremost of the holiest. Because it was established by me, it bestows emancipation.

3. "Some people here–Brāhmaṇas, Kṣatriyas or Vaiśyas–reach the highest abode by the very sight of the Liṅga.

4. "Everyday as the sun reaches the zenith, *Tīrthas* right from oceans and ponds come over to *Sthāṇu-tīrtha.*

5. "Those who eulogize me devotedly without fail, with this eulogy, to them I will always be easy of access; there is no doubt.

6. Having said so, venerable Lord Rudra disappeared. All gods and sages resorted to their respective places.

7. From then on the heaven was filled without leaving space by human beings. It is the efficacy of *Sthāṇu-liṅga* that (people) by its very sight, attain heaven.

8. At that all the groups of gods took refuge in Brahmā. And then Brahmā asked them: "Why have you come here?"

9. Then all the gods said this: "O Grandsire ! We have a serious threat from human beings. Please protect us."

10. Brahmā then told the leading god of the heavenly beings: "Fill the pond with dust quickly. Do favour to Indra."

11. After wards Lord Indra (the destroyer of Baka) poured dust (over the pond); the gods along with Indra are known to have filled (the pond) for seven days.

12. The Lord of gods, Maheśvara, observing the shower of dust held the *Liṅga,* the *Tīrtha* and the *Vaṭa* with his hand.

13. Therefore the *Tīrtha* where some water remained is the holiest one. A man taking bath therein is deemed to have bathed in all *Tīrthas.*

14. *Pitṛs* of a person who performs *Śrāddha* in the region between the *Liṅga* and the *Vaṭa,* will be very glad and bestow what is difficult to obtain on the earth.

15. Later having seen the pond covered, those sages too devotedly smeared their body with the dust.

16. Those ascetics also became cleansed of their sin by the dust and they, attended by gods, went to the abode of Brahmā.

17. Those who are eminent with superhuman power, and worship the *Liṅga,* attain the highest accomplishment from which there is no return.

18. Having known this, Brahmā then covered the primeval *Liṅga* and kept a *Liṅga* made of stone over it.

19. In course of time, (the stone *Liṅga* also) was illumined by its (original) enormous splendour. By touching even that, the seekers attained the highest abode.

20. O best Brāhmaṇas ! Then Brahmā was again intimated by the gods: "The people are attaining the highest abode by the very sight of (even) the (stone) *Liṅga.*"

21. Having heard it, venerable Brahmā, desirous of the welfare of the gods, placed seven *Liṅgas* one over the other (on the stone *Liṅga* he had earlier set).

22. Then those seekers of salvation who resorted to *Siddhāśrama,* attained the highest abode by zealously resorting to the dust (on the pond).

23. Even the dust scattered by wind in Kurukṣetra will lead even the most sinful to the final abode.

24. All sins committed consciously or unconsciously by a man or woman, will be destroyed by the efficacy of *Sthāṇu-tīrtha.*

25. Emancipation (is attained) by visiting the *Liṅga,* and by touching the banyan (*Vaṭa*) tree. By bathing in the water in its vicinity, one obtains the desired fruit.

26. He who offers libation in that water, will acquire infinite merit for every drop of his (libation) water.

27. He who performs *Śrāddha* with black sesamum in the region to the west of *Sthāṇu-liṅga*, and offers libation with faith, satiates (the *Pitṛs*) for three *Yugas.*

28. The *Liṅga* is spoken of as staying for a *Manvantara*; till then the satiated *Pitṛs* drink excellent water.

29. In *Kṛtayuga*, the pond was known as *Sannihatyā*; in *Tretā*, it was named *Vāyu*; between *Dvāpara* and *Kali*, it was spoken of as *Rudra-hrada.*

30. A worthy man by taking ablution in the *Rudrakara-tīrtha* on the fourteenth day of dark fortnight of *Caitra*, will reach the final abode.

31. He who meditates on Parameśvara sitting by the banyan tree, (will obtain) the cherished fruit by the grace of *Sthāṇu* and *Vaṭa.*

NOTES

(Numbers refer to Ślokas)

CHAPTER ONE

2. Sage Pulastya is one of the ten mind-born sons of Brahmā. Nārada is a celebrated sage; cf. ch. 2, śl. 29.

3. Vāmana, the fifth incarnation (*avatāra*) of Viṣṇu, is said to have occurred in the seventh *Tretāyuga* of *Vaivasvata Manvantara.* Birth etc., of Vāmana is described here in chapters 23 ff and 76 ff.

4. This is described in chapter 7 here.

5. Satī: Fem. of *Sat* meaning real or virtuous being, Śiva.

6-7. The event of Satī abandoning her body is related in chapter 4 and that of her birth as the daughter of Himavān in ch. 51 ff.

8. More than two hundred *Tīrthas* are glorified in the course of this Purāṇa. A few *Vratas* (see e.g. ch. 53) and the greatness of gifts (ch. 31) are also set forth.

11. Mandāra is a mountain situated to the east of Meru. Its celebrity is that it was selected as the churning rod when the Milk Ocean was to be churned for ambrosia. Identified with a hill in Bhagalpur dist (*Dowson* & Dey). For a different view, *see* Ali, pp. 41 & 180. *Haimavatī*: *lit.* means the daughter of Himavān. In this context, however, the term cannot be taken thus as the consort of Śiva is 'yet' the daughter of Dakṣa.

13. Bhavānī is the fem. form of Bhava meaning 'Lord Śiva'.

17. The metre of the stanza is Vaṁśastha. The last word in b, *Maheśa,* is to be amended to *Maheśvara,* which is, incidentally, the reading in Kashiraj edition.

18. Herons and cranes are said to conceive at the sound of thunders and they follow the clouds out of courtesy as it were. cf. *Meghadūta*: '*mandaṁ mandaṁ nudati pavanaś cānukūlo yathă tvām vāmaś cāyaṁ nadati madhuraṁ cātakas te sagandhaḥ: garbhādhāna-kṣaṇa-paricayān nūnam ābaddhamālās seviṣyante nayana-subhagaṁ khe bhavantaṁ balākāḥ.* (I. 10). The metre is Upajāti of Vaṁśastha (ab) and Indravaṁśā (cd). The reading in *mārutādinā* means 'shed by wind etc.', the reading in Kashiraj edn. *mārutahataḥ* is better.

19. ac: Indravaṁśā, b: Vaṁśastha, d: Upendravajrā

20. Upajāti metre: ab-Upendravajrā, cd-Indravajrā

21. Indravajrā metre except for b which is in Upendravajrā.

22. Upendravajrā (a), Vaṁśastha (bd), Indravajrā (c)

23. Vaṁśastha (ad), Indravaṁśa (b), Indravajrā (c).

24. Indravajrā (ad), Upendravajrā (b), Vaṁśastha (c).

25. Each pāda is in different metre: Vaṁśastha, Upendravajrā, Indravaṁśa and Indravajrā.

26. Upendravajrā (a), Vaṁśastha (bc), Indravaṁśā (d)

27. Six pādas: Indravaṁśā (acd), Vaṁśastha (b), Indravajrā (cf).

28. Mṛḍānī: fem. form of Mṛḍa, Lord Śiva. The metre is Śālinī.

31. Indravaṁśā (a), Vaṁśastha (bd), Upendravajrā (c). (Colophon: 'Haralalitam' is a very apt title for the chapter.)

CHAPTER TWO

2. The tense of the verb is not maintained in the original pādas—acd: Vaṁśastha; b: Indravajrā

3. Upendravajrā (a); Indravajrā (bcd).

4. ac: Vaṁśastha; b: Upendravajrā; d: Indravaṁśā.

7. *Keśava*: an epithet of Viṣṇu. The word means 'one having much or fine hair'. Viṣṇu sleeps for four months from the 12th day of bright half of Āṣāḍha (see here ch. 16, śl. 6) to the 12th day of bright half of Kārttika. Dakṣa: one of the ten sons of Brahmā, born of the thumb, was the chief patriarch of mankind; hence called' 'Pitāmaha'.

8. *Ādityas*: Though the word means 'sons of Aditi' and thus applicable to all gods, it applies particularly to the twelve solar deities. They are: Dhātṛ, Mitra, Aryamā, Śakra, Varuṇa, Aṁśa, Bhaga, Vivasvān, Pūṣan, Savitṛ, Tvaṣṭṛ and Viṣṇu. Sometimes, Jayanta, Bhāskara and Indra are mentioned instead of Vivasvān, Savitṛ and Śakra. *Kaśyapa*: The son of Marīci, the son of Brahmā. He married the thirteen daughters, Aditi, Diti, Danu, Vinatā and others, of Dakṣa, and begot from them all living beings. He is also called, therefore, Prajāpati. *Sadasya*: Sixteen *ṛtviks* are directly involved in a *soma* sacrifice. Some other scholars versed in the sacrificial lore are requested to be observers of the performance. These are called '*sadasyas*'.

9. The names of the spouses of some of the sages are: Vasiṣṭha-Arundhatī, Atri-Anasūyā; Kauśika-Dhṛti; Gautama-Ahalyā; Bharadvāja-Amāyā; Aṅgiras-Candrā.

13. *Ariṣṭanemi*, another name of Kaśyapa.

16. Dakṣa had numerous daughters: thirteen were married to Kaśyapa, twenty-seven (asterisms) were married to Moon. Satī, consort of Lord Śiva, Ahalyā and others were also his daughters.

20. Ādipurāṇa: Brahma-purāṇa.

21. Ekārṇava: the state of deluge when everything is submerged under water.

23. The predominance of any one of the three guṇas–*Sattva, Rajas* and *Tamas*–gives rise to a particular function; *Rajas* leads to creation, transformation; *Tamas* to destruction and *Sattva* is for maintenance.

27. Pitāmaha, grandsire, here is Brahmā, the creator, born of the primordial Lord referred to earlier (śl.23)

28. Brahmā here is the primordial being to be distinguished from Brahmā, the creator. In the sequel too 'Brahmā' is to be understood according to the context.

32. Parameṣṭhi is Pitāmaha, i.e. Brahmā (See śl. 27 above).

34. Upajāti—ac: Upendravajrā; bd: Indravajrā.

35. ab: Indravajrā; c: Indravaṁśā; d: Upendravajrā.

37. This is how Brahmā became four-faced one.

40. The mention of the beloved of Śaṅkara is rather out of place. The reading in Kashiraj edn. '*trapā*'(shame) for '*priyā*' is better.

42. Badari or Badarikā is the present Badrināth, the famous pilgrimage centre in the Himālayas.

48. Atri and Anasūyā got Durvāsa as their son after Atri received the stream emerging from the trident scar. Hence, Durvāsa was endowed with Śaṅkara's aspect also.

49. The skull that was on the palm of Śiva, *Indravajrā.*

50. Upajāti—ad: Indravajrā; bc: Upendravajrā.

51. Indravajrā.

52. *Ājagava,* the bow of Śiva. a: Indravaṁśā; bd: Upendravajrā; c: Indravajrā.

53. *śārva,* offspring of Śarva (Śiva). One divine year is equal to 360 human years. *Parivatsara,* one full year. abc: Indravaṁśā; d: Upendravajrā.

54. Nara is the one born of the shoulder. Upajāti—ab: Indravajrā; cd: Upendravajrā.

55. abd: Indravajrā; c: Indravaṁśā.

CHAPTER THREE

2. *Brahmahatyā,* the sin of killing a human being, particularly a Brāhmaṇa.

8. Kālindī or Yamunā is the river Jumna. Plakṣajā is the river Sarasvatī because its origin is near a Plakṣa tree.

9. *Puṣkarāraṇya,* the forest around Puṣkara, a place of Pilgrimage near modern Ajmer. *Magadhāraṇya,* the forest in modern south Bihar. *Saindhavāraṇya,* the forest in the Sindhu territory. *Kurujāṅgala,* the region near Hastināpura (modern north-western Uttar Pradesh).

10. *Naimiṣāraṇya,* on the river Gomatī near modern Lucknow; famous as the grove where Śakti, son of Sūta, told the Purāṇas to Ṛṣis. *Dharmāraṇya,* the forest near Bodhgayā or in Vindhyācala (See Dey, for this and other identifications).

11. Upajāti—ac: Upendravajrā; bd: Indravajrā.

14. Garuḍa is brahmini kite. But in the *Purāṇas,* Garuḍa is half-man and half-bird; is the son of Vinatā and Kaśyapa, hence called Vainateya; celebrated as the vehicle of Viṣṇu. Vāsudeva, son of Vasudeva, i.e. Kṛṣṇa.

17. *Adhokṣaja,* Janārdana-epithets of Viṣṇu.

21. The four *Vedas* are: Ṛgveda, Yajurveda, Sāmaveda and Atharvaveda. Six *Vedāṅgas*: Śikṣā, Vyākaraṇa, Nirukta,

Chandas, Jyautiṣa and Kalpa. Four *Upavedas*, one each of the four *Vedas* in order: Āyurveda, Dhanurveda, Gāndharvaveda and Sthāpatyaveda.

22. Upajāti—ab: Upendravajrā; cd: Indravajrā.

23. Upajāti—ad: Upendravajrā; bc: Indravajrā.

31. The reading is corrupt. Kashiraj edn. improves a little. However, see Satyavrat Sastri : *Poetry in Vāmana Purāṇa—Essays in Indology*, Meherchand Lacchmandass, Delhi, 1963, pp. 70 ff. abc: Upendravajrā; d: Indravajrā.

32. abc: Upendravajrā; d: Indravajrā.

33. abd: Indravajrā; c: Upendravajrā.

34. acd: Indravajrā; b: Upendravajrā.

35. Upajāti—ab: Upendravajrā; cd: Indravajrā.

36. Only wind entered the houses stealthily. *Dāna*: flow of ichor in sexually excited elephants. *Upendravajrā*: the figure of speech is Parisaṅkhyā.

37, 38. The figure of speech is Parisaṅkhyā. *Akulīnatva*: not lying on the earth (*ku*).

39. Figure of speech is double entendre.

41. *Daśāśvamedha*, a holy place in Vārāṇasī. Mani speaks of this as holy place in Kurukṣetra.

42. Upajāti—ad: Indravajrā; bc: Upendravajrā.

43. abc: Indravajrā; d: Upendravajrā.

44. *Hṛṣīkeśa*, an epithet of Viṣṇu, master of senses (hṛṣīka).

51. *Kapāla-mocana*, a *tīrtha* in Vārāṇasī. This episode is also found in *Kūrma, Nārada, Padma, Bhaviṣya, Matsya, Varāha, Śiva* and *Skanda Purāṇas*. In *Śiva Purāṇa*, Śaṅkara created Bhairava who burnt the head of Brahmā with ocular fire and was afflicted by *Brahmahatyā*. acd: Indravajrā; b: Upendravajrā.

CHAPTER FOUR

2. *Ahalyā*, princess of Puru dynasty (Mani). According to Vālmīki-Rāmāyaṇa, she is the first woman made by Brahmā. Here, she is the daughter of Dakṣa. Jayā is her daughter. Nowhere do we know about Jayā or her sisters Vijayā, Jayantī and Aparājitā as daughters of Ahalyā.

7. Wives of Moon, *see* note on 2-16.

17. Note Vīrabhadra is described here as lion-faced and as having born of the hairs of the body of Śaṅkara.

18. *Himasā* is Himālayas. *Kanakhala* is at the confluence of the rivers Gaṅgā and Nīladhāra, near Haridvār and to the east of it.

23. *Gaṇeśvara, Gaṇādhipa* and *Gaṇeśa*—all these refer to the leader of Śiva's troops, i.e. Vīrabhadra.

28. *Kiṁśuka*: the bastard teak tree with red blossoms.

29. Upendravajrā.

32. *Sādhyas, Siddhas, Gandharvas, Pannagas, Yakṣas* and *Kiṁpuruṣas*-are demigods.

33. The sons of Diti and Danu (*See* note on 2.8) are *Daityas* and *Dānavas* respectively. But the difference is almost ignored. They are also referred to as *Rākṣasas.*

49. Though the episode of Viṣṇu killing Madhu is well-known in the *Purāṇas*, devouring of Madhu by Viṣṇu as *Fish* is not found elsewhere.

50. abd: Indravajrā; c: Upendravajrā.

57. Upajāti—ac: Upendravajrā; cd: Indravaṁśā.

CHAPTER FIVE

1. *Kubjāmra*, identified with Hṛṣīkeśa near Haridwār (*Dey*). *See* also here 51.51; 79.3; 90.3.

2. *Sarasvatī* river, also called Sītā, manifested along the path made by the eight *Vasus* running away in fear from Śaṅkara. Identified with the river Sarsuti (*See De*, p. 180 f.).

Sītā is the name of one of the seven branches of Gaṅgā according to Mahābhārata (*De*).

4. *Puroḍāśa,* the sacrificial cake prepared from rice flour in the course of *Iṣṭis*; it is offered to deities and the remnant partaken of by the Yajamāna and the Ṛtviks (Śrauta).

6. *Śatarudrīya,* the Rudrādhyāya of Yajurveda; Tait. S. 4.5. 1-11; Vaj. S. 16.

18. *Vajra,* 'thunderbolt', weapon of Indra. The mountains, in the past, had wings. They could fly and land as they liked. This caused havoc to the people. So, Indra cut off their wings with the *Vajra.*

21. *Hutāśa,* sacred fire.

25. Reading in the first half seems to be corrupt.

27. i.e. ready to strike. The story is continued in śl. 43.

31. Here follows the description of the twelve constellations and their identification with the various parts of the body of 'Kāla'. cf. ch. 80. Some of the asterisms are named after their presiding deity, e.g. *Āgneya, Prājāpatya* which stand for Kṛttikā and Rohiṇī respectively. The deities for each of the asterisms are given in Nakṣatreṣṭi section, Tait. Br. 1.5.1; 3.1.1.

43. Śālinī metre.

45. In these verses, the characteristics of the twelve constellations, i.e., perhaps the characteristics of those born under them, are set forth. The basis for the description seems to be their respective names only.

49-50. Text seems to be corrupt.

58. *Skandha* also means a road.

61. acd: Indravajrā; b: Upendravajrā. The story of the destruction of Dakṣa's sacrifice is found in other *Purāṇas* too: *Mahābhārata, Bhāg, Vāyu, Kāli,* and *Śiva.* But, some of the details here seem to be peculiar. For example, the informant was Jayā, the daughter of Gautama. Satī fell dead at the very information. Vīrabhadra and his troops were born from the hairs of the enraged Śiva. Śiva also went with

Vīrabhadra to the venue of the sacrifice and it was Śiva who knocked down Pūṣan and Bhaga.

CHAPTER SIX

1. Dharma is an ancient sage, said to be one of the creators or one of the mind-born sons of Brahmā. From the Devībhāgavata and the Bhāgavata, we learn that Mūrli, one of the thirteen wives of Dharma begot him two sons, Nara and Nārāyaṇa.

6. *Apsarās* are nymphs, the female dancers of Indra's court of heaven. They are said to have been born of the Milk Ocean when it was churned for ambrosia.

7. *Kāma* or *Manmatha* or *Kandarpa* is Cupid or Eros. His weapon is a bow and five arrows. These arrows are all flowers: Aravinda (*red lotus*), Aśoka, Cūta (*mango*), Navamallikā (*a kind of jasmine*), and Nīlotpala (*blue lotus*). Hence, he is called Pañceṣu and Puṣpa-bāṇa. But here his three missiles are spoken of: Unmāda (*madness*), Santāpa (*torment*) and Vijṛmbhaṇa (*yawning*). See also Dowson, p. 145 f. His wife is Rati, and Vasanta (*spring season*) is his most intimate companion.

9-10. *Kiṁśuka* or *Palāśa* is the bastard teak. The leaves, fresh or dried, are stitched in a round shape to be used as dining plates. During summer, the tree is full of red flowers.

11. *Lodhra* is a tree with red or white flowers.

12. *Karṇikāra* is Oleander.

13. *Nīpa* or *Kadamba* plants blossom in rainy season.

19. *Bandhujīva* is the red variety of *Nīpa*. *Sindhuvāra* is the five-leaved chaste tree.

21. The reading *bhṛṅga* (bee) in Kashi edition for *saṅga*, is better.

22. The story is resumed in ch. 7.

24. Mention of Kāma as the son of Harṣa is rather peculiar.

26. *Death of Satī, see* here 4.9; *Destruction of Dakṣa's sacrifice, see* 4.18 ff.

27. Unmāda is one of the arrows of Kāma. The two others mentioned here are Santāpana (śl. 43) and Vijmbhaṇa (śl. 45).

43. Indravajrā (acd), Upendravajrā (b).

44. Indravajrā.

45. Indravajrā (a), Upendravajrā (bcd).

46. Six pādas: Upendravajrā (a), Indravajrā (bcdef)

47. Indravajrā (acd), Upendravajrā (b).

48. Indravajrā (ab), Upendravajrā (cd).

49. Upendravajrā (a), Indravajrā (bcd).

50. Indravajrā.

51. Indravajrā (acd), Upendravajrā (b).

52. Indravajrā (acd), Upendravajrā (b).

53. Indravajrā (ab), Upendravajrā (cd).

54. Upendravajrā (acd), Indravajrā (b).

55. The holy place of Pañcālikeśvara is situated to the north of Kālañjara (modern Kalinjer) and to the south of the Himālayas. Indravajrā (acd), Upendravajrā (b).

56. Indravajrā.

58. Dāruvana episode occurs in several *Purāṇas.*

59. That means Śiva was naked.

86. The promulgators of the four *śāstras-āgamas* for the worship of Śivaliṅga are spoken of. The *āgamas* are associated with the four *varṇas* respectively: Śaiva-Śiva himself as *Sakti,* son of Vasiṣṭha; his disciple, Gopāyana (Brahmaṇa). Pāśupata-Bharadvāja; his disciple, King Somakeśvara (Kṣatriya). Kāladamana-Āpastamba; his disciple, Kratheśvara (Vaiśya). Kāpālika-Dhaṇada; his disciple, Arṇodara (Śūdra).

107. The story of the burning of Kāma is told in other *Purāṇas* also: *Brahma Purāṇa, Brahmavaivarta Purāṇa, Liṅga Purāṇa,* and *Skānda Purāṇa.*

CHAPTER SEVEN

1. Story continued from 6.22.

2. Sage Nārāyaṇa created from his thighs, a damsel of rare beauty who came to be called Urvaśī, thigh-born. Even Kāma felt whether she was his wife Rati.

6. *vadana* (Kashi edition) should be read for *vacana.*

20. *dharmajābhyām* (Kashi edition) is a better reading for *dharmajñābhyām.*

22. Dānava-son of Danu, one of the wives of Kaśyapa. Diti is another wife and her children are *Daityas.* But Dānava and *Daitya* are synonyms and refer to *Rākṣasas,* the enemies of *Devas,* heavenly beings. They are also called *Asuras.* The term *asura* which in the *Veda* meant "one possessing divine power" came to mean 'one having physical power', and gave birth to a new word *sura.*

26. *Vainākuleśvara* a holy place on Narmadā river.

32. The *reading-putro* is incorrect. Kashi edition reads*-putre.*

46. *Śārṅga* is the bow of Viṣṇu and *Ājagava* that of Śiva.

53. Indravajrā (a), Upendravajrā (bcd).

54. Upendravajrā (ac), Indravajrā (bd).

55. Indravajrā (ab), Vaṁśastha (c), Upendravajrā (d).

56. Indravajrā (abd), Upendravajrā (c).

57. Upendravajrā (ad), Indravajrā (bc).

58. Upendravajrā (acd), Indravajrā (b).

59. Upendravajrā (abc), Indravajrā (d).

61. Vaṁśastha (ac), Indravajrā (b), Upendravajrā (d).

62. Indravajrā (ab), Upendravajrā (cd).

65. Vaṁśastha (a), Upendravajrā (b), Indravaṁśa (c), Indravajrā (d).

CHAPTER EIGHT

10. The reading *deveṣu* (Kashi) for daityeṣu is better.

14. Crescent moon-like, i.e. the arrow having the tip shaped like crescent.

51. *Hṛṣīkeśa,* master of senses (hṛṣīka-īśa). The 'Fish' and 'Tortoise' incarnations are referred to Viṣṇu is spoken of as having horse-headed incarnation to kill a horse-headed *Daitya* (Devībhāgavata and Mahābhārata-Śāntiparva).

52. Viṣṇu as 'Boar' killed Hiraṇyākṣa who was the elder brother of Hiraṇyakaśipu who was killed by Viṣṇu as Narasimha. Prahlāda was the son of Hiraṇyakaśipu.

53. Indravajrā (abc), Upendravajrā (d).

71. Indravajrā (acd), Upendravajrā (b).

72. Indravajrā (abd), Upendravajrā (c).

CHAPTER NINE

6. The office of *Purohita* is an important one in the administration of a State. A person deeply learned in the Veda and the practical aspects thereof, is eligible for the office. He has to advise the king on all religious and legal matters.

9. *Amarāvatī,* the capital of Indra.

20. Reading doubtful.

26. Nalva is an unit of linear measurement, equivalent to 400 hastas or cubits (about 18 inches).

27. Prahlāda is evidently different from the well-known son of Hiraṇyakaśipu. cf. 8. 72. But there seems to be a confusion because of the name. See, for example, 10.15.

41. Vaṁśastha (a), Upendravajrā (bd), Indravajrā (c).

42. Upendravajrā (ac), Indravajrā (bd).

43. Indravajrā. The reading *patanti* (Kashi edition) for *pibanti* is better.

44. The reading in d here is better than that of Kashi edition. Indravajrā (ac), Upendravajrā (b), Indravaṁśā (d).

45. Vaṁśastha (abd), Indravaṁśā (c).

46. Upendravajrā (abd), Indravajrā (c).
47. Upendravajrā (ad), Indravajrā (bc).
48. Indravaṁśa (ad), Upendravajrā (b), Vaṁśastha (c).
49. Indravajrā (abd), Indravaṁśa (c).
50. Upendravajrā (a), Indravajrā (bcd).
51. Indravajrā (a), Upendravajrā (b), Vaṁśastha (c), Indravaṁśā (d).
52. Indravajrā (ab), Upendravajrā (cd).

CHAPTER TEN

5. The reading *nagān* (Kashi edition) is better than *nāgān*, though the latter reading may refer to the movement of the arrows.
15. cf. note on 9.27.
31. Indravajrā (abc), Upendravajrā (bd).
32. Indravajrā.
33. Indravajrā (abc), Upendravajrā (d).
34. The episode of Sukeśī is given a detailed treatment in ch. 11 ff. Indravajrā (ac), Upendravajrā (bd).
35. Upendravajrā (abc), Indravajrā (d).
36. Indravajrā (acd), Upendravajrā (b).
37. Upendravajrā (ad), Indravajrā (bc).
38. Indravaṁśā (ab), Vaṁśastha (cd).
39. Indravajrā (abd), Upendravajrā (c).
40. Indravajrā (abc), Upendravajrā (d).
41. Indravajrā (ab), Upendravajrā (cd).
42. Upendravajrā (a), Indravajrā (bcd).
43. Dākṣāyaṇī is Aditi, Varuṇa is her son. *Upendravajrā.*
44. Viśvakarmā is the architect of gods and Maya is the architect of *Daityas.* There are some instances in the *Purāṇas* wherein it is described that either of them has worked for the other. But here both the terms are used together. Hence, the term Viśvakarmā is to be understood as a common noun meaning architect.

45. Upendravajrā (abc), Indravajrā (cd).

46. The reading-*kāyā* (Kashi edition) for *kopam* is better. Indravaṁśā (a), Upendravajrā (bc), Indravajrā (d).

47. Upendravajrā (abd), Indravajrā (c).

48. Indravajrā (abc), Upendravajrā (d).

49. Upendravajrā (abd), Indravajrā (c).

50. Indravajrā (ac), Upendravajrā (bd).

51. Indravajrā (abc), Upendravajrā (d).

52. Upendravajrā (abd), Vaṁśastha (c).

53. Upendravajrā (abc), Vaṁśastha (d).

54. Vaṁśastha (ad), Indravajrā (b), Indravaṁśā (c).

55. Upendravajrā (ad), Indravajrā (bc).

56. Indravajrā (abd), Upendravajrā (c).

57. Indravajrā (abd), Upendravajrā (c).

CHAPTER ELEVEN

1. The reference is to 10.34.

6. *Rākṣasas* are a class of beings that are mostly nocturnal. Hence, they are also called *niśācara, kṣaṇadā*-(night)-*cara* etc. And they are treated as not different from *Daityas* etc. *See* also note on 7.22.

15. The *Dharmas* of various beings are set forth in this and the following verses.

16. *vandanam* should be read as *vedanam* (Kashi edition).

18. The object of intense meditation is not given.

22. *Japa* is repeating the name/s of a deity, or a *mantra* or a formula. Repetition is normally counted with a rosary.

24. It is curious to note that another popular deity that goes with these four, viz., *Gaṇa*pati is not added.

29. It is worthy to note that Sukeśī himself of Rākṣasa order, desired to know about the *Dharmas* of human beings. He along with his followers even put them into practice. *See* 15.5.

30. *Dvīpa* is an island. The universe is spoken of as having seven divisions and each of them is understood as an island.

An account of these *dvīpas* (*Bhuvanakośa*) is a topic found in almost all the *Purāṇas.* However, there is no agreement among the *Purāṇas* in regard to details. *See* Ali, S.M.: *Geography of the Purāṇas,* and also Agrawal: *Vāmana Purāṇa— a study.*

31. *Yojana* is a linear measurement equivalent to about 14 kms.

50. Crore Yojanas come to about 700 million Kms.

51. Almost all the names of the hells are descriptive.

58. Vaṁśastha (ab), Indravajrā (cd).

CHAPTER TWELVE

2. *Karmavipāka,* fruits of one's actions is dealt with in *Dharma-Śāstra* texts also. Some of the lines here are common with them. E.g. Verse 7 is the same as Manu 12.76.

Śālakaṭaṅkaṭa, matronymic of Sukeśī.

17. Fire of the eye, i.e. brightness, eyesight.

28. Dried by fire, i.e. hot.

31. '*Adhaḥ Kṛtya*' is understood by some as 'making one sit below'; others take it as 'despising'. It is not clear why the teacher should be punished if the student disregards him. Does it mean that the teacher who teaches under duress is punishable? Or it is the new teacher that is punishable, as made out in the translation here.

44. 6 pādas: Vaṁśastha (ac), Upendravajrā (bdef).

45. Upendravajrā (ab), Indravaṁśa (cd).

46. Vaṁśastha (ab), Indravajrā (cd).

47. Upendravajrā (acd); Indravajrā (b).

48. Indravajrā (ab), Upendravajrā (c), Vaṁśastha (d).

49. Indravajrā (abd), Upendravajrā (c).

50. Kāñcī, the modern Kāñcipuram near Madras, was once a famous city as well as a centre of learning. Indravajrā (acd), Upendravajrā (b).

51. *Kālasthalī*, a misreading for *Kuśasthalī*, modern Thanesvar. Upendravajrā (ac), Indravajrā (bd).

52. Indravajrā.

53. *Kācamācī*, a solanaceous plant. Upendravajrā (ad), Indravajrā (bc).

54. *tuṅgeṣu* (Kashi edition) is a better reading for *phaleṣu*. *Phala* has already been spoken of in 51 above. Upendravajrā.

55. Upendravajrā.

56. Vaitaraṇī is the river of the hell. Indravajrā (acd), Upendravajrā (b).

57. Indravajrā (a), Indravaṁśā (b), Upendravajrā (c), Vaṁśastha (d).

CHAPTER THIRTEEN

14. For identification of mountains etc., see Ali, *op. cit.* For janapadas, see also Agrawal, *op. cit.* For rivers, see also Dave, S.K.: 'The Rivers in the Vāmana Purāṇa', *Purāṇa*, January 1970.

36. Indravajrā (a), Upendravajrā (cd). b is metrically defective;

it becomes Indravajrā if *saha-kauśikaiś ca* is amended to *sakauśikāś ca*.

59. Vaṁśastha (a), Indravajrā (bcd).

CHAPTER FOURTEEN

17. Importance of good conduct is stressed here. cf. *ācārahīnam na punati vedāḥ*—Āpastamba.

19. Indravajrā (abd), Upendravajrā (c).

20. *Brāhmamuhūrta*, last quarter of night, period just before dawn. Indravajrā (ac), Upendravajrā (bd).

23. Indravajrā (abd), Upendravajrā (c).

24. Bhṛgu and others are the seven Great Sages. Upendravajrā (a), Vaṁśastha (b), Indravajrā (cd).

25. Sanatkumāra and others are the four mind-born sons of Brahmā. Vaṁśastha (a), Upendravajrā (b), Indravajrā (cd).

26. The five great elements and their chief characteristics. Indravajrā (abd), Upendravajrā (c).

27. Indravajrā.

28. Indravajrā (ac), Upendravajrā (bd).

29. Upendravajrā (a), Indravajrā (bcd).

30. Upendravajrā (ab), Indravajrā (cd).

31. Vaṁśastha (ac), Upendravajrā (b), Indravajrā (d).

32. Indravajrā (a), Upendravajrā (b). cd are metrically defective. c is Indravajrā verse but needs one syllable at the end. Kashi edition reading *śaucanāya* for śuddhaye is not happy. d has thirteen syllables; by omitting the first two (*sadā*)-it is so in Kashi edition, it becomes a normal Indravajrā verse.

33. Upendravajrā (acd), Indravajrā (b).

34. Upendravajrā (ad), Indravajrā (b), Indravaṁśā (c).

35. Upendravajrā (ad), Indravajrā (bc).

36. Indravajrā.

37. Indravajrā (ac), Upendravajrā (bd).

38. Indravajrā (acd), Upendravajrā (b).

39. Upendravajrā (a), Indravajrā (bcd).

40. Indravajrā (abc), Upendravajrā (d).

48-9. The days (*tithis*) of the lunar fortnight are grouped into 5 groups of 3 days each. *Nandā-tithis* are the first, the sixth and the eleventh. *Bhadrā-tithis* are the second, the seventh and the twelfth. *Jayā-tithis* are the third, the eighth and the thirteenth. *Riktā-tithis* are the fourth, the ninth and the fourteenth. *Pūrṇā-tithis* are the fifth, the tenth and the fifteenth. Indravajrā (both).

50. Citrā and others are asterisms. Upendravajrā (a), Indravajrā (bcd).

51. Mūla etc. are asterisms. Indravajrā (ab), Vaṁśastha (c), Upendravajrā (d) *-ne udak-*, hiatus is archaic; it is avoided in Kashi-reading.

52. Indravaṁśā (acd), Upendravajrā (b).

53. Indravaṁśā (a), Vaṁśastha (b), Indravajrā (c), Upendravajrā (d).

54. Upendravajrā (a), Indravajrā (bcd).

55. Indravajrā (ab), Upendravajrā (cd).

56. Indravaṁśā (a), Upendravajrā (b), Indravajrā (cd).

57. Vaṁśastha (a), Upendravajrā (bcd).

61. The reading *-ratna-* (Kashi edition) for-*vastra-* is better.

62. *Saṁhata* means, 'well-knit', 'close' an it is interpreted as 'brand new'. But it can also mean 'heaped', 'destroyed' *i.e.* 'used'.

63. *bahir ambunā* (better than Kashi edition reading: *sahabhasmanā*) means 'outside water' *i.e.* of a tank or a river and the like.

64. The reading *takṣaṇāt* (Kashi edition) meaning 'by scraping, planing' is better than *tatkṣaṇāt.*

66. Reading doubtful.

72. In other words, the milk obtained after the suckling of a calf, a fruit felled by a bird, a load carried by an ass, a deer caught by a (hunting) dog-are not defiled.

75. A person should first of all know that he has eaten defiled food and then only can he attend to the expiation. And a person either comes to know of the defilement after eating or will have known it earlier. Both the alternatives are spoken of as having no expiation. Hence, it is to be understood that expiation is to be undergone if one eats defiled food wantonly though it is known as such. And one need not undergo expiation if one was forced by circumstances to eat defiled food or one came to know of it later.

78. *Kṣipet,* 'should be thrown out', is to be understood on the basis of the context, that 'proper arrangement of drains are to be there.'

79. The idea is not clear.

80. *Vīra* means both son and husband; therefore *vīra-hīnā* may also mean 'issueless woman.'

84. *śeṣatva*, the state of being residue, *i.e.* having had sexual intercourse (extra-marital).

100. The expression 'mentioned earlier' refers to the four forms pointed out in the earlier half of the stanza and detailed in the next.

121. Indravajrā (acd), Upendravajrā (b).

122. Indravajrā (a), Upendravajrā (bcd). Almost all *purāṇas* have devoted some space to good conduct.

CHAPTER FIFTEEN

5. Thirteen parts out of sixteen (*kalās*).

22. The vow of Aśūnya-Śayana-Dvitīyā is described in 16.20 ff.

25. The vow of *Akṣaya Aṣṭamī* is described in 16.30 ff.

62. Indravajrā (ad), Vaṁśastha (b), Upendravajrā (c).

63. Indravajrā (abd), Upendravajrā (c).

CHAPTER SIXTEEN

1. Question refers to 15.22, 25.

5. Āṣāḍha: when the sun appears starting to move southwards from the Tropic of Cancer—roughly July.

8. The twelfth day of bright half of Āṣāḍha is called even today, Śayana-dvādaśī.

22. Upendravajrā (abc), Indravajrā (d).

23. Upendravajrā (ab), Indravajrā (cd).

39. Reading in cd is corrupt.

46. Pāda c is metrically bad and the reading is corrupt. The reading here *bhavāṁstvamīśa* is better in way than *bhavantam īśa* (Kashi edition). An emendation may be suggested: *bhavāṁstvadhīśaḥ*. Indravajrā.

48. *Pañca gavya*: the five products from the cow—milk, curds, ghee, urine and dung.

CHAPTER SEVENTEEN

25. See 15.22, 24.

26. Viṣṇu-pañjara is a prayer to Viṣṇu to give protection in all directions. This prayer is found in other *purāṇas* like *Agni, Brahmāṇḍa, Brahmavaivarta, Bhāgavata* and *Viṣṇu-dharmottara.*

38. See 19.40.

42. *sarvadā* mean 'giver of anything', as well as 'always'.

44. *Pañcanada,* the place where there are five rivers flowing towards west Panjab. The five rivers are— Śatadru, Vipāśā, Irāvatī, Candrabhāgā and Vitastā.

53. It was Mahiṣāsura. The reading in the second half is doubtful.

55. *Padmanidhi,* one of the nine *nidhis* (treasures) of Kubera.

67. Reading corrupt.

72. Indravajrā (abc), Upendravajrā (d).

73. Reading in d corrupt. Upendravajrā (ad), Vaṁśastha (b), Indravaṁśā (c).

CHAPTER EIGHTEEN

1. Vaṁśastha (a), Indravaṁśā (b), Indravajrā (c), Indravaṁśā (d).

2. Indravaṁśā (ac), Upendravajrā (b), Vaṁśastha (d).

3. Vaṁśastha (a), Upendravajrā (bd), Indravaṁśā (c).

4. Indravajrā (abd), Upendravajrā (c).

5. Indravajrā.

6. Upendravajrā (abc), Vaṁśastha (d).
7. Indravaṁśā (ac), Vaṁśastha (b), Upendravajrā (d).
8. Indravajrā (acd), Upendravajrā (b).
9. Indravajrā (abc), Vaṁśastha (d).
10. Indravaṁśa (ab), Vaṁśastha (c), Indravajrā (d).
11. Indravajrā (a), Indravaṁśā (b), Vaṁśastha (c), Upendravajrā (d).
12. The term Prajāpati is applied most commonly to the sages who are the mind-born sons of Brahmā, like Marīci, Atri, Aṅgiras, Pulastya, Pulaha, Kratu, Vasiṣṭha, Pracetas or Dakṣa and Bhṛgu. Their number varies from seven to twenty-one and their names too vary from authority to authority. (Dowson, p. 239, *Vettam Mani*, p. 599). Vaṁśastha (a), Indravaṁśā (bcd).
13. Indravaṁśā (a), Indravajrā (bcd).
14. The reading *tūnau* (Kashi edition) for *tūṇam* is better as it goes with *-s'arau*. Upendravajrā (a), Indravajrā (bcd).
15. Indravajrā (acd), Upendravajrā (b).
16. Indravajrā.
17. Indravajrā (a), Indravaṁśā (bd), Upendravajrā (c).
18. Upendravajrā (a), Indravajrā (bc), Vaṁśastha (d).
19. Upendravajrā (a), Indravajrā (bcd).
20. Indravajrā (abc), Upendravajrā (d).
21. Upendravajrā (ad), Indravajrā (bc).
22. Upendravajrā (a), Indravajrā (bcd).
23. Upendravajrā (abc), Indravajrā (d).
24. Upendravajrā (ab), Vaṁśastha (cd).

25-26. Vasantatilaka.

27. Metrically interesting, the *Gaṇa* scheme of a and d is na-na-ra-ja-ga-ga; c agrees with this if Kashi reading bhaviṣyate for bhaviṣyati is accepted; b has na-ja-ja-ra-ga. Velankar (*Chandānuśāsana*, App.) records the latter but not the former. Dwivedi also notices the stanza (*Purāṇa*, 1963, p. 151).

28-29. Indravajrā.

30. Indravajrā (ad), Upendravajrā (bc).

31. Indravajrā (c), Upendravajrā (bcd).
32. Indravajrā (acd), Upendravajrā (b).
33. Indravajrā (abc), Upendravajrā (d).
34. Upendravajrā (ab), Indravajrā (c), Vaṁśastha (d).
35. Indravaṁśa (a), Indravajrā (bc), Upendravajrā (d).
36. Indravajrā (acd), Upendravajrā (b). The episode of Agastya sub duping Vindhya is found in *Devībhāgavata, Padma, Viṣṇu-dharmottara* and *Skānda Purāṇas* also.

CHAPTER NINETEEN

1. Upendravajrā (ac), Indravajrā (b), Indravaṁśā (d). Kashi reads *tām* for *bhṛṣam* in d, making it Indravajrā. Read *caṇḍaśca* for *caṇḍa* in d.
2. Indravajrā.
3. Indravaṁśā (a), Indravajrā (bcd).
4. Upendravajrā (abd), Indravajrā (c).
5. Vaṁśastha (a), Upendravajrā (bd), Indravajrā (c).
6-7. Indravajrā (ad), Upendravajrā (bc).
8-9. Indravajrā (acd), Upendravajrā (b).
10. Mekhala is a girdle, figuratively, it is anything that surrounds; here it is likened to a rampart round a city. Upendravajrā (ab), Indravajrā (cd).
11. Indravajrā (abc), Upendravajrā (d).
12. The knees are fancied as the palms of the creator. Indravajrā.
13. The avagraha(s) after *ye* in c is unnecessary; *sūpa* is an arrow; arrows of Kāma are of flowers only. Indravajrā (acd), Upendravajrā (b).
14. Indravajrā (acd), Upendravajrā (b).
15. Indravajrā (ac), Upendravajrā (bd).
16. Indravaṁśa (a), Indravajrā (bc), Upendravajrā (d).
17. Indravajrā.
18. Indravajrā (abc), Upendravajrā (d).
19. Upendravajrā (ad), Vaṁśastha (b), Indravajrā (c).

20. Indravajrā.

21. Dundubhī is a large war-drum. Upendravajrā (acd); Indravajrā (b).

22. Indravajrā (ad), Upendravajrā (bc).

23. Indravajrā (abc), Upendravajrā (d).

24. Upendravajrā (ac), Indravajrā (bd).

25. Indravajrā (ab), Upendravajrā (cd).

26. Indravajrā.

27. Reading in ab doubtful. Upendravajrā (a), Indravajrā (bcd).

28. Indravajrā (abc), Upendravajrā (d).

29. Indravajrā.

30. Indravajrā (abc), Upendravajrā (d).

31. Indravajrā.

32. Indravajrā (ab), Upendravajrā (cd).

33. Upendravajrā (ab), Indravajrā (cd).

37. An army consisted of four divisions—chariots, elephants, cavalry andinfantry.

40. For Viṣṇu-pañjara, see 17.26-27.

42. Indravaṁśā (a), Indravajrā (bc), Upendravajrā (d).

43. Indravaṁśā (a), Indravajrā (bcd).

CHAPTER TWENTY

3. Devayuga is Kṛtayuga, the first of the four eons. Dharma was supposed to be on all its four feet then. Incidentally it may be mentioned that Kṛta, *i.e.* four, is the maximum score in dice play.

5. Reading doubtful.

11. *Rudrāsyā* is not in instrumental case; *asi* is masc., it is to be taken with *dānavāḥ.* Kālarātrī is a name of Durgā.

16. Better to read *madhye* (Kashi edition) for *yuddhe.*

33. Ḍamaru is a small drum held in one hand and shaken to play.

36. Upendravajrā (acd), Indravajrā (b).
37. Vaṁśastha (a), Indravajrā (b), Upendravajra (cd).
38. Indravajrā.
39. Upendravajrā (ac), Indravajrā (bd).
40. Upendravajrā (a), Indravajrā (bcd).
41. Indravajrā (a), Upendravajrā (bcd).
42. Upendravajrā (ab), Indravajrā (cd).
43. The reading *vacakratvam* is not intelligible. Kashi reads *tvacakratvam.* Indravajrā (abd), Upendravajrā (c).
44. Upendravajrā (abc), Indravaṁśā (d).
45. It should not be forgotten that the *Asura* was in buffalo form. Indravajrā.
46. Indravajrā (abc), Upendravajrā (d).
47. Upendravajrā (ac), Indravajrā (c), Indravaṁśā (d).
48. Indravajrā (abd), Upendravajrā (c).
49. *Pramathas* are the groups (*Gaṇas*) of demi-gods that attend on Śiva. Upendravajrā (ab), Indravajrā (cd).
50. Indravajrā (acd), Upendravajrā (b).
51. Indravajrā. Mahiṣāsura-vadha is recounted in *Devībhāgavata, Mārkaṇḍeya, Varāha, Śiva* and *Skānda Purāṇas.*

CHAPTER TWENTY-ONE

4. *Vadhiṣyati* is future tense verb.
9. The birth of Skanda as son of Pārvatī was for killing the *Asura* Śuṁba here *(see* below śloka 20) and not Tāraka.
13. Haṁsa stands for the soul.
15. *Athā surendreṇa* may be a misprint for *sthāsu*-kashi. reading *Mahiṣa* for *Niśumbha* here and in earlier passages, does not appear cogent.
17. Agniśvāttas are a class of *Pitṛs.* Menā is the mind-born daughter of these *Pitṛs* according to *Śiva Purāṇa* also.
18. Mahātithi or the most auspicious period is that when the Sun, the Moon and Jupiter are in the Mṛgaśirā constellation. It is also called Akṣayā (see 50.3).

21. Reading doubtful.

26. After expounding the greatness of the holy spot Pṛthūdaka, it is continued in ch. 50. The other question in śloka 25, about the *tithi* is answered in 50.3.

31. Vaibhrāja is the celestial garden. The Kashi edition reading *athonmādanam abhyayat* for d appears better; but *atha* gets repeated.

39. Pratiṣṭhāna near Hastināvatī was the capital city of Saṁvaraṇa. It is identified with Bithoor near Delhi.

45. The reading *argha-*(Kashi edition) for *arca* is better.

47. Upendravajrā (abc), Indravajrā (d).

48. Vasiṣṭha returned to his hermitage along with Tapatī, the daughter of Sun.

48-49. Indravajrā (ac), Upendravajrā (bd).

50-54. Features that distinguish an eminent person. Many of the details here are based on *Bṛhatsaṁhitā* as well as *Sāmudrika-Śāstra* of Prahlāda.

50. Indravajrā (abd), Upendravajrā (c).

51. Indravajrā (acd), Upendravajrā (b).

52. Indravajrā.

53. Six features that are to be prominent: sides, belly, chest, nose, shoulders and forehead. Three that are to be deep: voice, strength and navel. Three that are to be long: eyebrows, arms and scrotum. Seven spots that are to be red: soles of the feet, palms, corners of the eyes, nails, teeth-ridge, tongue and lips. Four features that are to be black: pupils of the eyes, eyebrows, beard and hairs of the head. Three features that are to be stooping: breasts and their nipples and lines on the foot. Upendravajrā (ab), Indravajrā (cd).

54. Two spots that are to be white: teeth and eyes. Face, breath, armpit, sweat or semen: these four are to be sweet-smelling. Tongue, upper lip, palate, mouth, face: eyes, breasts, nails, hands and feet: these ten are to resemble lotus. Indravajrā (abd), Upendravajrā (c).

55. The reading in the latter half is not clear enough. Upendravajrā (ab), Indravajrā (cd).

56. *jāne* in c to be substituted by *jñātvā* (Kashi edition) Indravajrā (ac), Upendravajrā (bd).

57. Vaṁśastha (a), Indravajrā (bd), Upendravajrā (c).

58. Upendravajrā (abd), Indravajrā (c).

59. Indravajrā (ac), Indravaṁśā (b), Upendravajrā (d).

60. Upendravajrā (a), Indravajrā (bd), Vaṁśastha (c).

61. Indravajrā.

62. Indravajrā (abc), Vaṁśastha (d).

CHAPTER TWENTY-TWO

1. Indravajrā (ab), Vaṁśastha (c), Upendravajrā (d)

2. Upendravajrā (ac), Upendravajrā (bd).

3. Upendravajrā (a), Indravajrā (bcd).

43. Indravajrā (acd), Upendravajrā (cd).

44. Indravajrā (ac), Upendravajrā (bd).

45. Indravajrā (ab), Upendravajrā (c), Indravaṁśā (d).

46. Indravajrā (abc), Upendravajrā (d).

48. The text suggests that a new chapter should have begun here. Kashi makes it a new one. Attention must be drawn to the point that the narrator from here on is Lomaharṣaṇa, and the audience are the sages, and not Pulastya and Nārada.

50. Indravajrā.

60. Vaṁśastha (abd), Indravaṁśā (c).

Kurukṣetra is also described in other Purāṇas like *Agni, Nārada, Padma, Brahma* and *Brahmāṇḍa. See* also Agrawala, pp. 46 ff.

CHAPTER TWENTY-THREE

5. Hiraṇyakaśipu was killed by Narasiṁha.
6. Influence of *Daityas* was very conspicuous.
8. As the Sun was in his courses, *i.e.* when it was regular.

CHAPTER TWENTY-FOUR

1. *me* to be substituted by *naḥ* (Kashi edition) as the sages are the speakers here and not Nārada.

7. *Deva* and *sura* are synonyms. Here *sura* should be taken in the sense of 'celestial beings in general', to include demigods also.

9. 'Resting on the staff'. To keep the back of the body straight during meditation, a forked support-crutch-is used. It is also called *daṇḍa.*

14-17. Text is corrupt.

18. Muhūrta is the period of 48 minutes; here it is used figuratively.

20. Reading is doubtful.

21. *Bahvṛca* is one versed in *Ṛgveda. Krama* and *Pada* are modes of reciting a *vedic* text.

22. *sa* is a misprint for *sā.*

24. Lokāyatika is a materialistic philosopher. Here, it may be understood as philosopher in general.

34. Reading doubtful.

CHAPTER TWENTY-FIVE

3. *surārīṇām* should be *surādīnām* (Kashi edition).
6. *Carati* must be *carata* (Kashi edition).
8. Brahmavādin is a knower of Brahman, Vedāntin.
13. Reading unsatisfactory.
21. *sthāna* refers to postures while standing.

CHAPTER TWENTY-SIX

Whole of this is in prose and is the prayer of Kaśyapa to Lord Viṣṇu. It is a series of names of the Lord, used in the vocative case. Each name brings out an aspect of the glory of the Almighty.

śata-... babhūva—reading doubtful.

bhūtādi etc. —Ahaṅkāra and the great elements, the tattvas of the Sāṅkhyas.

ghṛtārchiḥ—lit., 'flame of ghee'.

ūrdhvakarman— 'moving upwards', a name of Viṣṇu.

anantaeḥ-reading doubtful.

caturbhis' ca etc.— Śloka metre.

The numbers refer to the number of syllables in the five formulas which are the essential ones in the course of a *homa.* They are in order: āśrāvaya (4) astu śrauṣat (4), yaja (2), ye yajāmahe (5), and Vauṣaṭ (2). When the formula Vauṣaṭ is uttered, the *Havis* is offered to Fire.

CHAPTER TWENTY-SEVEN

6. The *Visarga* after *maheśvara* should be dropped.

7. *svayameva:* The gods did not put forth any specific plea (śloka 6). But Viṣṇu himself assured them help in clear terms.

14. *-bhojanāḥ* should be *-bhojana.*

25. Those actions by which the cycle of birth and death goes on, are *pravṛtti-karmas.* Those that break the cycle are *nivṛtti-karmas.*

26. Harimedhase: Viṣṇu addressed as *Aśvamedha.* cf. *Bṛhadāraṇyaka Upaniṣad.*

31. Read *-jāla-samu-* for *-jālam samu.*

32. Reading in 'c' doubtful.

CHAPTER TWENTY-EIGHT

4. 'my grove', grove sacred to Viṣṇu, i.e. Kurukṣetra.

11. Born as Vāmana.

CHAPTER TWENTY-NINE

2. *Brahma-daṇḍa*: Curse of a Brāhmaṇa which is effective instantaneously.

10. Instead of saying that Prahlāda visualised Viṣṇu lying in the womb of Aditi in the form of a dwarf, it is said that he saw the entire universe within the *Dwarf*.

Vasus: the terrestrial gods in the Veda go by this name. In *Puranic* mythology, they are a set of divine beings born of Dakṣa Prajāpati and Vasu. Their number is usually eight (in a system of expressing members through words, Vasu is eight).

Rudras: in both *Vedic* and *Purāṇic* mythology, the number of Rudras is infinite. However, figure eleven is often associated with them (in fact, in classical literature, the word Rudra stands for eleven).

19. ab: Upendravajrā, cd: Indravajrā.

20. ad: Upendravajrā, bc: Indravajrā.

21. a: Upendravajrā, bcd: Indravajrā.

22. ad: Indravajrā, bc: Upendravajrā.

23. Indravajrā.

24. ad: Indravajrā, bc: Upendravajrā.

25. ad: Indravajrā, bc: Upendravajrā.

26. *Anantam*: not limited by space, time and relation.
a: Indravajrā, bcd: Upendravajrā.

27. *Ṣoḍaśa-aṁśa*: sixteenth part; based on Moon's digits.
a: Indravajrā, bcd: Upendravajrā.

CHAPTER THIRTY

12. ab is not syntactically related to cd.

13. *Govinda*: Cow-keeper, an epithet of Kṛṣṇa; hence a name of Viṣṇu.

20. *Sthiti*: preservation stage, the other two being *sṛṣṭi* (creation) and *laya* (destruction).

22. *Damādiguṇa*: *dama* (restraint), *dāna* (charity) and *dayā* (compassion). *Bṛhadāraṇyaka Upaniṣad*, 2. 5-2-3.

24. *Śeṣa-bhoga-śaya*: Viṣṇu is conceived as reclining on the coils of the Great Serpent called *Ādi-śeṣa*, having a thousand hoods which are spread providing shade to Viṣṇu's head. 24 cd has reference to Viṣṇu's form of Varāha. Hiraṇyākṣa, a formidable Asura threw the earth into the ocean. Then Viṣṇu in the form of the Great Boar-Ādi-varāha-lifted it up with the tusks and also killed the *Asura*.

25. *Nṛkesarin* obviously refers to *Nara*-(or *Nṛ*-)-*siṁha*, Man-lion form of Viṣṇu.

26 & 27. Textual reading not clear.

32. *Hṛṣīkeśa* (*hṛṣīka*: sense organ, *īśa*: lord) is an epithet of Viṣṇu.

36. Deer skin, *Yajñopavīta*, etc. form the features of a Brahmacārin.

41. *Saparvatam* and *sādri* are repetitive.

42. Vāmana's movement, i.e. sluggish.

44. Reading doubtful.

CHAPTER THIRTY-ONE

18. *Saṁsāra*, cycle of birth and death. *Deveśa*, reading doubtful.

37. *Purohita* is the King's adviser on matters of *Dharma* and such.

37 & 38 ab. Seem out of place.

43. *Ṛtvik*, a participant in a *Vedic* sacrificial performance.

46. *Kupya*, any metal other than gold and silver. In Kauṭilya, it refers to forest produce.

53. Pouring water on hand registers gift or promise.

64. *Iṣṭi* is a type of *Vedic* sacrifice in which the chief offering is either *puroḍāśa*, cake-made of rice-flour or *caru*, cooked rice. *Paśubandha*, a *Vedic* sacrifice with a *paśu* as the chief offering.

73. One *kalpa* is one day and night of Brahmā. In terms of mortal years it is two thousand *mahāyugas*. A *mahāyuga* consists of 4,320,000 years, the sum of the four *yugas*, *Manvantara*, the period of time ruled over by a Manu of whom there are 14; *Vaivasvata Manu* is the 7th (current).

83. *Śrāddha*: Etymologically anything done in faith (*śraddhā*); generally, obsequies.

88-89. See infra, ch. 36. vv. 68-69.

CHAPTER THIRTY-TWO

6. *Araṇī* is a piece of Śamī tree useful in churning fire; usually two pieces are employed. Hence, *source*.

9. The three components of *Om* are *a, u* and *m*.

10. Earth (*bhūḥ*), atmosphere (*bhuvaḥ*) and heaven (*svaḥ*) are the three *lokas*; *ṛk, yajus* and *sāma* are the three *Vedas*; recitation of hymns, performance of sacrifices, singing of *sāmans* are the three *vidyās*. Three fires: *Āhavanīya*, *Gārhapatya* and *Dakṣiṇā*. Three lights: Sun, Moon and Fire. Dharma, Artha and Kāma are the three human values (*puruṣārtha*).

11. *Sattva, Rajas* and *Tamas* are the three *guṇas*. The three varnas are Brāhmaṇa, Kṣatriya and Vaiśya. Agni, Vāyu, Āditya are the three *Devas*. *Vāta, Pitta* and *Śleṣma* are the three *Dhātus*. *Jāgrat* (Conscious), *Svapna* (dream) and *Suṣupti* (deep sleep) are the three states. The three *Pitṛs* are: *Vairājas, Agniṣvāttas* and *Barhiṣadas*. *Aṇimā* etc. cannot be construed; Kashi edition reads *evam ādayaḥ*.

13. *Somasaṁsthā* and others are the three types of *Vedic* sacrifices.

14. *Ardhamātra*: anusvāra, nasal sound of '*om*'.

15. Tongue, palate, lips, velum and teeth are the places of origin of phonemes.

18. Six qualities: knowledge (*jñāna*), power (*śakti*), might (*bala*), prosperity (*aiśvarya*), prowess (*vīrya*), effulgence (*tejas*)—these are the foremost of the supreme of infinite qualities (*ViṣṇuPurāṇa*). The three guṇas are *sattva, rajas* and *tamas.*

21-22. Metre is Śālinī. *Vinaśyanti* in 21 b cannot be construed.

22. Vowels and consonant i.e. language.

CHAPTER THIRTY-THREE

6. Today too this verse is employed in purification rites and repeated as a *Mantra.* Kashi edition reads Kurukṣetra for *puṇḍarīkākṣa.*

8. *Mukti* is of four types, i.e. the means of liberation is fourfold.

15. *Sannihita* pond. See infra 41.9.

CHAPTER THIRTY-FOUR

3. *Śṛṇu* is singular but refers to 'sages' (*pl.*). Kashi edition also has the same reading. cf. 6 which has *Śṛṇuta.*

7. Kashi edition reads Vasunadī for Amlunadī.

9. The *tīrtha* is Kurukṣetra.

21. *dvijottamaḥ* to be read as *dvijottamāḥ.*

22. The five great worships (*yajñas*) are: worship of gods (*Deva-yajña*), of manes (*Pitṛ-yajña*), of beings (*Bhūta-yajña*), of guests (Human beings, *Manuṣya-yajña*) and of *Veda* (*Brahma-yajña*).

30. Soma (Moon) married the twenty-seven Aśvinī and other daughters of Dakṣa; but was mostly attached to Rohiṇī.

On the plea of others, Dakṣa cursed Moon to be afflicted with disease.

36. *tat* (*ca*) *liṅgam* to be read as *tau* (*ca*) *liṅgam.*

CHAPTER THIRTY-FIVE

7. The reading of b is doubtful.

16. Reading not clear.

30. Surabhi, the divine cow.

32. The reading *brahmaṇā* (Kashi edition) is better for *brāhmaṇaḥ.*

36. Perhaps this verse should have come after 39.

37. Read *sarasvatyām* for *sarasvatyā.*

42. *dharmajña* is vocative; it should be nominative.

48. *Prāṇāyāma,* control of breath.

CHAPTER THIRTY-SIX

1. *Krośa* is a measure of distance, about a little more than four kilometres ($2^3/_4$ miles).

8. Each of the three types of sacrifices has eight types. The seven *Soma* sacrifices are: *Agniṣṭoma, Atyagniṣṭoma, Ukthya, Ṣoḍaśa, Atirātra, Vājapeya* and *Āptoryāma.*

9. Bharadvāja and others are the seven great sages.

10. Read *etaiḥ* for *ete.*

16. Kedāra, the holy mountain Kedāranātha.

18. Kātyāyanī, Bhadrā, Nidrā, Māyā and Sanātanī are names of Durgā.

33. Read *vipraḥ* for *vipro.*

42. *Japa,* repetition of a holy name, syllable/s, etc.

50. i.e., *Śrāddha* at Phalakīvana is equal to Śrāddha at Gayā.

62. *Prastha* is a vessel of measure, as well as the quantity.

68-69. See supra ch. 31.88-90.

CHAPTER THIRTY-SEVEN

2. Sentence incomplete. Read -*saṁyutaiḥ* for-*saṁyutaḥ*. Hanūmān as child jumped at the sun thinking it to be his food; then, at Rāhu who appeared bigger than the sun; then on to Airāvata when Indra struck him with *Vajra.* Hanūmān fell down wounded. Vāyu carried him off and hid himself. He came back after Brahmā and other gods, revived Hanūmān and conferred boons on him. (*Vālmīki- Rāmāyaṇa*, Uttara-kāṇḍa, sargas 35, 36).

8ff. Vedavatī was the daughter of Kuśadhvaja, son of Bṛhaspati. Her father desired Viṣṇu to be his son-in-law but he was killed by a *Daitya* King Śambhu. Vedavatī took to austerities in Himālaya to realise her father's wish. Rāvaṇa who came there saw her and asked her to marry him. On her refusal, he dragged her. At this she felt defiled. She vowed to kill him and burnt herself up. She became Sītā, the daughter of Janaka. (*Vālmīki Rāmāyaṇa*, Uttara-kāṇḍa, Sarga 17. Also *Devī-bhāgavata* 9. 15-16)

12. Read *ātmavatā* for *ātmavanam.*

16. The reading *candramā* (Kashi edition) for Vāmana appears better.

29. Yajamāna is the chief sacrificer in a vedic sacrifice.

38. Sentence incomplete. cf. 38. 1

CHAPTER THIRTY-NINE

10. *Auśanasa-tīrtha.* See 42.25

25. b. Reading doubtful.

CHAPTER FORTY

12. Maiṭrāvaruṇa is son of Mitrāvaruṇa, Vasiṣṭha

30. cd. Reading doubtful.

33. *dainya* is perhaps a better reading for *daitya* in b.

CHAPTER FORTY-ONE

9. Sentence is not complete.

20. *Kurukṣetram* in d cannot be the correct reading. Kashi edition reads *Kuru-tīrtham.*

25. *turya-bhāgena* in d cannot be construed.

28. *Ṣaṣṭhī*: the half-month is not specified.

31. Savitṛ and Pūṣan are synonyms of Sūrya in classical Sanskrit. But they are specific aspects of sun in the *Veda.*

CHAPTER FORTY-TWO

16. Kashi edition reads *Kūpa* for *Kūla* (d).

21. d. *ravi* (Kashi edition) appears better for *ṛṣi.*

25. ff. 39. 1 ff repeated.

CHAPTER FORTY-THREE

15. *Paryaṅka,* a type of yogic posture of sitting. cf. Kalidāsa: *Paryaṅka-bandha-sthira-pūrva-kāyam. Kumārasambhava.* 3. 45.

17. *Ekārṇava,* one watery mass; *arṇava* can, perhaps, be interpreted as nebulous.

25. ab: Indravajrā; c: Śālinī; d: Upendravajrā.

26. acd: Indravajrā; b: Upendravajrā.

27. a: Indravajrā; b: ja. bha. ta. ga.ga; c: Indravaṁśa; d: Upendravajrā. Reading doubtful. *daṇḍa-vidhāna* may refer to infliction of prāyaścitta.

33. The reading *tasyām* (f.) and *aṇu* doubtful.

41 & 42 ab. To be dropped; cf. 40 cd and 44.

50. The reading *pātitāntaka,* feller of Death, would have been better.

52. Read *saṁśita-vratān.* The reading *-vratam* is perhaps the result of misconstruing *mām evam* instead of *nā mā evam.*

57. *Vanamālā* is a garland extending upto knees; made of all-seasonal flowers with a large bunch in the middle (see the quotation in Apte).

58. Reading doubtful.

60. *Proktvā* is archaic form.

66. b: split: *vā ākhyā* or read *vyākhyā.*

71. Add a verb form like *agāt* or *iyāt.*

CHAPTER FORTY-FOUR

7. Padmagarbha is an epithet of Brahmā, Viṣṇu and Sun.

19. c: Read *pātitam.*

38. Prose. All 93 epithets are in vocative case. Saṁvarta, one who does periodical destruction; also a name of deluge cloud. *muñja-keśa,* yellow-haired one.

CHAPTER FORTY-FIVE

5. *tasya* (c) does not go with *ye* (b).

11. *pāka-śāsana,* Indra, Killer of Pāka. See ch. 70 of *Vāyu-Purāṇa* (Vettam Mani, p. 545).

28. *manvantara,* cycle of four *yugas*; has a total of 43,20,000 years; also called *mahāyuga.*

30. Read *kūpam rudra-hradam*; cf. 29.